Between the Lines

Portraits of Authors

CHRIS CLOSE

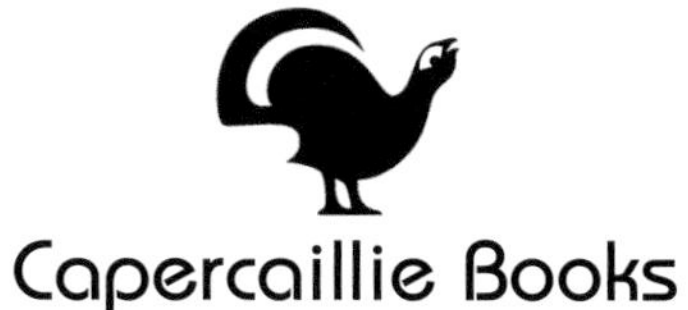

Capercaillie Books

First published by Capercaillie Books Limited in 2015.

Registered Office Summit House, 4–5 Mitchell Street, Edinburgh

A catalogue record of this book is available from the British Library

ISBN 978-1-909305-81-6

www.capercailliebooks.co.uk

Peter Ackroyd · Patience Agabi · Tariq Ali · Martin Amis · Simon Armitage Iain Banks · Steve Bell · Tom Benn · Fatima Bhutto · Mark Billingham Malika Booker · Christopher Brookmyre · John Burnside · Jessie Burton Peter Buwalda · John Byrne · Lydia Cacho · Simon Callow · Melanie Challenger · Tracy Chevalier · Eoin Colfer · Teju Cole · Nick Cope · Frank Cottrell Boyce · Mackenzie Crook · Nicola Davies · Alain de Botton · William Dalrymple · Carol Ann Duffy · Phil Earle · William Fiennes · Frederick Forsyth Michael Frayn · Diana Gabaldon · Neil Gaiman · Janice Galloway · Dave Gorman · Alasdair Gray · Bonnie Greer · Nick Harkaway · Seamus Heaney Richard Holloway · Emmanuel Jal · Gabriel Josipovici · A L Kennedy · Judith Kerr · Karl Ove Knausgaard · Hanif Kureishi · Irma Kurtz · Phyllida Law Kathy Lette · Nicolai Lilin · John Lloyd and Jon Canter · Adam Marek Benjamin Markovits · George R R Martin · Alexander McCall Smith · Val McDermid · Ian McEwan · William McIlvanney · Jonathan Meres · Ben Mezrich · China Miévelle · Denise Mina · Nicola Morgan · Kate Mosse Paul Muldoon · Jo Nesbo · Patrick Ness · Ben Okri · Sharon Olds · Michael Palin · David Peace · DBC Pierre · Philip Pullman · David Rain · Ian Rankin Griff Rhys Jones · Nile Rodgers · Jon Ronson · Michael Rosen · Meg Rosoff James Runcie · Salman Rushdie · Marcus Sedgwick · Will Self · Sara Sheridan · John Gordon Sinclair · Sjon · Ali Smith · Neal Stephenson · Adam Stower · John Taylor · Adam Thirlwell · Kim Thuy · Colm Toibin · Chika Unigwe · Irvine Welsh · Tobias Wolff · Luke Wright

Every August, the Edinburgh International Book Festival presents an unforgettable literary adventure in the heart of the city. Hundreds of authors and thousands of visitors come together for the festival in Charlotte Square Gardens. Visitors relaxing in the Gardens often find themselves in close proximity with authors who are also household names.

These writers, whose ideas and whose worlds readers have shared so intimately, live an increasingly public life and perhaps this is one reason why the photographs in this book have a special quality. Chris Close's images are often captured immediately after the authors have been on stage, where they have shared their ideas in an intense atmosphere with an audience of hundreds. Looking into the eyes of the authors, I think you can see some of the adrenaline coursing in their veins. What's clear from these photos is that writers understand the need to learn a very 21st century skill: as well as being good at communicating via the written word, they must be performers too. I think Chris' great skill is to capture that mood, that sense of the writer in a mode of public portraiture. To me these images carry with them an unusual quality: they don't feel remotely like straightforward studio shots, and they carry within them something more like live action photography. These pictures unquestionably capture a moment in the authors' life that they are sure they'll remember. Yet oddly enough, somehow Chris manages to make them feel intimate at the same time. I've watched countless authors being photographed by him and it nearly always looks as though they are having the time of their life.

Over the years, Chris' ever-changing exhibition of writers has become an important part of the Edinburgh International Book Festival experience. As the festival unfolds, hundreds of authors arrive and leave, bringing with them their stories and their experiences from around the world and creating an incredible buzz. But when each author departs, thanks to Chris they leave behind more than just a memory. By the end of the seventeen-day festival, Chris has helped us build a vast portfolio of faces that represent the year's literary celebrations. Even if visitors don't arrive until the final day, it's still possible to see all the great writers who have shared the experience of the Gardens.

It is fitting that some of the most interesting of Chris' photographs have been brought together in this book. They provide a snapshot not only of some memorable literary faces, but also of a moment in history when book festivals have exploded in popularity. Taken together, these portraits represent an intriguing portrait of 21st century literary life in Britain.

Nick Barley, June 2015

Introduction

In 2009 I took an idea to the Edinburgh International Book Festival. I wanted to photograph a selection of authors appearing that year and produce a 'live' exhibition of the work. The portraits of the authors would be captured one day and on display the next, in an ever growing body of work.

Some logistical problems were overcome and at 5.30pm on 15 August 2009 Emmanuel Jal, a former Sudanese child soldier, now musician and author, was the first person I photographed in what has gone on to become an annual exhibition and to the best of my knowledge the only one of its kind.

It took almost three minutes from the first exposure to the last and it was a swift lesson in working fast that was to become so important. Afterwards Emmanuel beamed at me and simply said,

'You're the man, you are the man.'

High five.

I have now photographed well over five hundred authors.

* * *

The concept behind the work is unusual in that it is both a 'live' exhibition and that it is shot and displayed outdoors. There was simply no indoor space available either to take the photographs or display them. However this lead to a unique style of portraits of authors.

The studio, a simple white backdrop on the side of one of the marquees and some lights.

'Well at least the overheads are low,' retorted Simon Callow.

Each day I photograph a small selection of authors and by night select and print them onto sheets of canvas ready for hanging the next day. Every author who is photographed will be on display, unlike other exhibitions where work is carefully curated. The process is mentally and physically exhausting. Whilst authors may be allowed their off days it is much harder as a photographer to be allowed an off day. You must perform and performing is what it is, at least with my approach. The energy I bring is often reflected in the final image.

The works are printed onto canvas and hung along the open air walkways within the festival venue at Charlotte Square Gardens in Edinburgh. They have to withstand the rigours of whatever the weather may bring.

The style of work developed part by chance, part by circumstance. Unlike shooting in a studio, which immediately isolates the subject from their surroundings, shooting outside allows for much greater freedom of expression and elements of randomness. Noises off, the weather etc., all lead to unexpected results. As the exhibition progresses there is a dual dynamic that becomes apparent from the authors. Some, on seeing the work, can become more and more extreme, wanting to out do the others, whereas some become more intimidated. The former politician, Shirley Williams said she loved the work but would never pose for me.

Portraiture is all about humanity, trying to portray the person, either in a different light or as a real person. Many portraits are created before the photographer has met the subject. I can't do that. I often have preconceived ideas of how a person should be and almost invariably I am wrong. Sometimes I photograph people on more than one occasion. One year they may be gregarious and outgoing the next shy and introverted. I take people as I find them.

I am often asked the name of my favourite author or the one I enjoyed photographing the most. I have to be horribly political in my answer. Rather like Audrey Hepburn in the film *Roman Holiday*, who, when asked by the press which country she had most enjoyed visiting was prompted to say, 'Each in their own way.'

* * *

What follows is a selection of some of the photographs and the stories behind them.

Chris Close, 2015

Peter Ackroyd

Peter braved the rain, worried perhaps not so much about getting wet as diluting his wine. Not true, but in many ways he is the archetypal English writer. Specialist subjects Dickens, Sir Thomas More, T.S. Elliot and a 'starter for ten' on William Blake. Visually a kind of Captain Mannering meets Sir David Niven and with a CBE to boot Peter is a one off.

Start to finish exactly two minutes or in the words of Mohammed Ali, 'Fast, I'm so fast I hit the switch in my room and I'm in bed before it's even dark.'

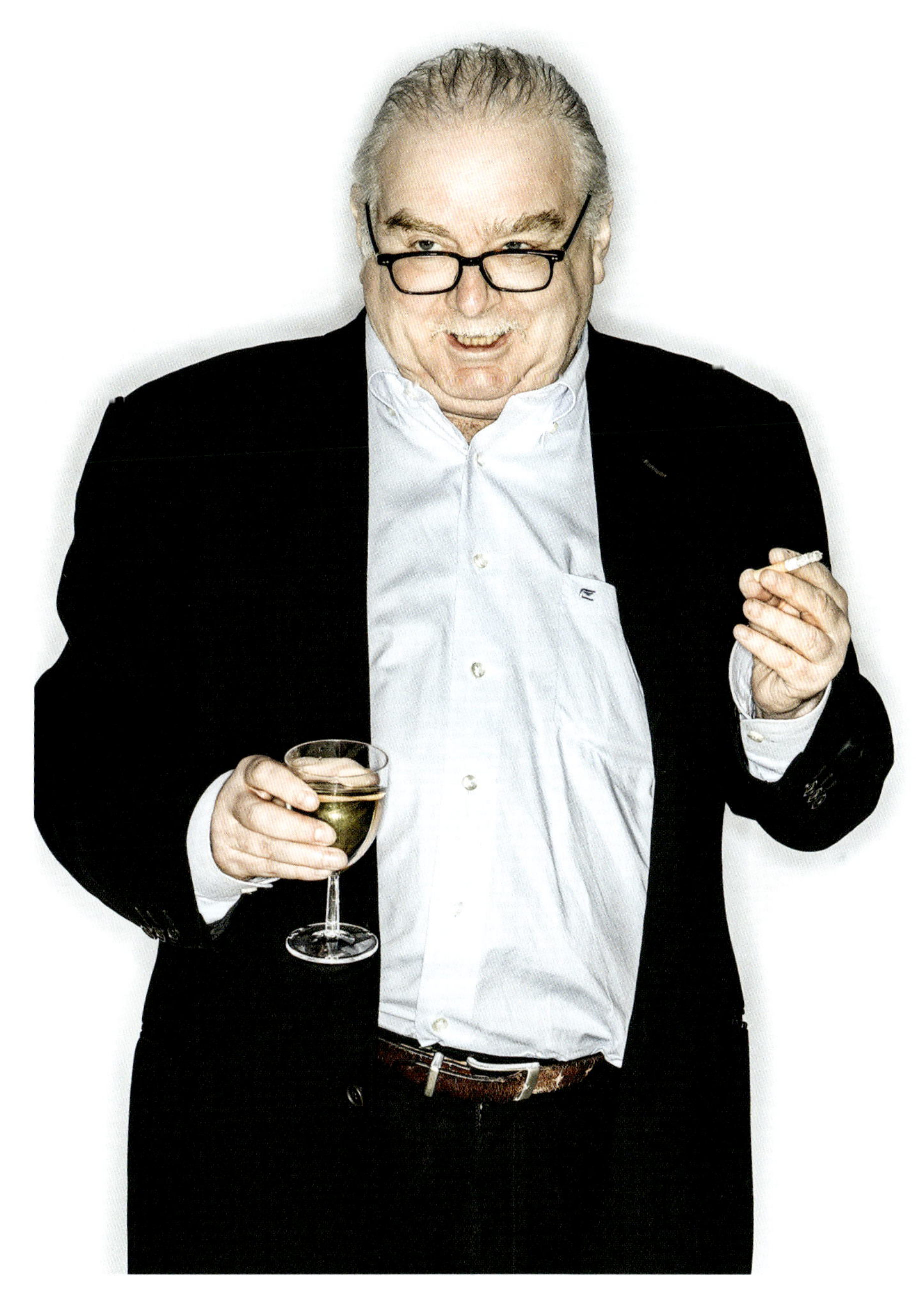

Poet, performer. Patience by name, patient by nature? Perhaps not but like her poetry she has a stylish elegance with an edge, sporting as she did a large tattoo on her back. I photographed this during the session, her dress cut to show it off but I opted for the simplicity of this image.

Although this is not directly about Patience it seems appropriate,

> *'She was tall and dark-skinned and looked like a Nigerian sculpture.'*

BONNIE GREER, *A Parallel Life*

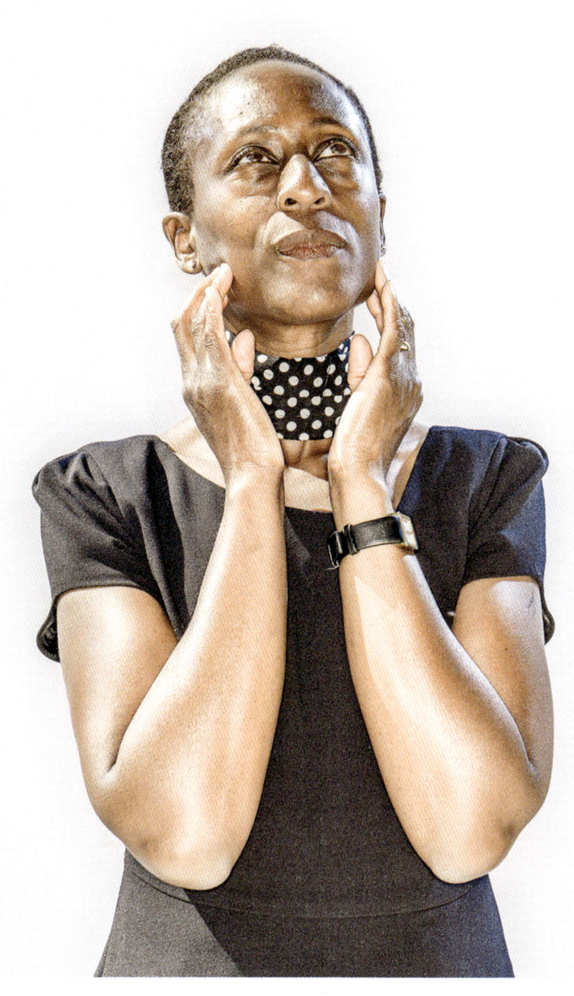

Tariq is from Pakistan but has spent most of his life in the UK. Political commentator, left leaning intellectual, Tariq has a very direct stare: a mixture of confidence and curiousity, reflecting his own fusion of multi-cuturalism.

This more off-guard image seems to have a human and humane quality.

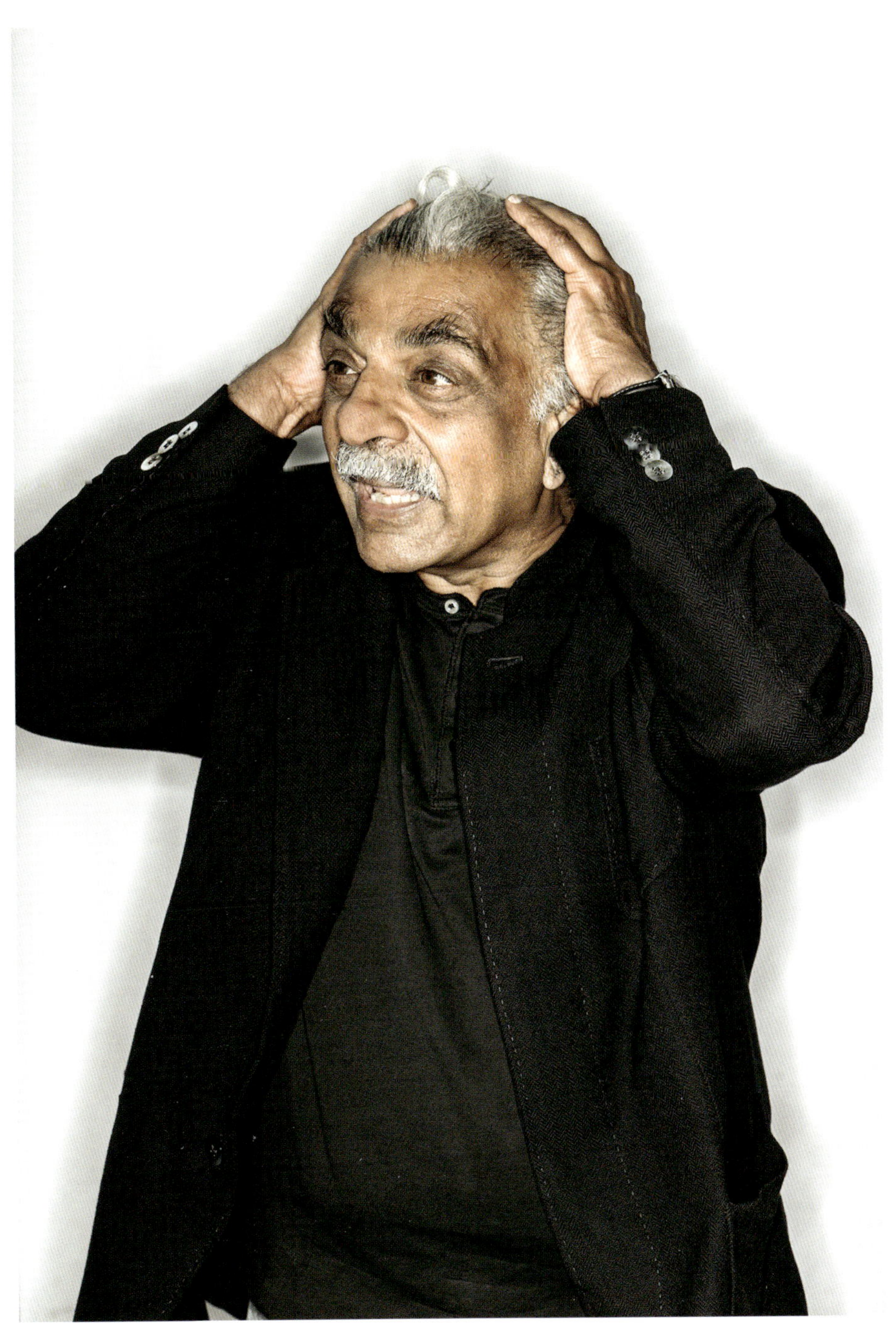

If writing were pugilism Martin would be Cassius Clay. Thankfully boxing gloves are not de rigour for writing novels and I understand Martin is a pen and paper man before committing to the keyboard so I imagine they would have slowed him down somewhat. There were elements of discomfort, embarrassment and disdain at being photographed which I attempted to capture in one image.

> *'I am the only writer to have received the Somerset Maugham award twice – the first time for my first novel, the second time for my second first novel.'*
>
> MARTIN AMIS

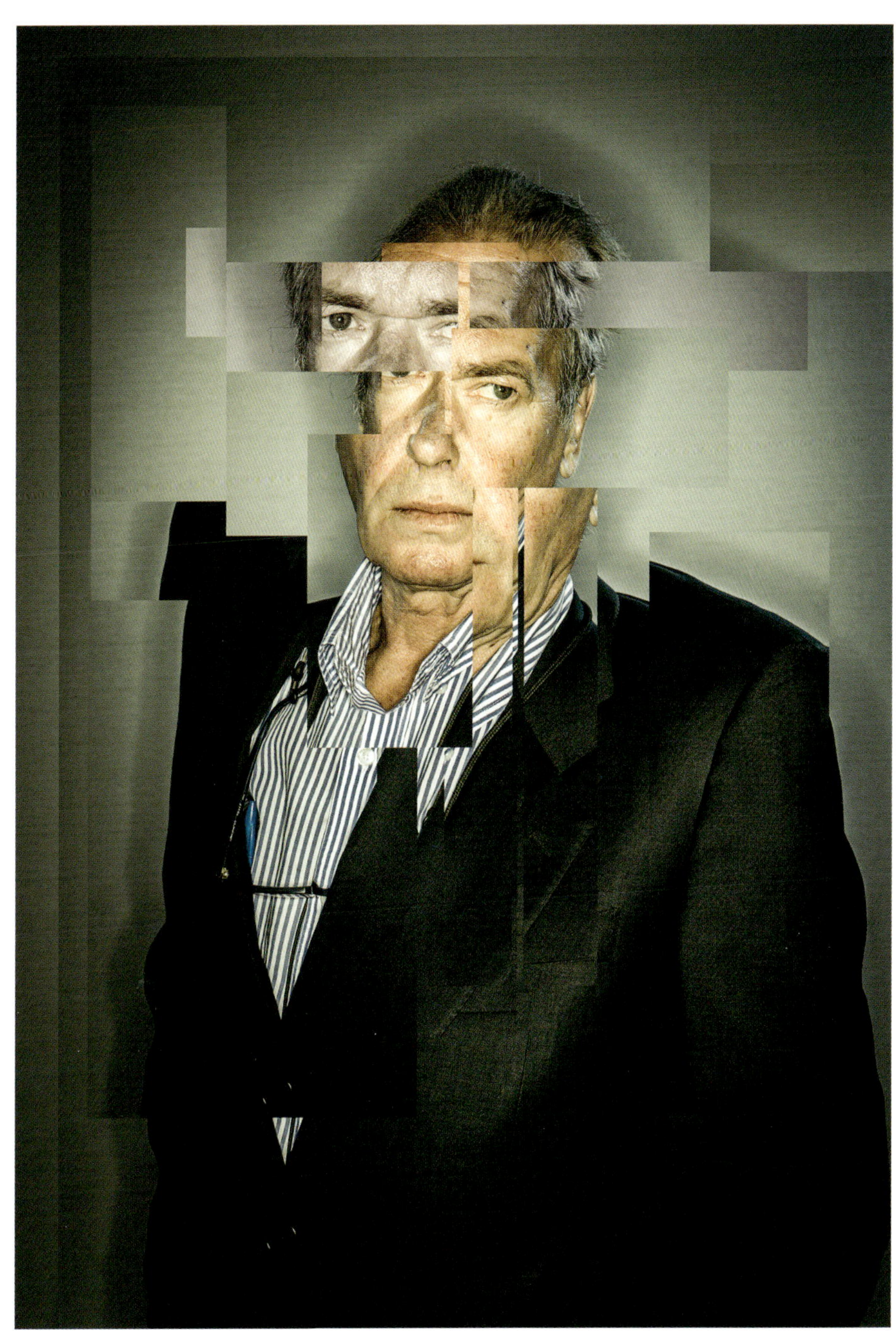

The highly accomplished but still youthful Simon Armitage, clearly an afficionado of style, donned my hat, which like Hitchcock in his movies keeps cropping up in my photographs.

One of the UK's most prominent poets and playwrights, who along with at least three others in this book has his portrait in the National Portrait Gallery, London. I don't know if this is akin to having a portrait in the attic.

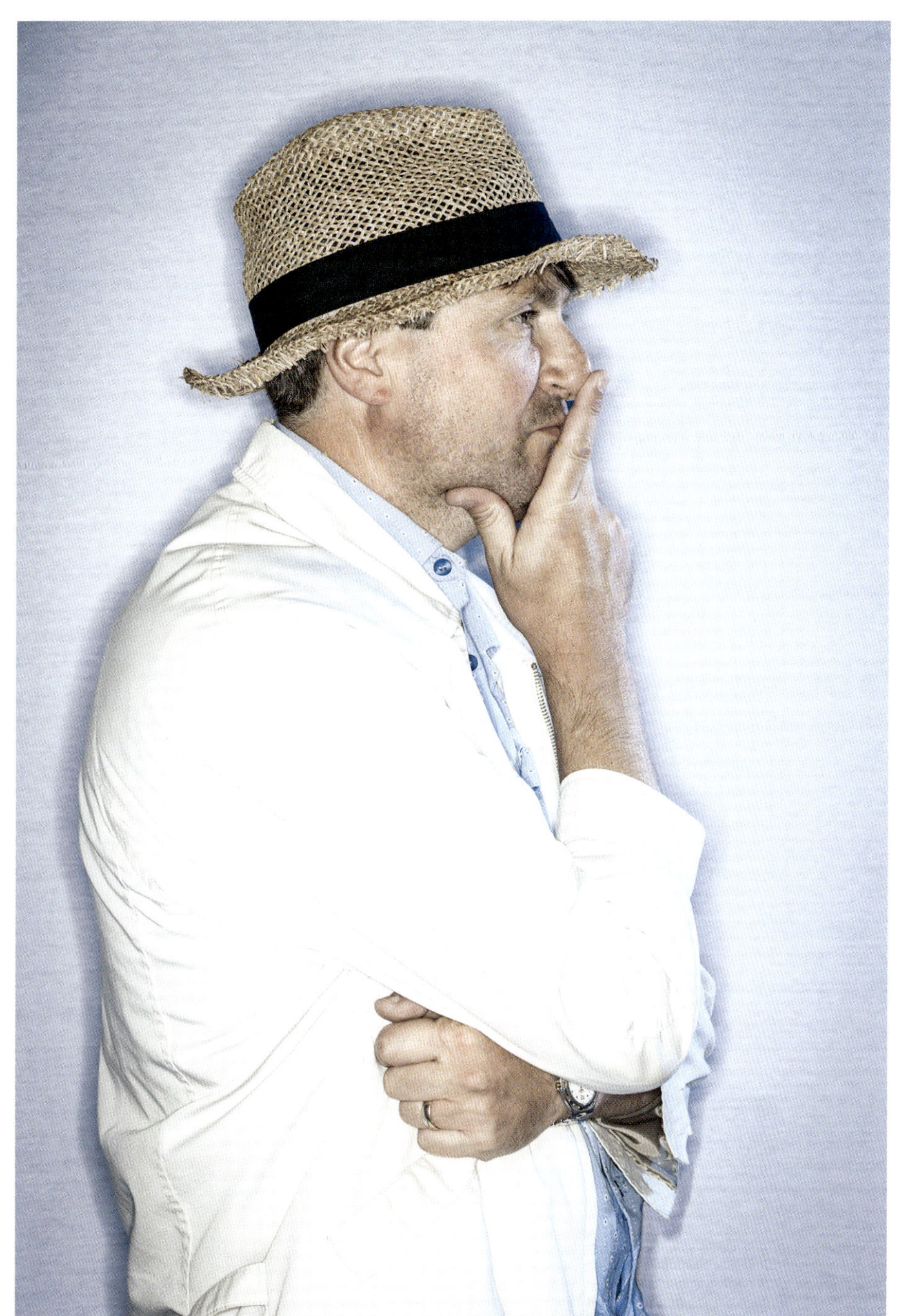

Iain Banks, Iain M Banks neither, sadly no longer with us except in literary form. The 'M' used to differentiate his science fiction from his other writing; 'M' standing for 'Menzies'. This now seems the most poignant image from the series. I have photographed a number of authors on more than one occasion but sadly only photographed Iain once.

A man who proposed to his wife with the words 'Would you do me the honour of becoming my widow?' having been diagnosed terminally ill.

'Empathize with stupidity and you're halfway to thinking like an idiot.'

IAIN BANKS, *Consider Phlebas*

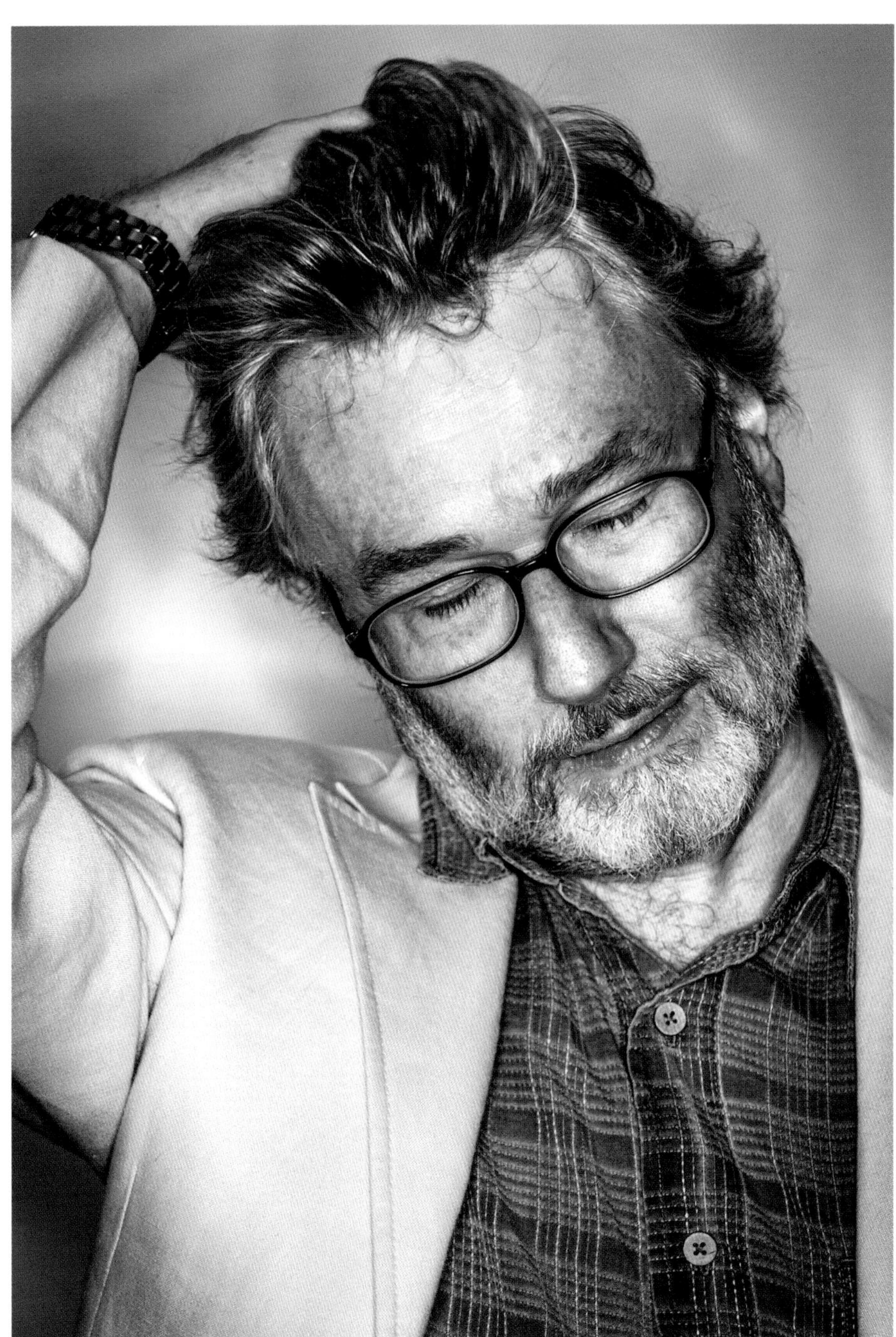

Satirical cartoonist, Steve Bell. I asked if he ever drew himself and am pleased to say he was happy to oblige. I think this was the first time I used illustrations in a photograph and it was late and dark by the time this was shot, the only illumination a few overhead low wattage bulbs. I could hardly see Steve as the camera hunted for focus. The result is part photo, part graphy.

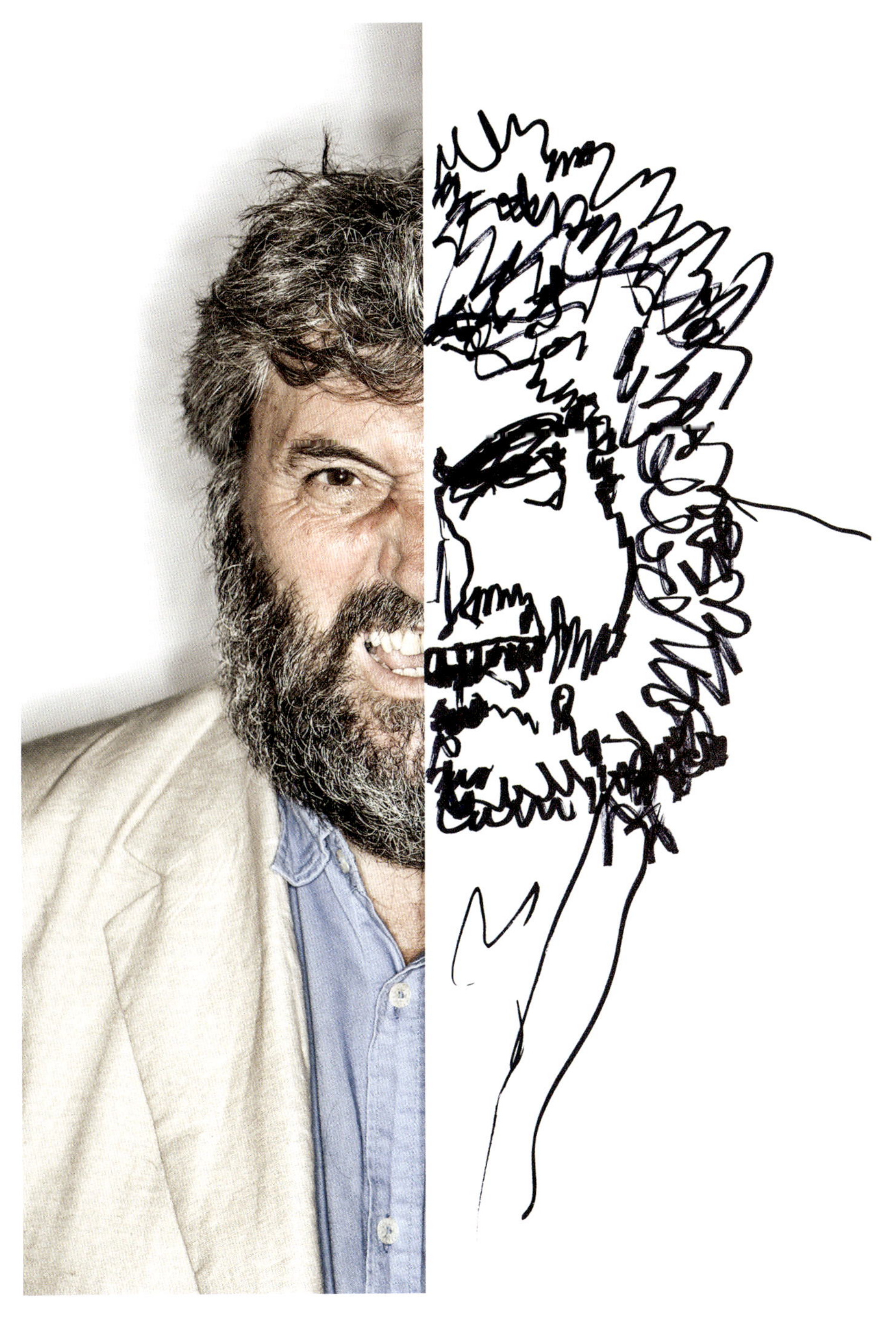

Crime writer Tom Benn has a distinctive look, 'the best a man can get'!

'Generally, I'm not interesting or uninteresting enough to be a recognisable character.'

TOM BENN

He struck me as having the demeanour of a man who did not want to draw attention to himself but would stand out in a crowd nonetheless.

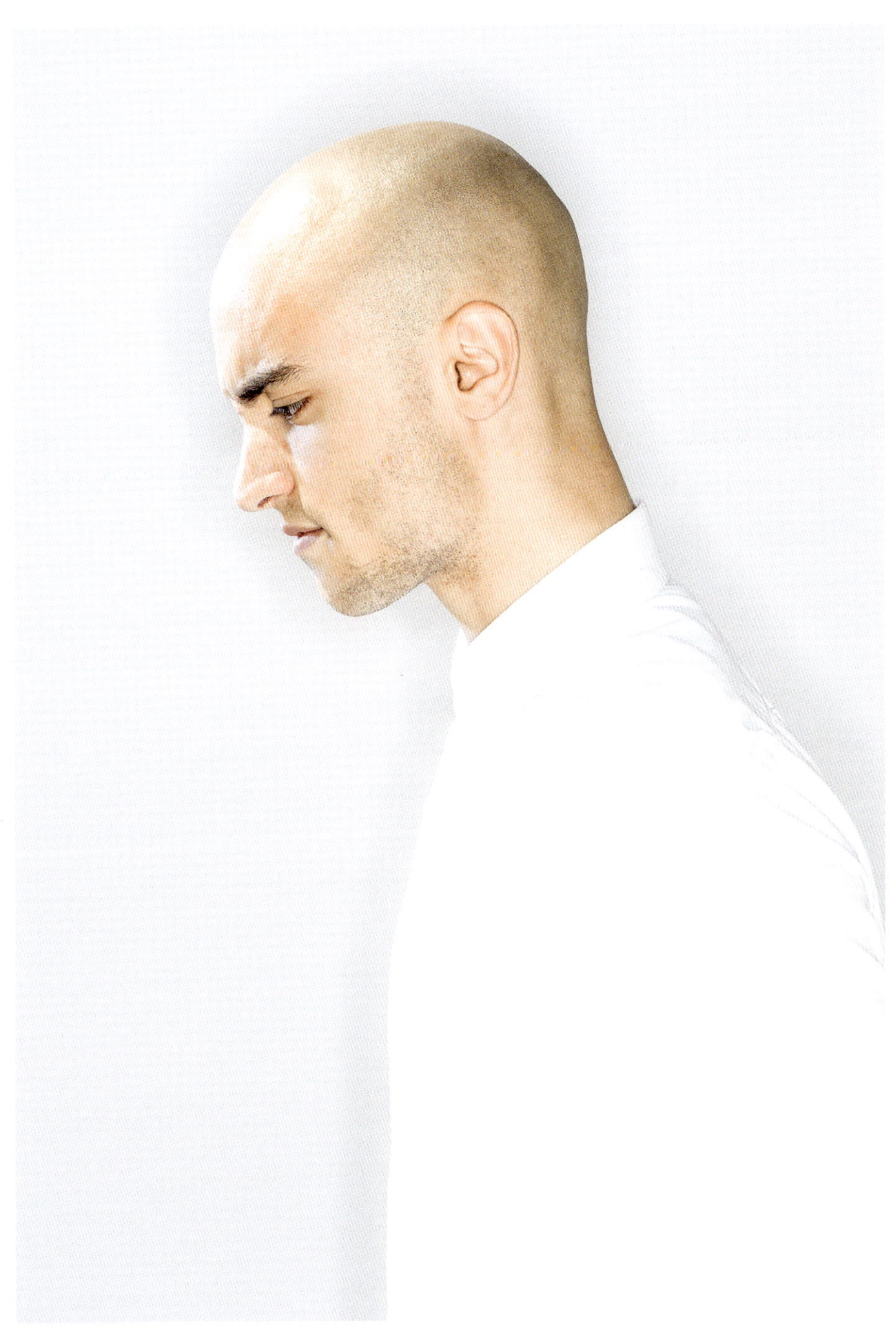

The name Bhutto carries with it a good deal of history. Fatima is a poet and the niece of former Prime Minister Benazir Bhutto. Normally before I photograph someone I try to find out something about them. (It does not always happen that way. People often arrive unexpectedly in my 'studio'.) However I had been scheduled to shoot Fatima and she drifted in like a serene vision and everything I had been reading about her drifted out! All except her rumoured romantic links with one George Clooney and so, struggling for words, I bumbled into some conversation where my mouth was saying one thing and my brain was desperately trying to give my jaw cramp. Fatima subsequently did come over to say she liked the picture and said 'Call me sometime'. Ok the first part is true!

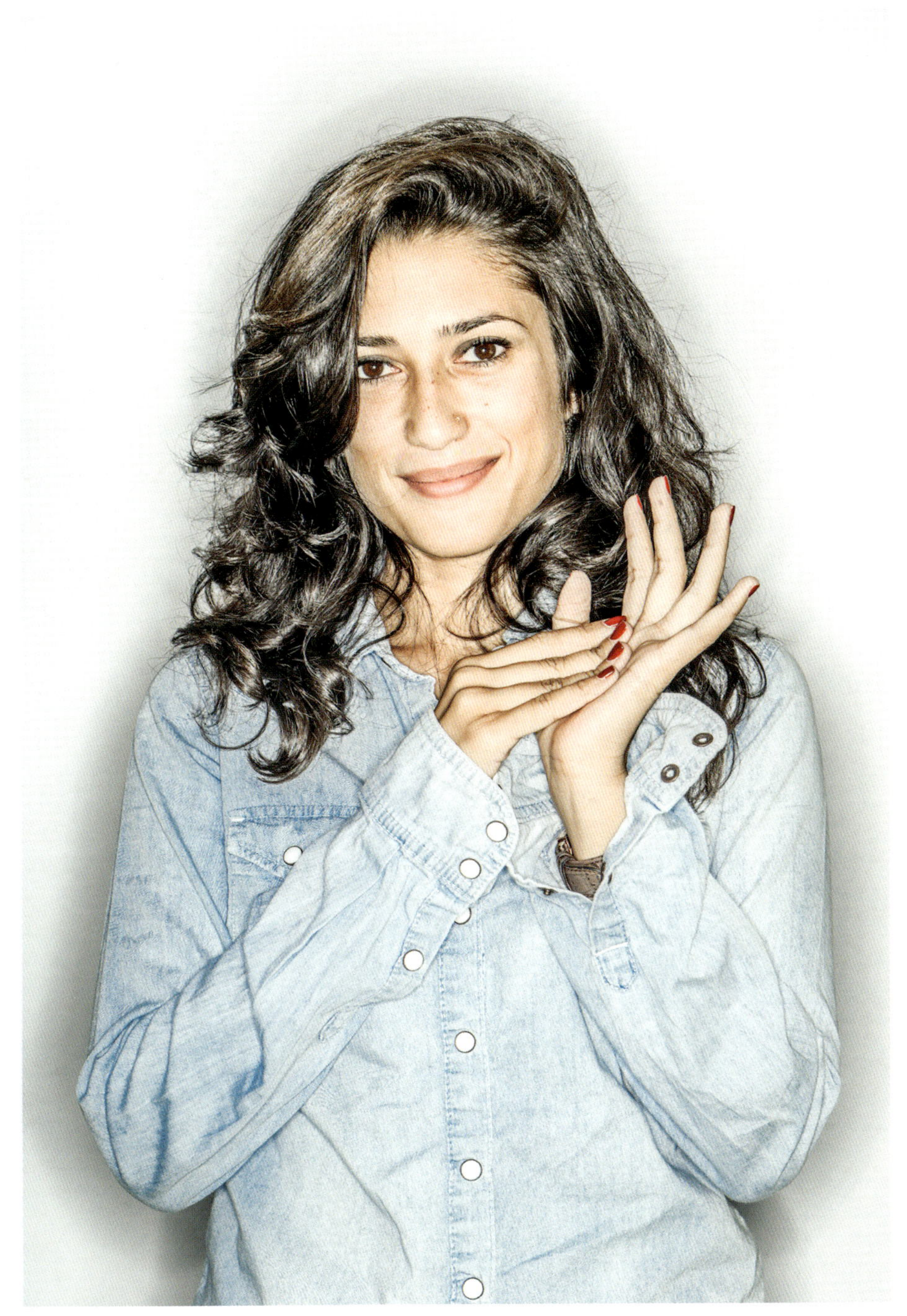

'Ok Mark, as you are best known as a crime writer lets do a serious picture this time.'

Well that was the intention. I have photographed Mark several times in the past so was looking for a new slant. I managed a couple of frames before the eyes twitched, his mouth twisted . . .

'I'm not going to get this am I?' I said. 'Maybe I should have brought some rope or a candlestick or lead piping.'

'I could shoot myself,' he replied. 'Perfect.'

The water was from a previous shoot. I could have made it red but that would have been too Tarantino.

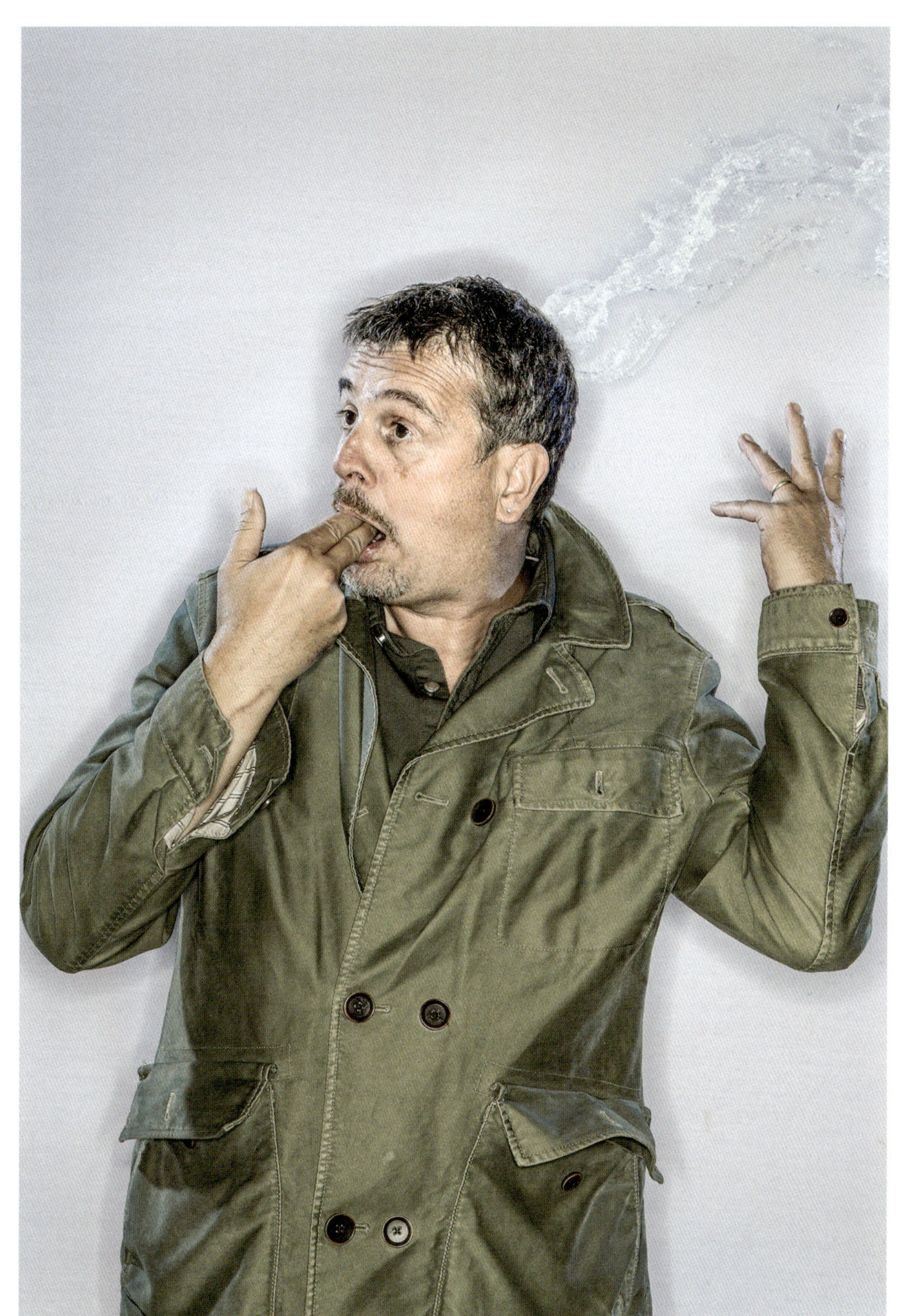

Malika Booker, now there's a perfect name for a writer to have.

Fun, happiness, joy are as important attributes to the human condition as any, so in the words of Heath Ledger, playing The Joker, 'Why so serious?' There's a lot of fun in my portraits but rather like photographing a landscape on a sunny day, that can be trickier than the more traditional serious portrayal of authors. The way I work is to plan little, improvise lots. I don't think it is possible to plan spontaneity.

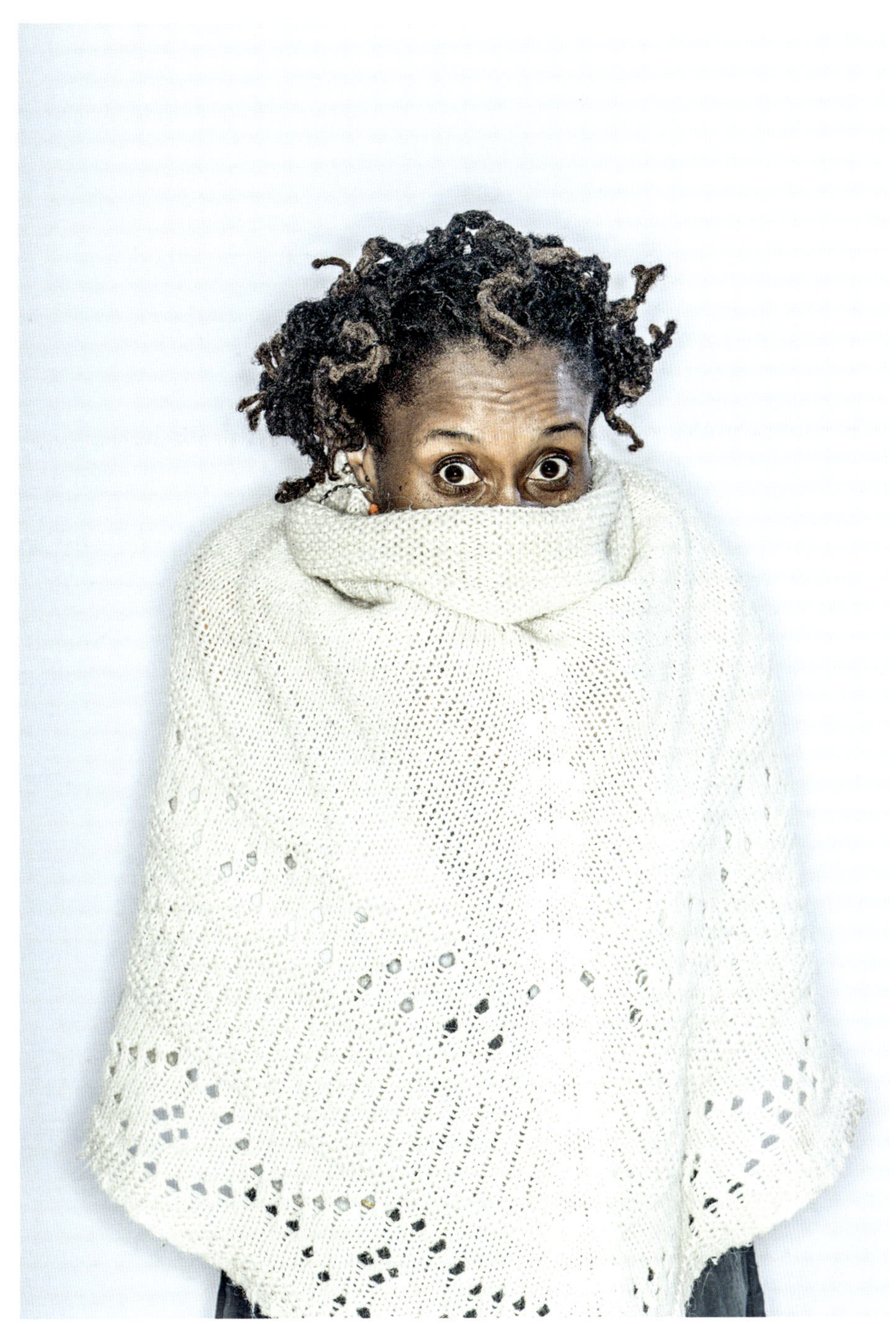

The devil may wear Prada but I can't vouch for Christopher's attire. With nineteen books thus far to his name, his work has some unusual titles from 'Quite Ugly One Morning' to 'All Fun and Games Until Someone Loses an Eye', and then what could almost be a children's book, 'Attack of the Unsinkable Rubber Ducks'. There is a comic malevolence to the titles and a few demons and devils lurking in there too.

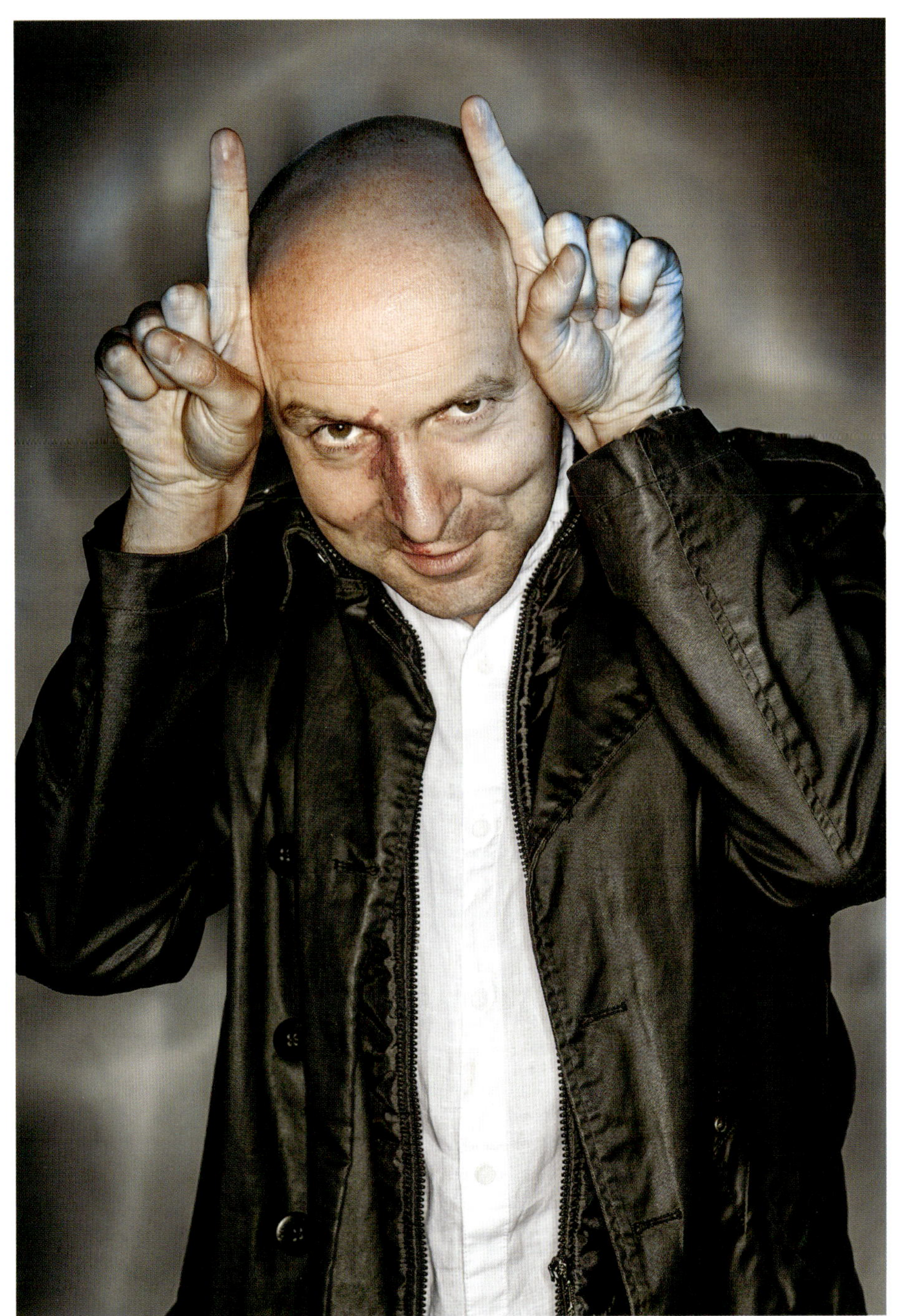

This was one of the portraits when displayed seemed to prompt lots of people to come to me and say words to the effect, 'That's so John'. When you read John's memoirs about his battles with his own demons and difficult family situations this portrait may seem at odds with his account but this is a further example of how preconceptions are often misleading.

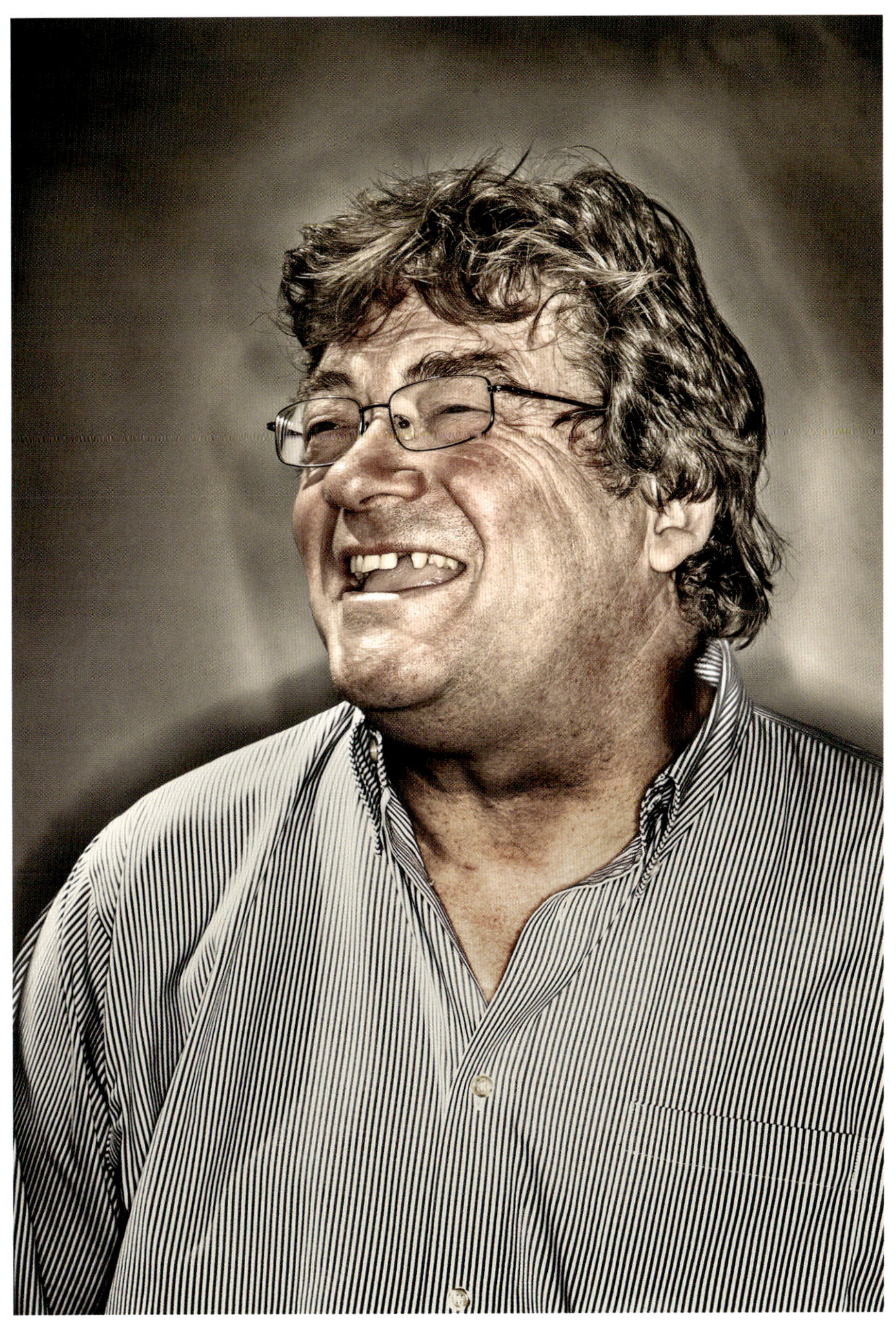

Author of *The Miniaturist* which had the publishers in a bidding war. The face emerging from the wall was her publicist. A former actress, Jessie also won the 2014 National Book Awards 'New Writer of the Year' and the impact of her book, something other authors could only dream of. Partially inspired by a 1963 film, *The Haunting*, the concept of the face emerging also portrays how fictional characters emerge from the author's imagination to become believable and three dimensional.

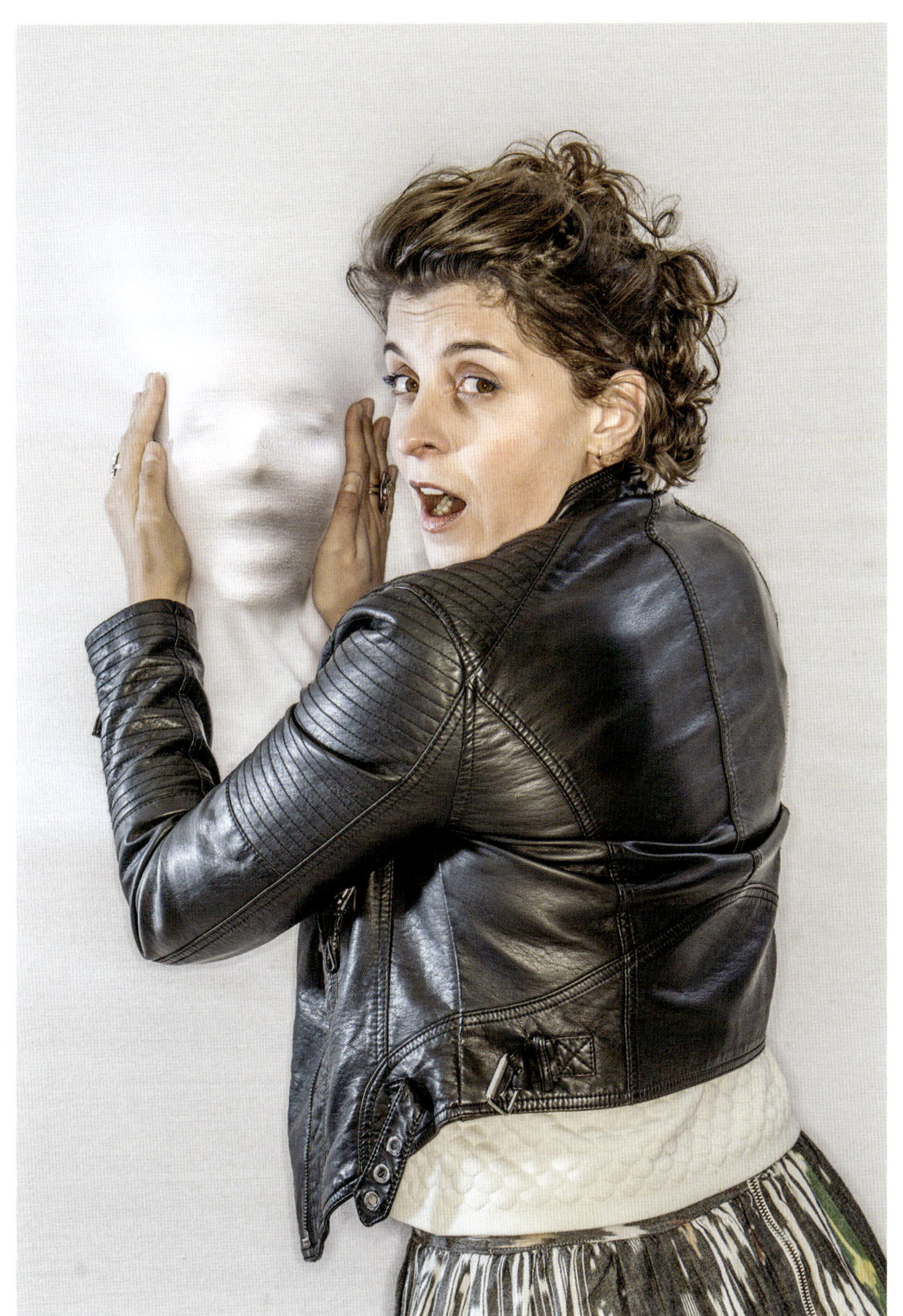

Peter is Dutch. He has the look of a man recently out of the shower, with a wonderfully expressive face: Mick Jaggeresque. Tall and slender with hair to match what is seemingly going on inside his head. His first novel a crazy mixture of fiction set amidst factual backdrops. Flash backs, flash forwards and flash bang wallops from the main character, a photographer. I took this image of Peter as we discussed his book.

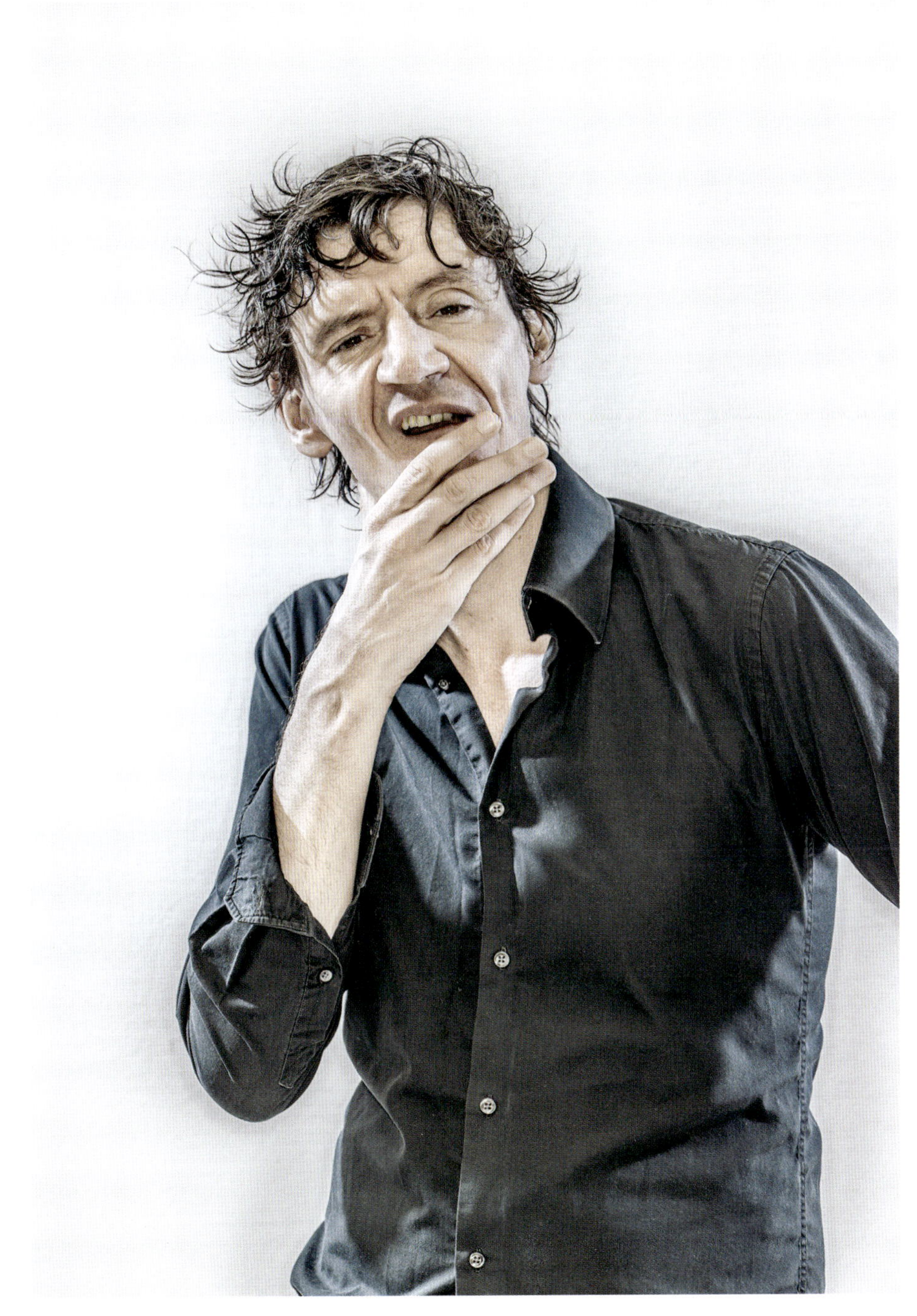

Maestro Mr Byrne: writer, artist, composer. John is one of the jewels in the crown of the art and literary world. It was hard to know how to portray such a figure and which of his multiple talents to latch onto. His eyes wide and his demeanour that of someone fascinated by the world. I left thinking he was like an artistic version of Columbo. You can interpret that how you like.

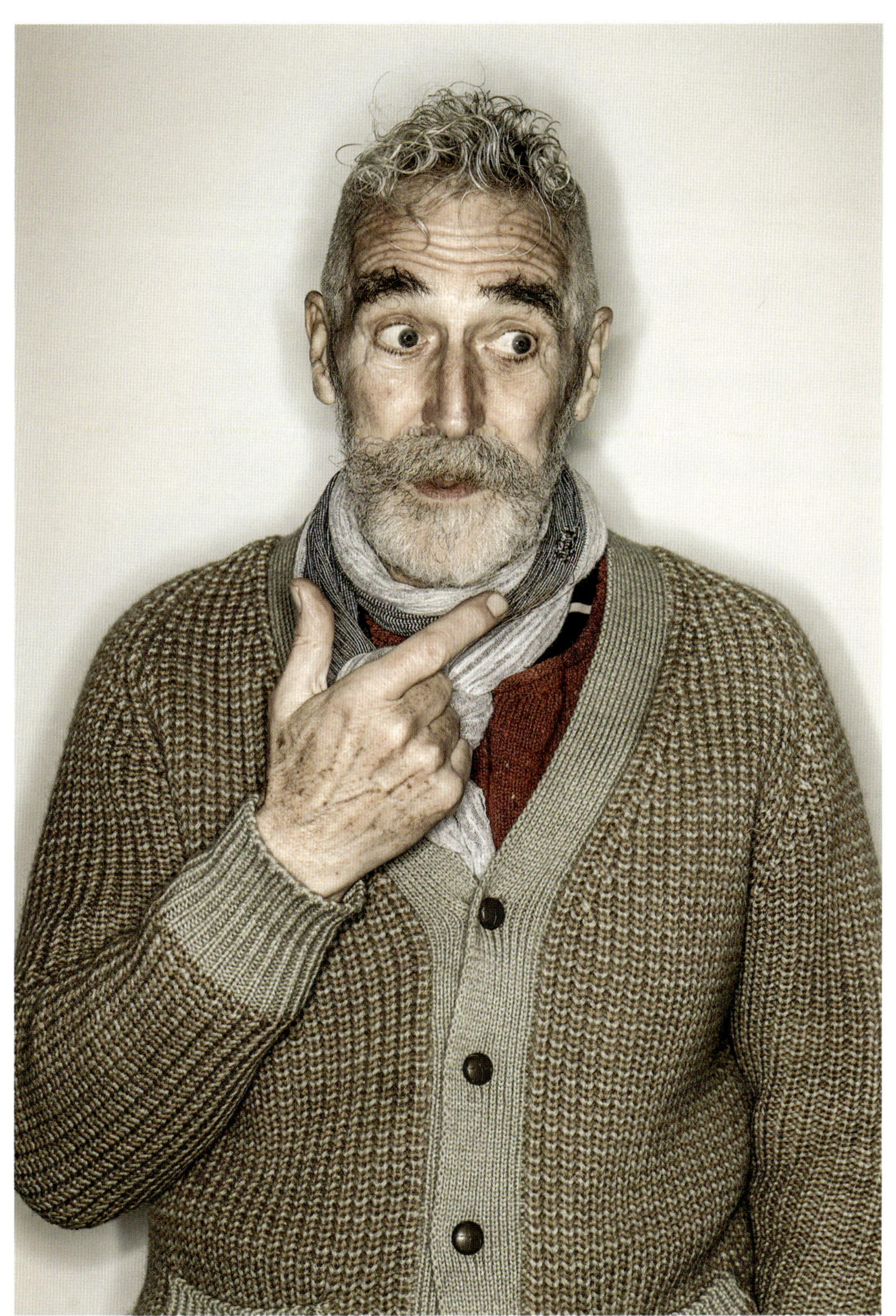

Lydia is a Mexican journalist who writes about the mafia, the sex trade, abuse of women and children and other niceties of the criminal underworld. She has visited over a hundred countries in pursuit of these fine upstanding citizens. Least favourite was Japan and most favourite was Columbia but as she rightly pointed out, she isn't exactly on the tourist trail.

For her troubles she has been attacked, raped, had bones broken and almost been killed after the wheel nuts on her car were loosened. This is no ordinary women. She was however absolutely charming and a joy to photograph. I did question whether I should be photographing her, in case there was a price on her head, hence the idea of her face being partially obscured.

She shrugged, 'Life's too short not to make a difference.'

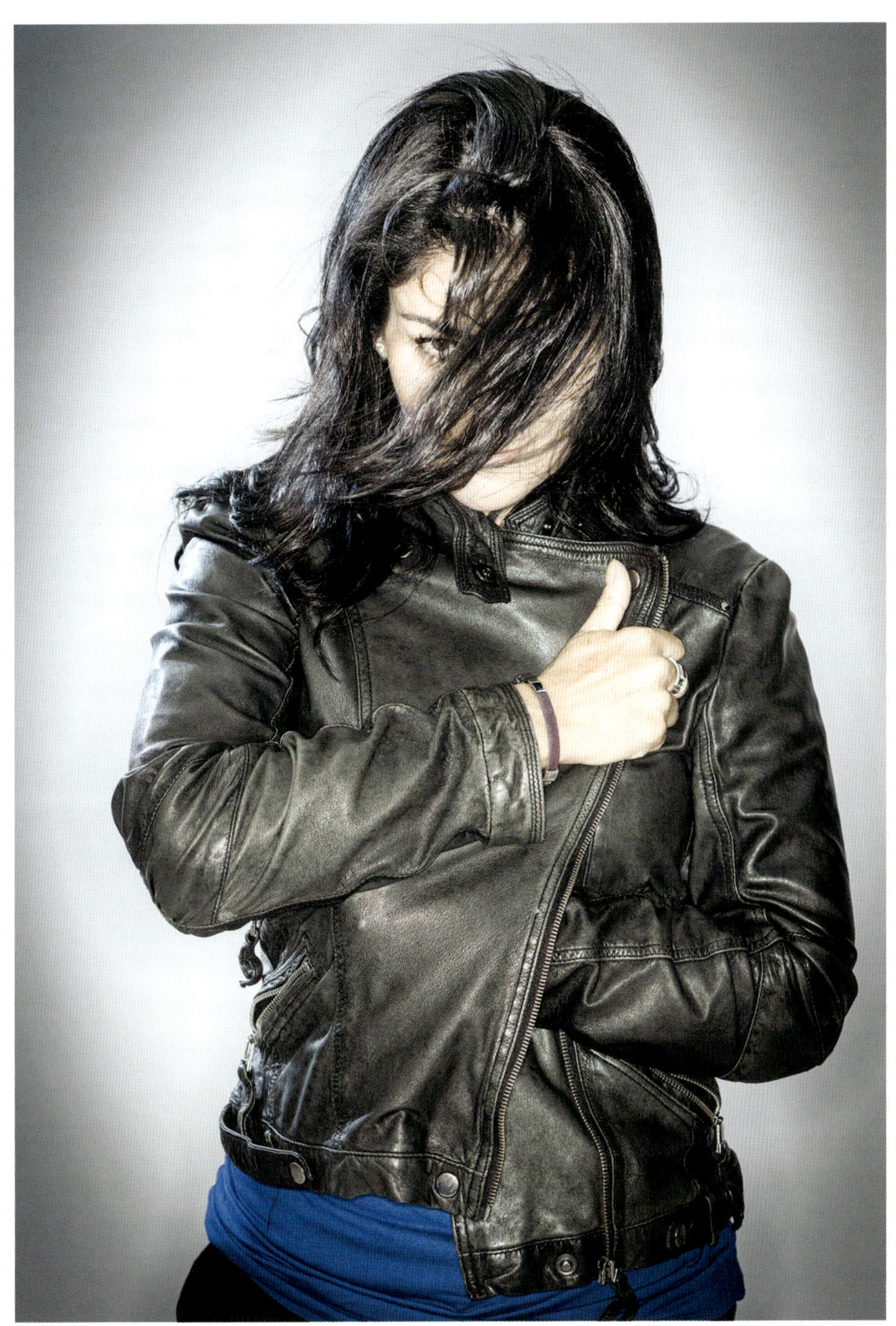

'Well at least the overheads are low,' retorted Simon Callow as I invited him to the 'penthouse studio' on ground level in a garden. The 'penthouse studio' became a standing joke after I met a member of the public who asked if I was the photographer who had taken the portraits. When I replied, 'Yes', she exclaimed, 'I thought you'd be in a penthouse studio somewhere.' Ah Scotland and New York so very, not the same!

I have worked with Simon on a couple of occasions and he is a delight. Extrovert, clever, and good humoured. I had the *brilliant idea* he could portray some Shakespearian characters. I would throw them out there and he would do them. The result was mildly chaotic but this was the result somewhere betwixt Falstaff and Puck!

> *'Callow is not simply a terrific actor who happens to write – you could as well call him a terrific writer who happens to act.'*
> THE TIMES

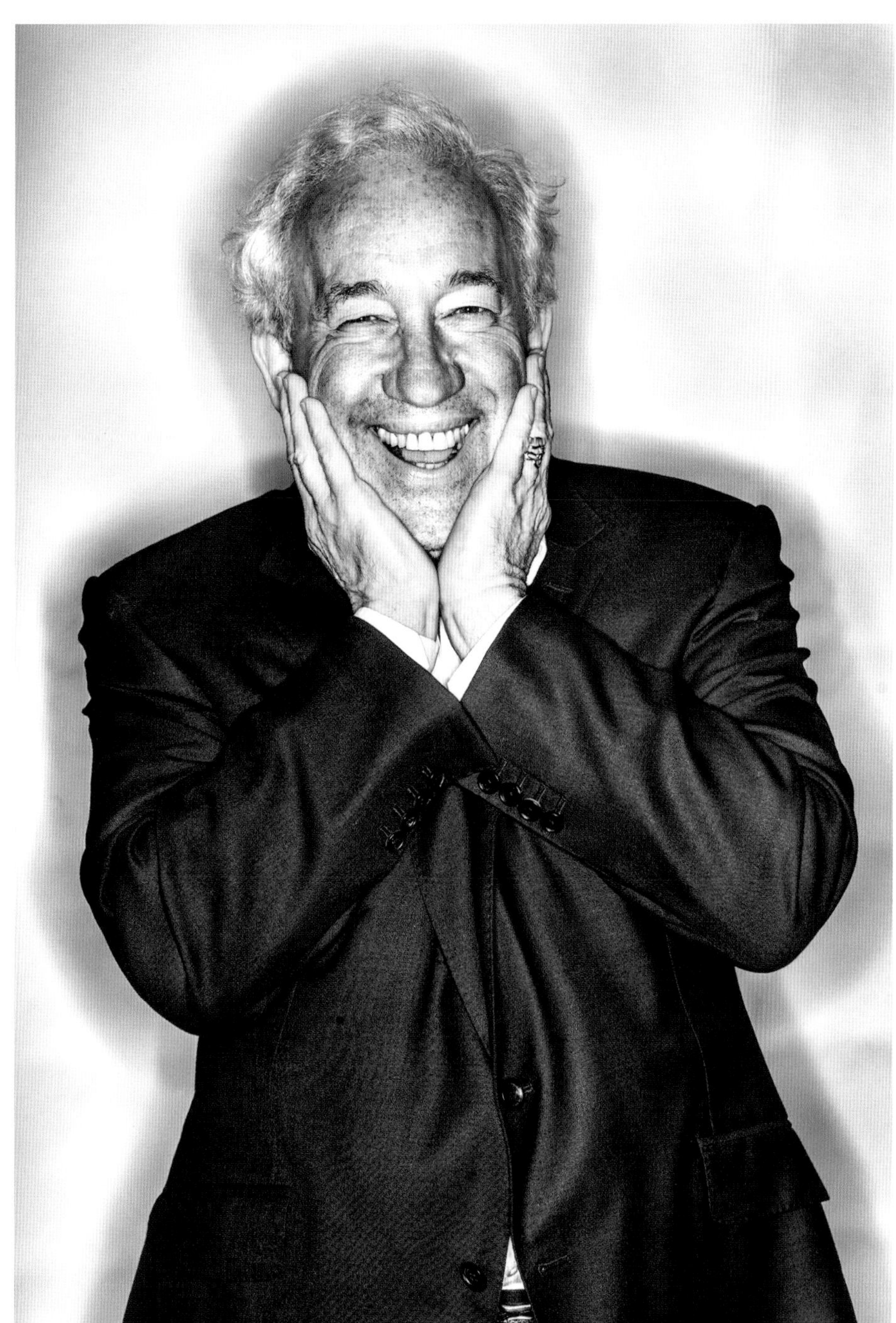

Poor Melanie was rather poorly when this was shot. A writer on environmental issues hence the leaves, which were taken from a nearby tree in a rather unenvironmental way. Photographically this feels like my homage to the singer Kate Bush. It has a sensual serenity that appeals, we are both fans and our conversation about the singer led to this picture.

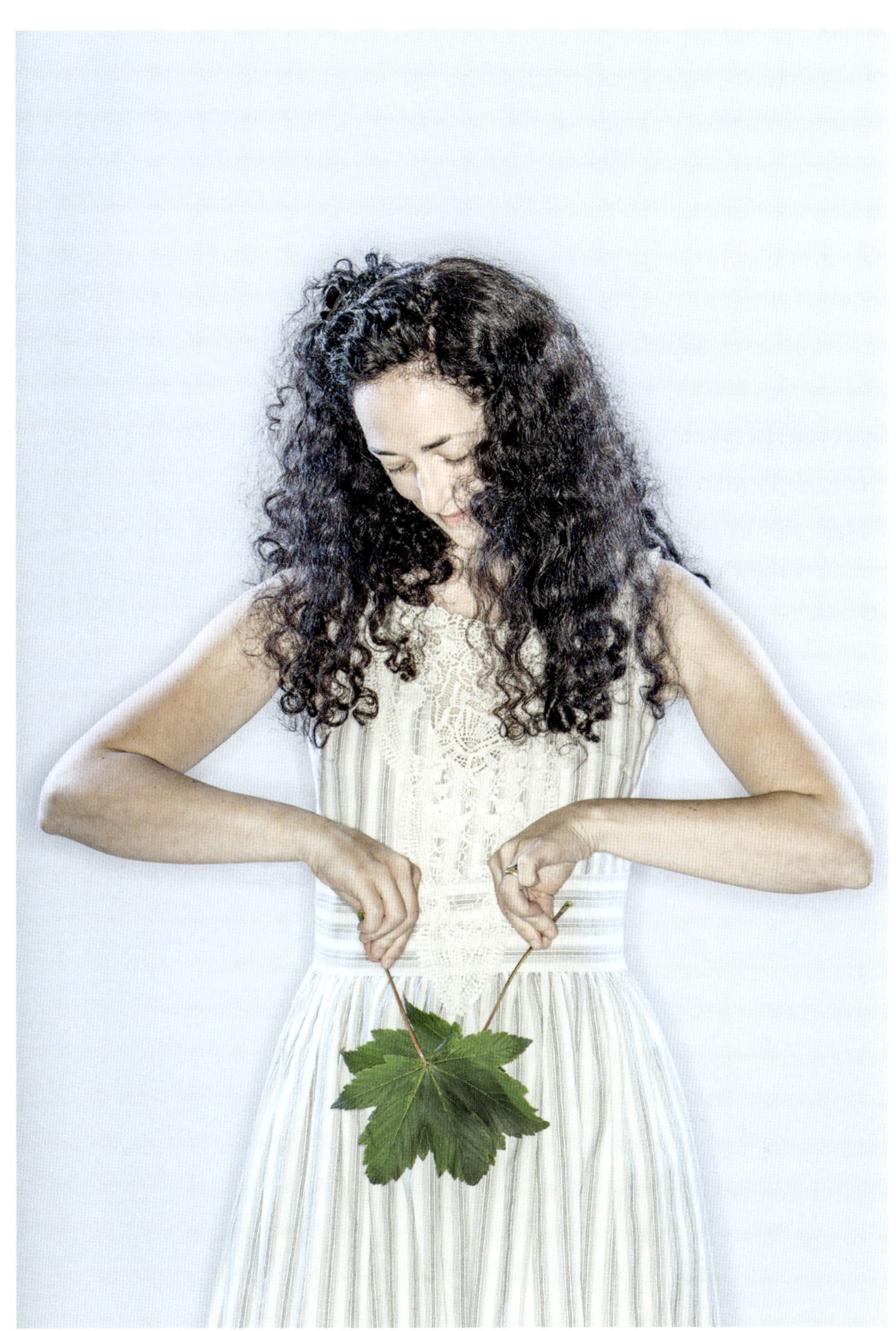

Most famous for her book the *Girl with the Pearl Earring* she has also written about female fossil hunters in Regency times on the Dorset Coast, *Remarkable Creatures*.

I wish I could recall what I said to Tracy at the time of taking this but it may or may not be repeatable.

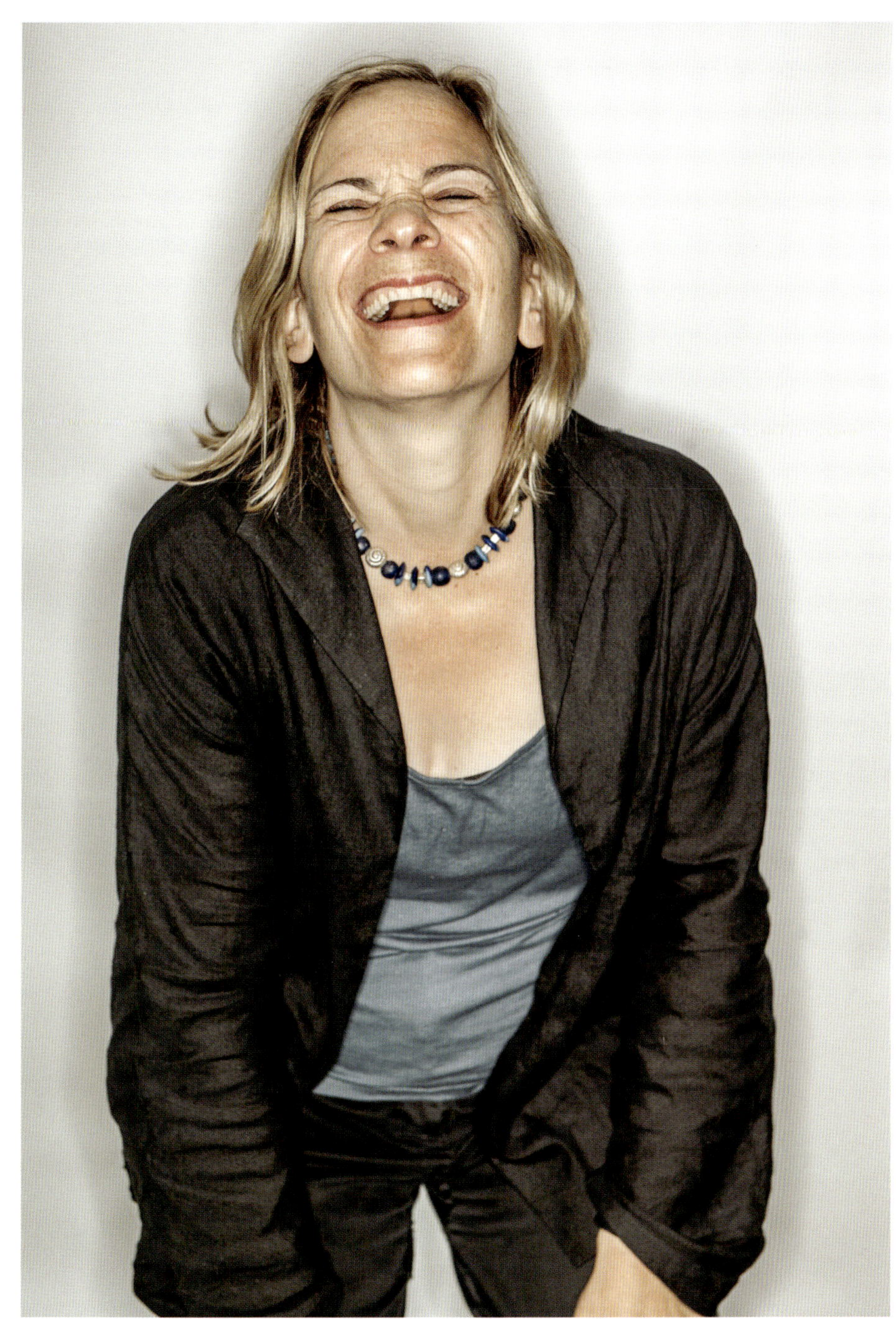

I showed Eoin this picture which drew the response:

> *'I wish I still looked that angsty and grainy. I just look contented now.'*
>
> EOIN COLFER

Well that's the result of writing a worldwide successful series of *Artemis Fowl* books, described as 'Die Hard with Fairies'. Eoin writes both children's and adult fiction. He has one of those faces where the older he gets the more photogenic he will become, contented or otherwise.

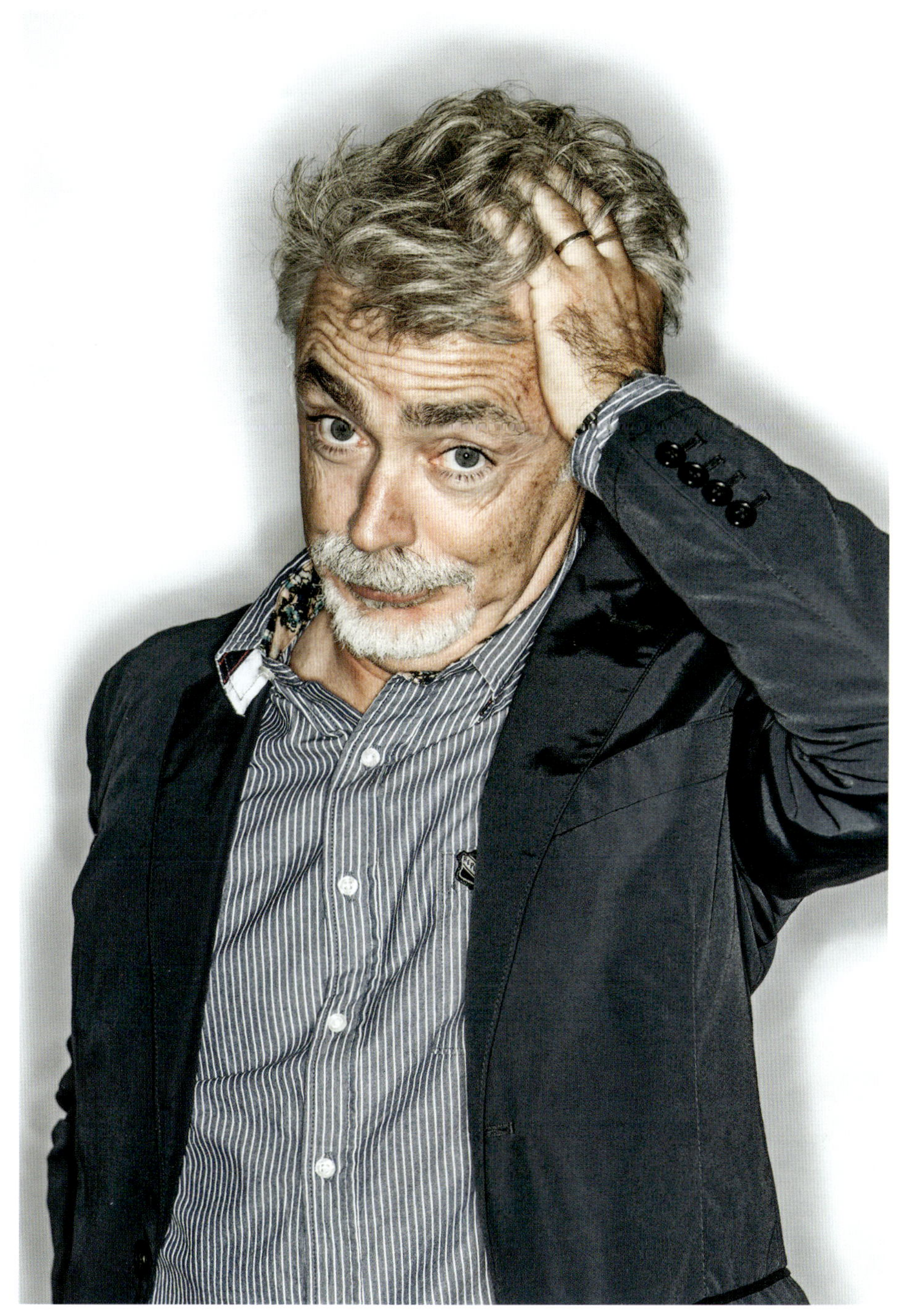

'Teju Cole is among the most gifted writers of his generation.'

SALMAN RUSHDIE

A portrait does not need to include the person's face. I have photo-graphed the backs of heads, faces hidden behind clocks or cloths, people with hands in front of their faces.

However to me a portrait should be of a person. I struggle with the idea of a portrait of animals. Anthropomorphism of animals I understand but is that a portrait?

Teju is a keen photographer himself being, as he is, the photography critic of the *New York Times* magazine.

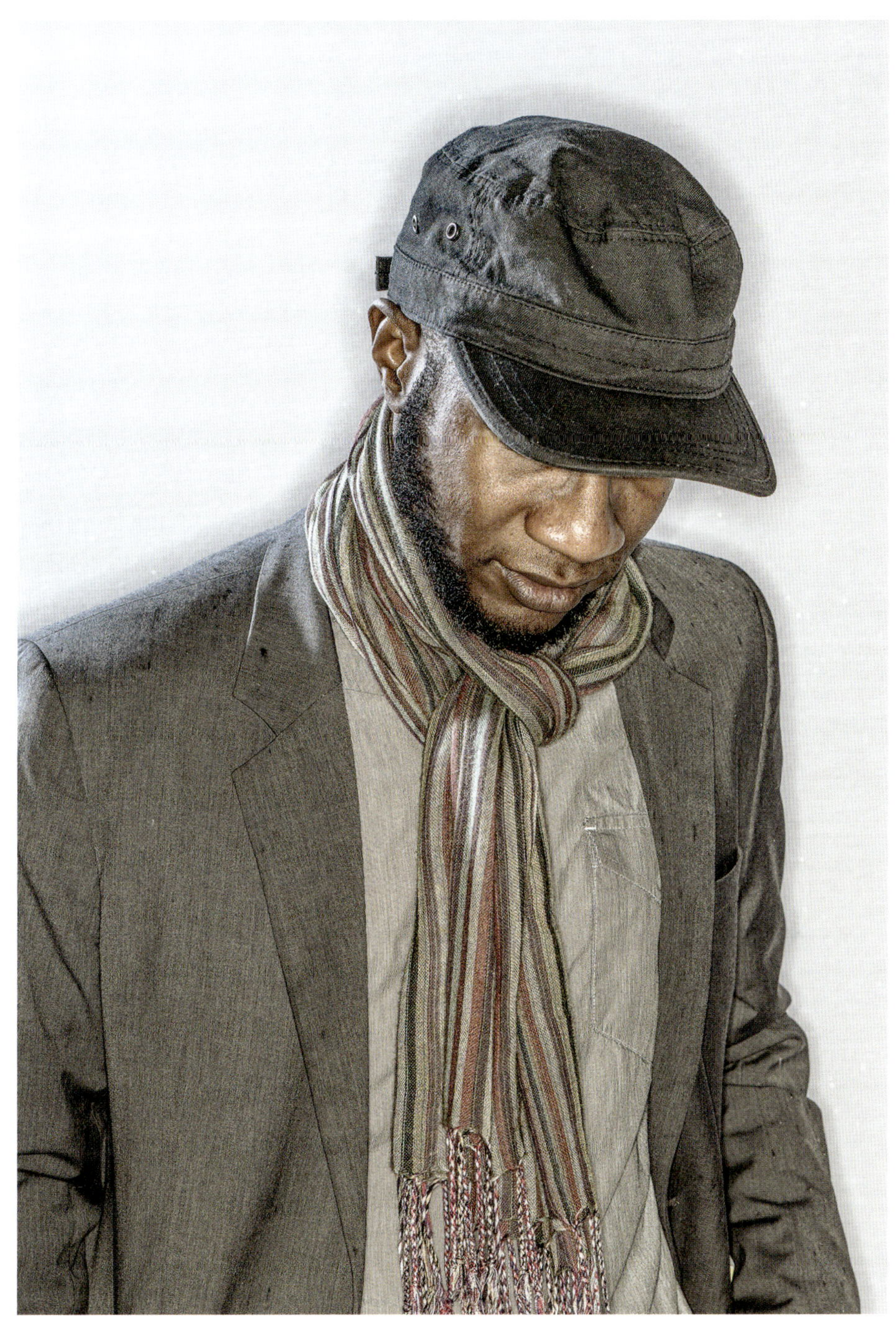

Nick Cope arrived and after talking for a few minutes said he had some glasses with him. Some? We began with two pairs then the challenge became how many he could wear at once. Risk visiting Nick's website and you may soon be singing along to his addictive tunes. The reason is he was originally lead singer of Britpop band The Candyskins. No relation to Julian Cope who also wears glasses and sings a bit.

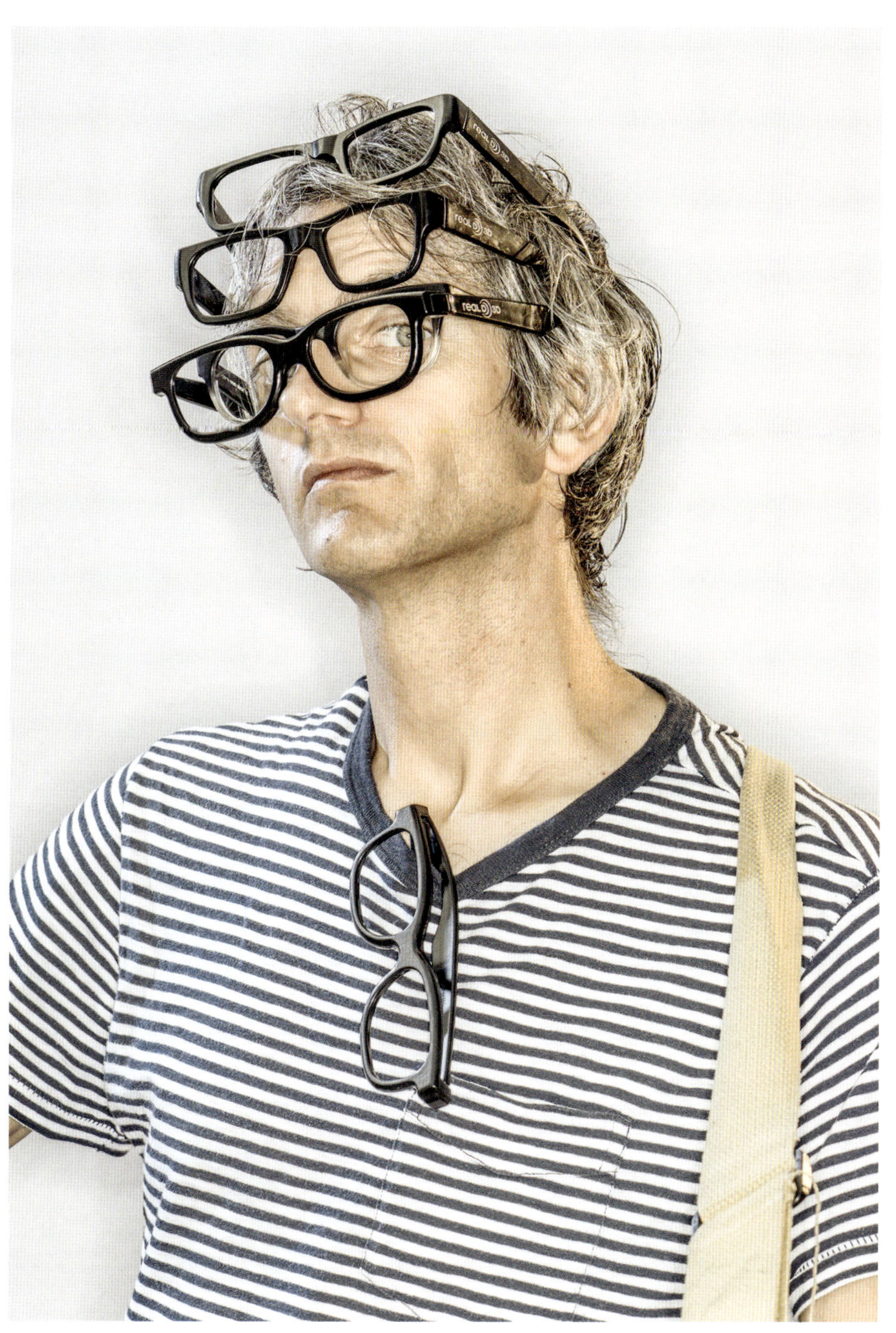

Frank has written for *Dr Who*.

He is also screenwriter, novelist and collaborator with filmaker, Michael Winterbottom and Danny Boyle with whom he wrote the opening ceremony of the London 2012 Olympics, based on *The Tempest*.

All very good but did I mention he has written for *Dr Who*.

Oh and it was raining . . . a lot. So no, he is not portraying a sea devil or other such, he is merely protecting himself from the deluge, such is one of the random elements thrown in to shooting studio portraits outside. Glamourous? No. Game? Yes.

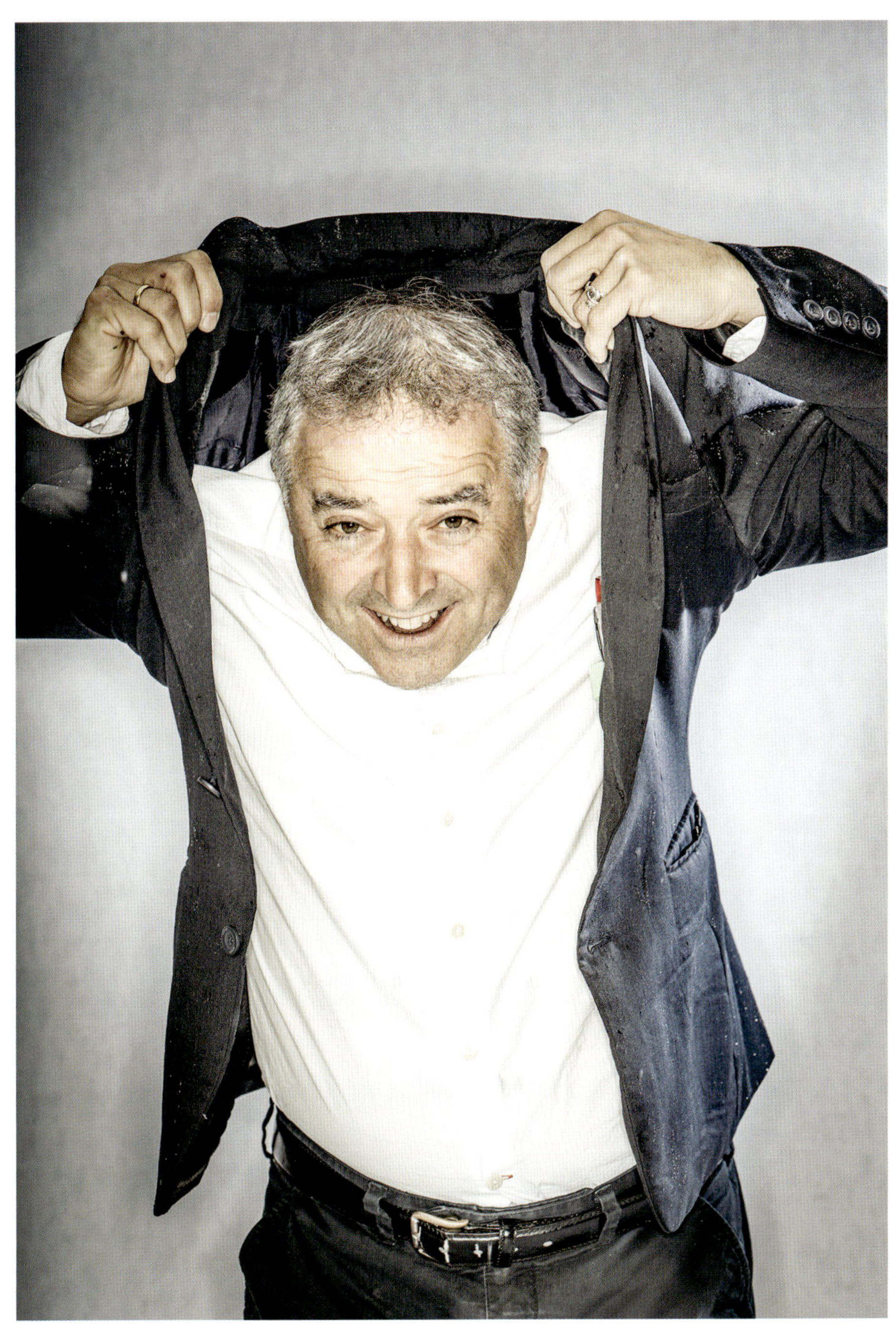

Mackenzie took his first name from a Scottish relative as there was an equity listed actor with his birth name, Paul James Crook.

'Have you heard of him?', he asked.

'Nope.'

'Exactly.'

Mackenzie is perhaps best known for *The Office* and chasing his eyeball around the decks in *Pirates of the Caribbean* films.

With authors I very often have to work hard to get them to relax and bring something of themselves to the surface. With actors almost the opposite is true. They are so used to portraying different characters in front of cameras that you question whether they are revealing their true selves.

Generally when things are going well I do not art direct people too much but this felt like a genuine portrait.

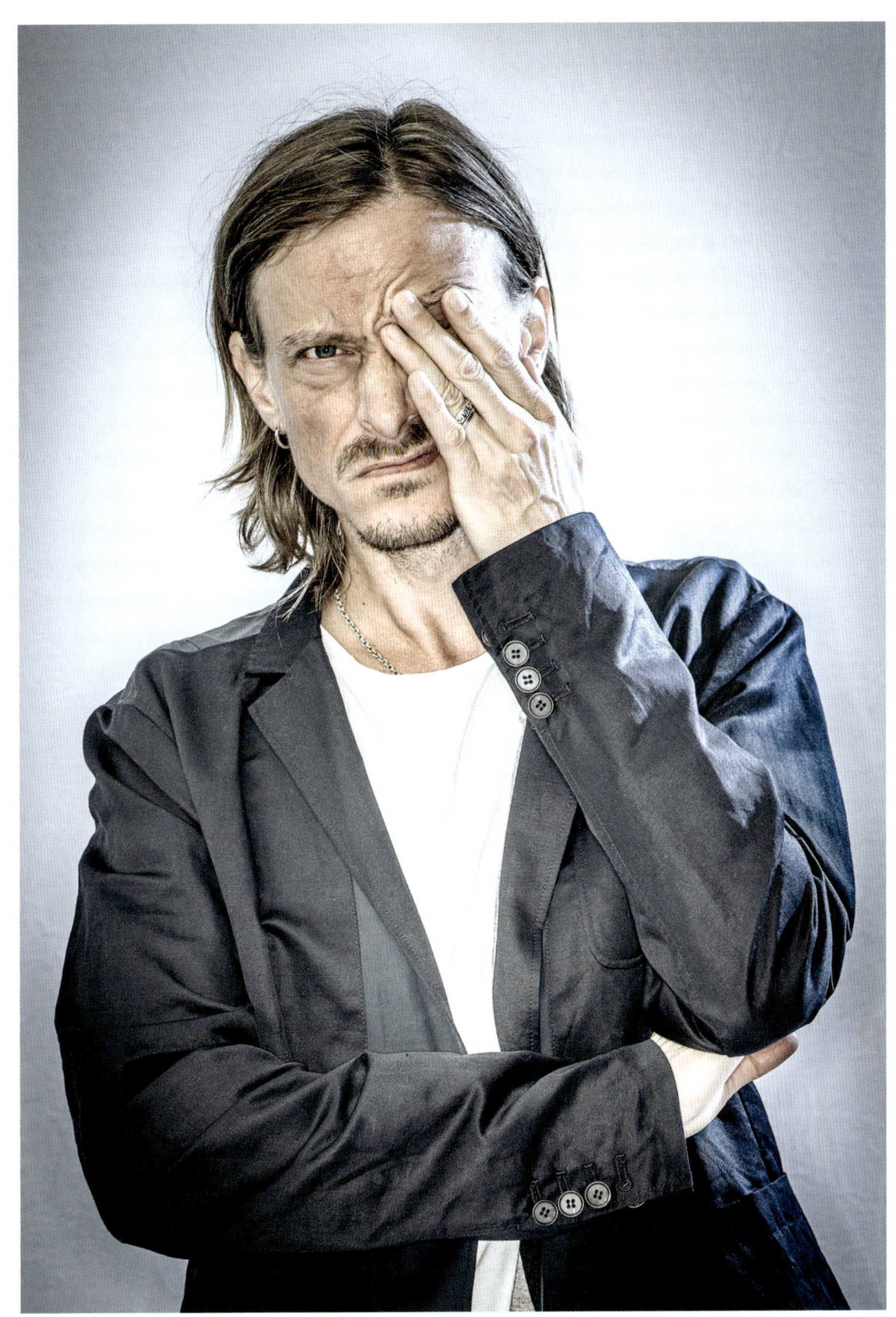

Children's authors often resonate to the energy of their youthful audience. It is one of the reasons I enjoy photographing them. There is almost a child-like vivacity to this picture. That said, Nicola was initially a reluctant model but was soon embracing the moment and forgetting to be shy.

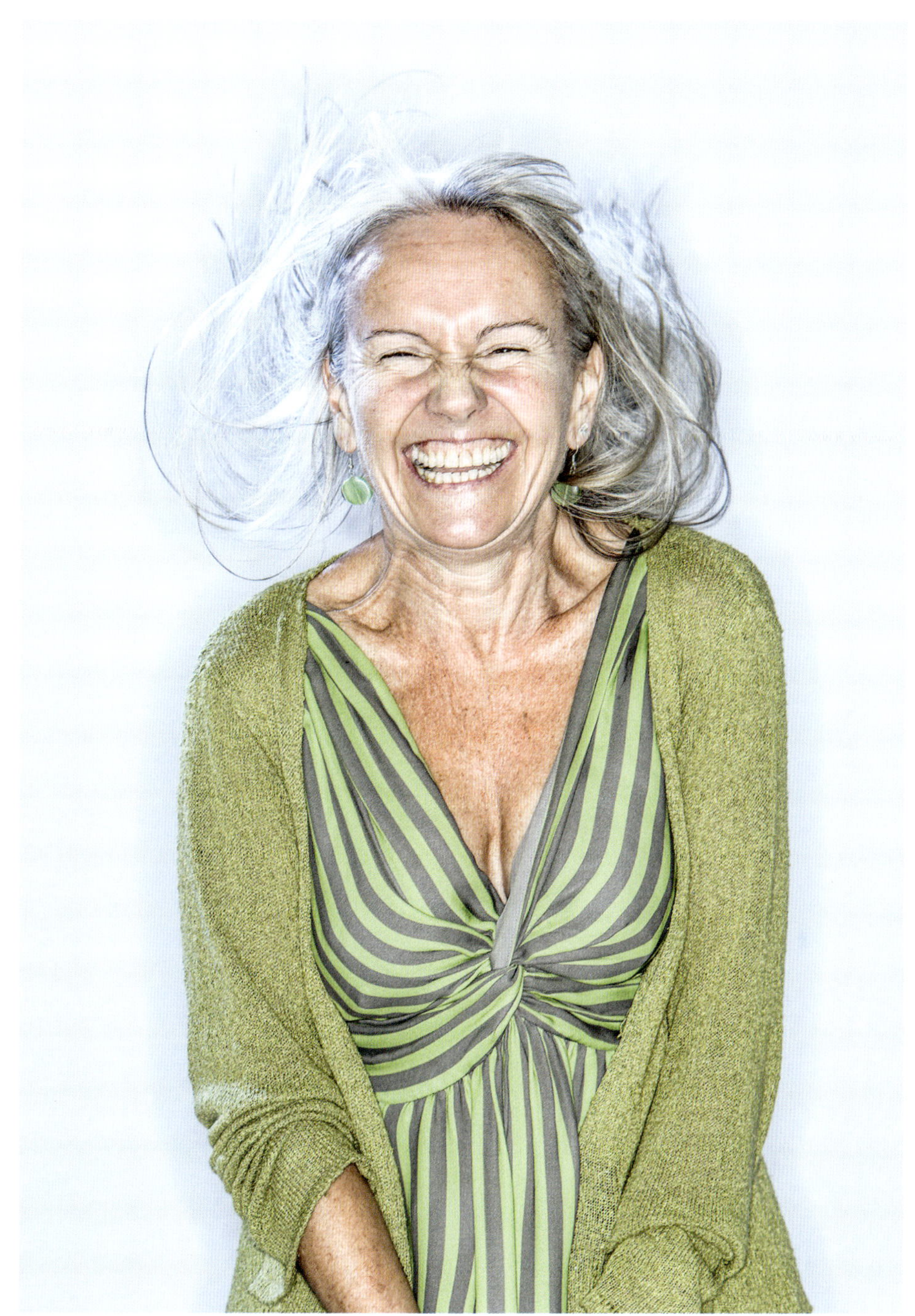

Writer, Philosopher. I opted for a cubist approach to Swiss born Alain de Botton, breaking up this picture of Alain to try and represent a philosopher whose work also draws on influences from artists and thinkers. It combines several images from the series.

'My greatest joy comes from creativity: from feeling that I have been able to identify a certain aspect of human nature and crystallise a phenomenon in words.'

ALAIN DE BOTTON

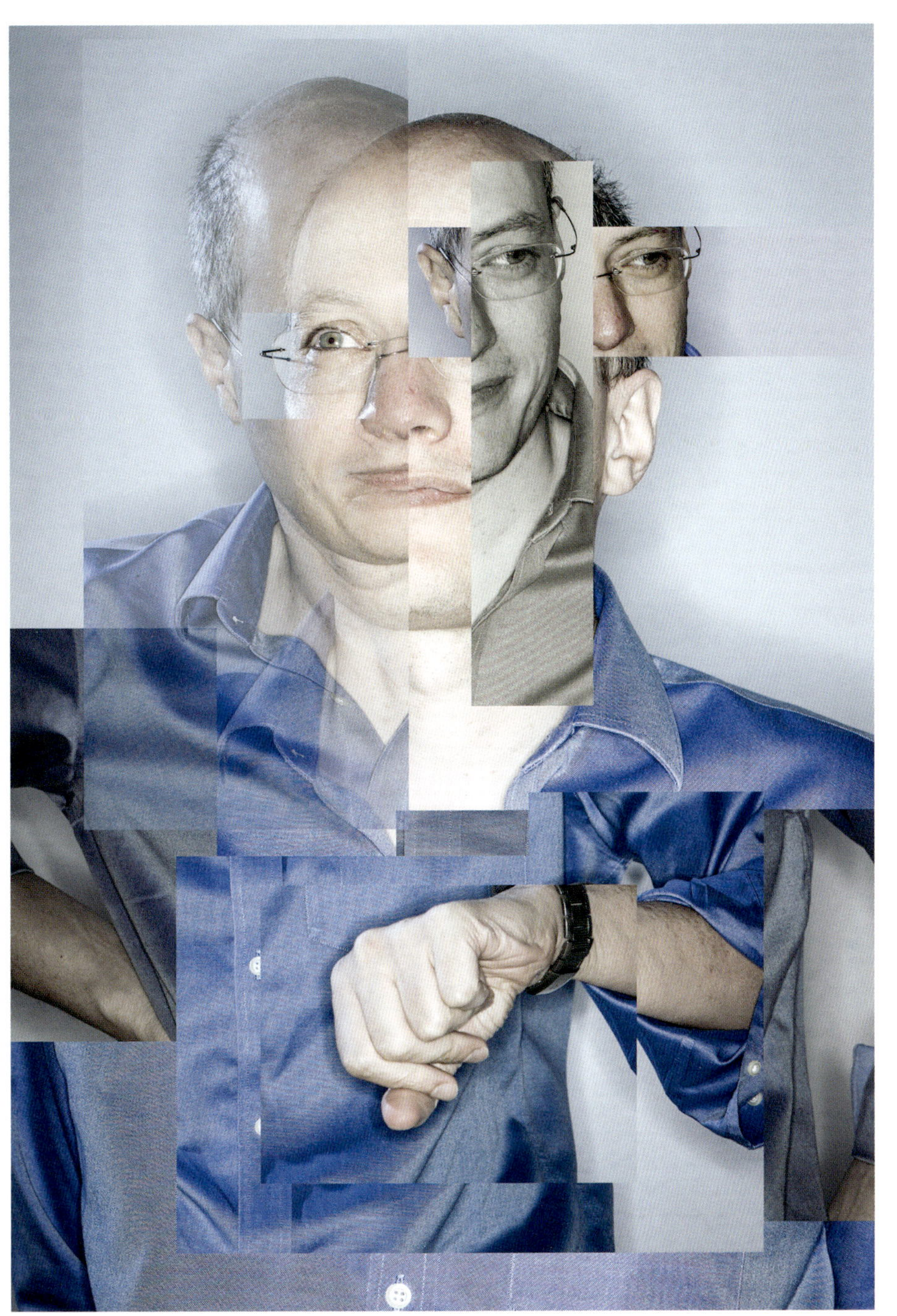

William Dalrymple

'India has always had a strange way with her conquerors. In defeat, she beckons them in, then slowly seduces, assimilates and transforms them.'

White Mughals: Love and Betrayal in Eighteenth-Century India

William lives outside Delhi so like Fatima Bhutto finds the outside temperatures in Scotland somewhat lacking. It also means he has an inside-outside perspective on both Asia and the UK. 'Mr William, he said, in my life six times have I crashed, and on not one occasion have I ever been killed,' said a taxi driver from city of Djinns.

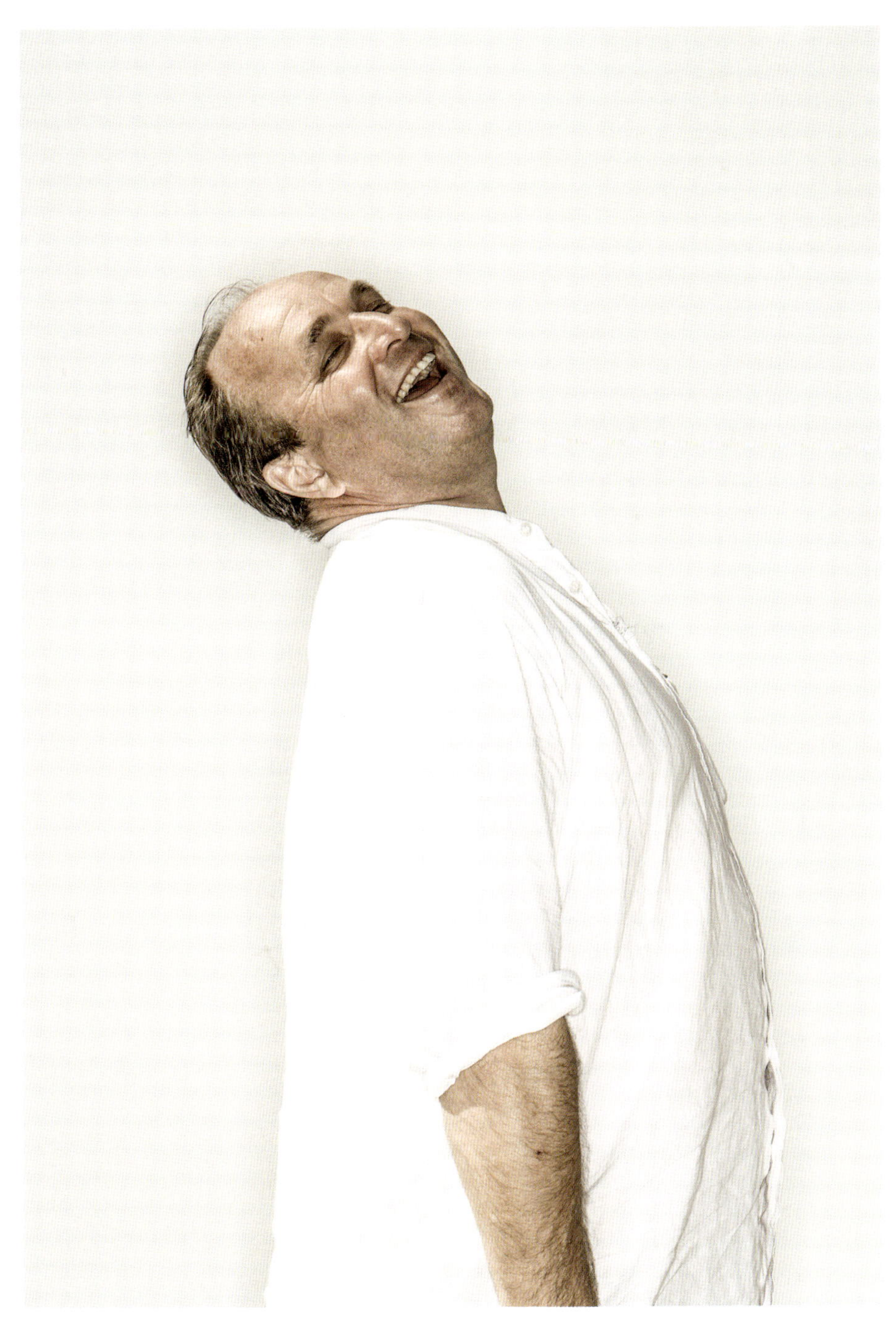

Britain's Poet Laureate whose wonderful poem called 'Valentine' features the line 'I Give You an Onion' and so, I gave her an onion!

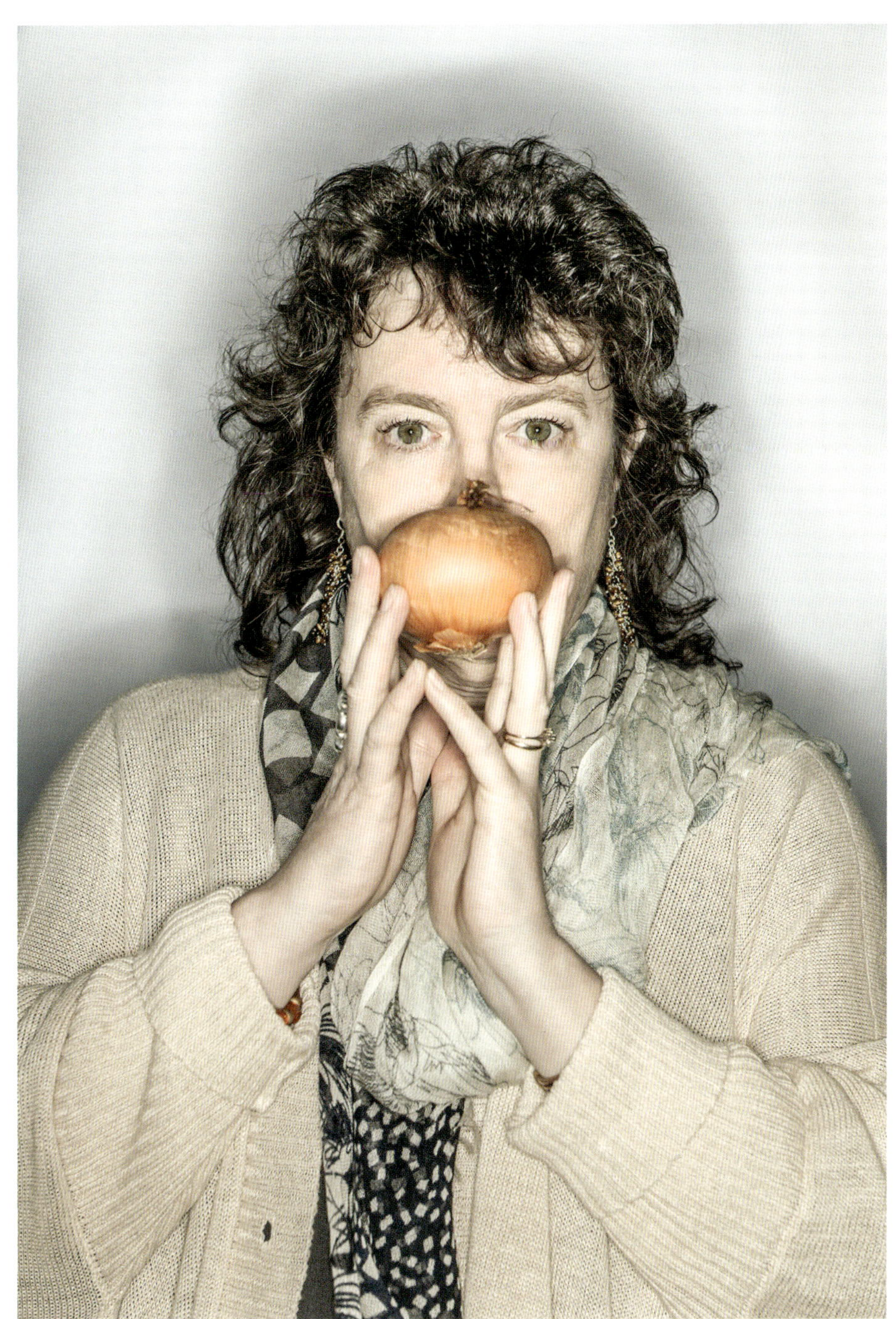

The Bubble Wrap Boy is the title of one of Phil's books. He mentioned this as we chatted beforehand. Perfect. Stage left there was some bubble wrap and after nearly suffocating Phil, (I am allowed a certain amount of collateral damage annually!), I managed to allow him some air to breathe and tears so that he could see.

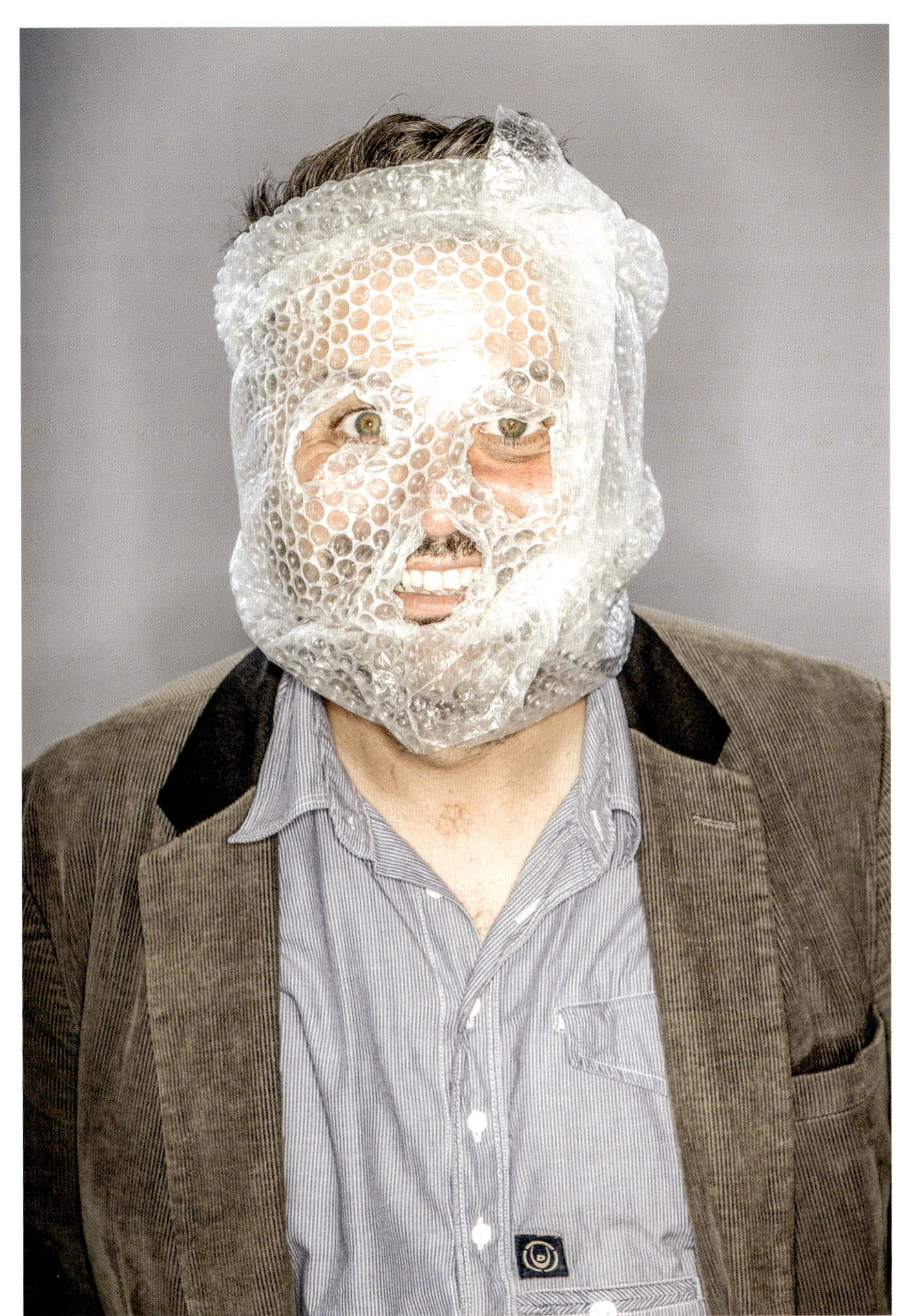

'So when you arrived in Edinburgh and saw the castle did you think that was your B&B?' was my opening gambit with Will Fiennes. Will had grown up on a large private estate in England although often wished for a more humble abode, akin to his peers. I love the lack of vanity in this image. We spoke about castles, epilepsy and girls. As you do.

To the best of my knowledge he has only written two books, *The Snow Geese* and *The Music Room*. I went walking with Will in the South of France and asked him about it, to which he replied, 'If the internet had existed in Dickens' times, he would never have written as much either.'

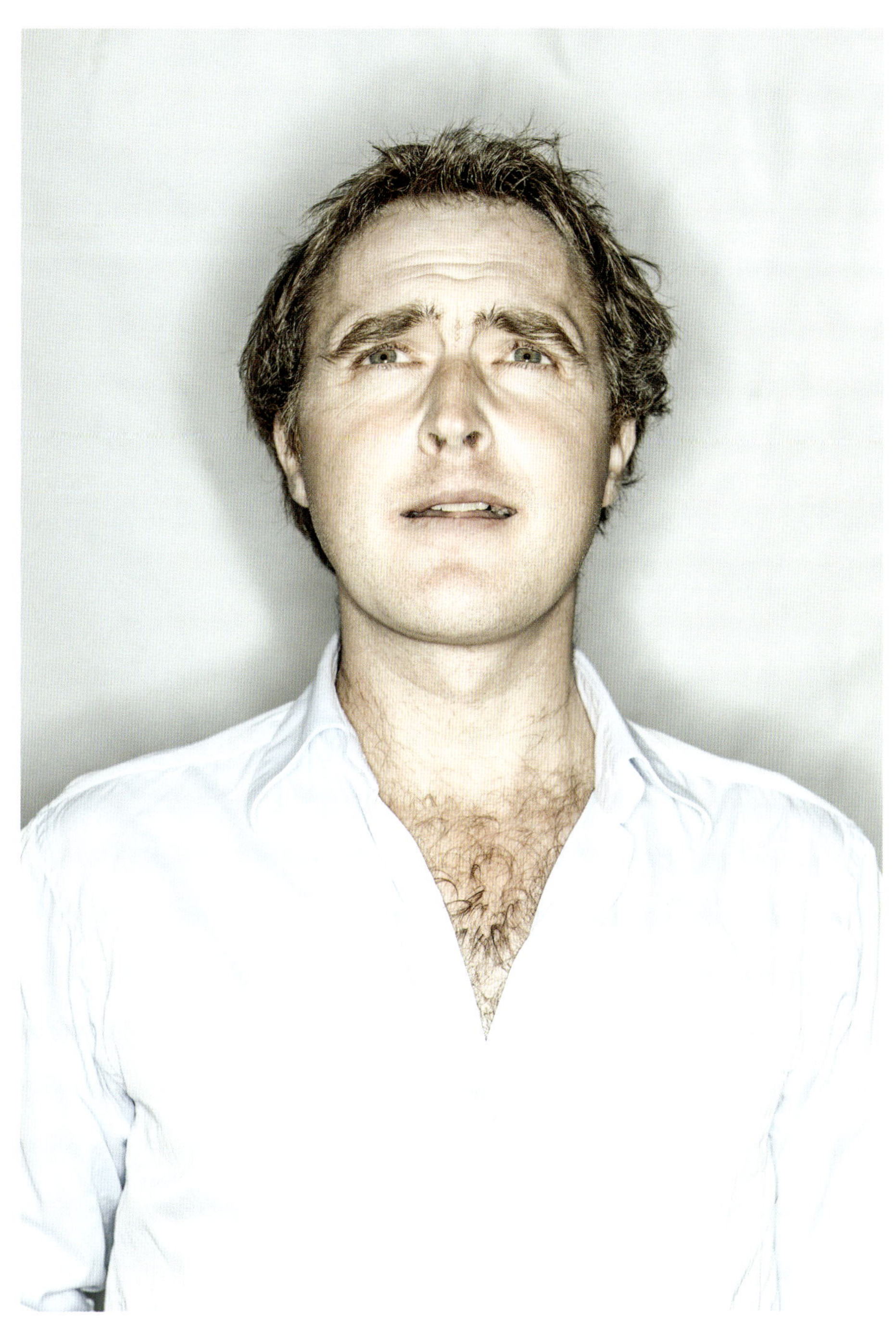

Best selling thriller writer, Frederick's background in the RAF and diplomatic service was ideal training ground for writing cold war novels, some of which have made the silver screen, although parts of his own life would make a good screenplay too.

I was once on the film set of *The Fourth Protocol* which featured the Russians trying to break up NATO by exploding an atomic bomb in the UK. In fact they were trying to blow up Milton Keynes where it was filmed!

He is almost Churchillian in demeanour.

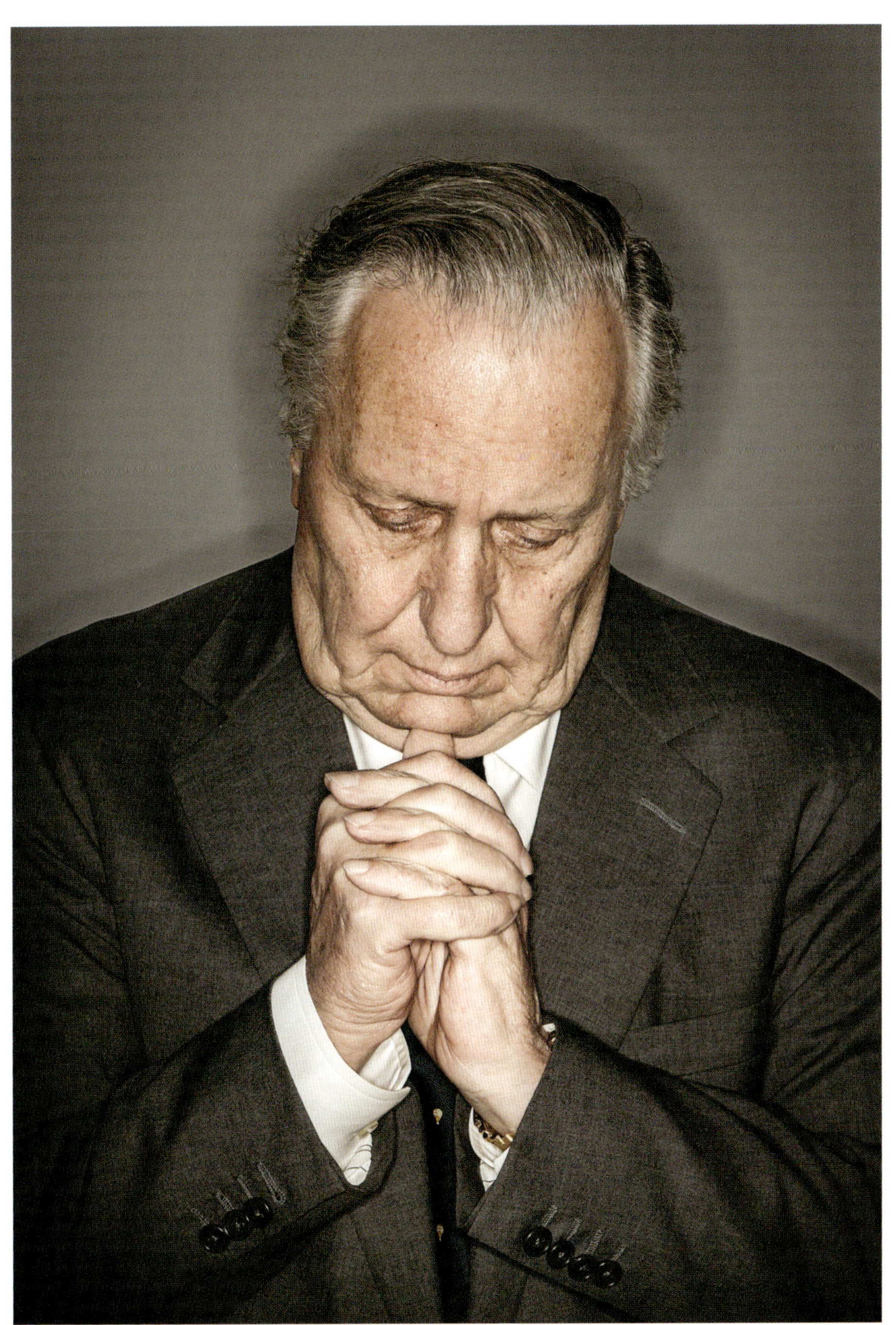

'*Cambridge produces in abundance talents with the ability to please, but few with that greater ability to disregard whether they please or not.*'

MICHAEL FRAYN

I am not sure whether it is a greater ability but I think in true portraiture, pleasing the subject should be far from your mind. Sometimes it works out that way, people like to look at others in my pictures and not themselves.

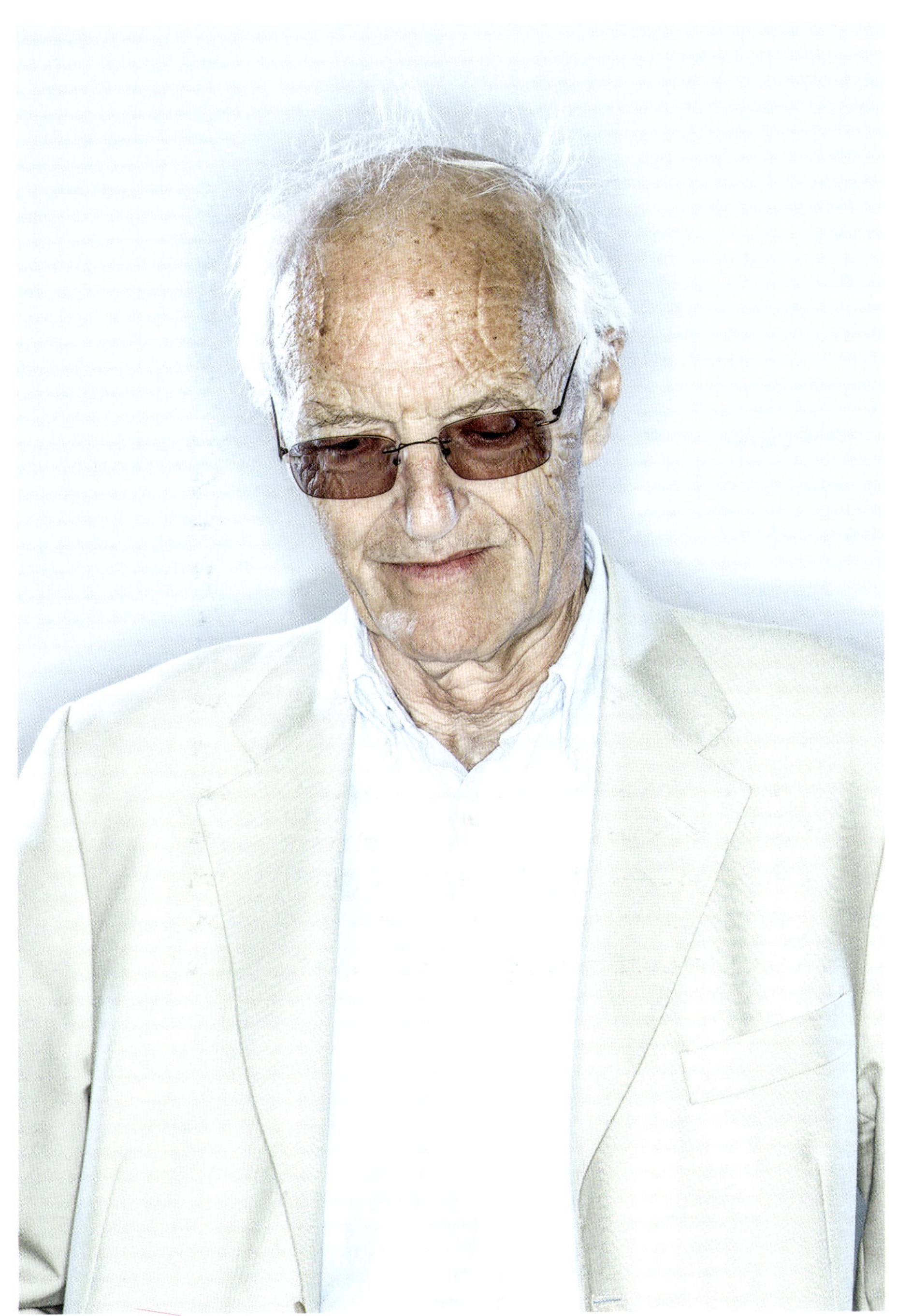

I have never been greeted by cheers and a round of applause to revealing a portrait before.

The Outlander series made Diana massive and I mean that purely in the terms of her fan base. She wrote the global best seller without having visited Scotland. She was very much in demand and so my time was very short.

I managed to shoot this and an hour later it was on view at the exhibition before her adoring fans.

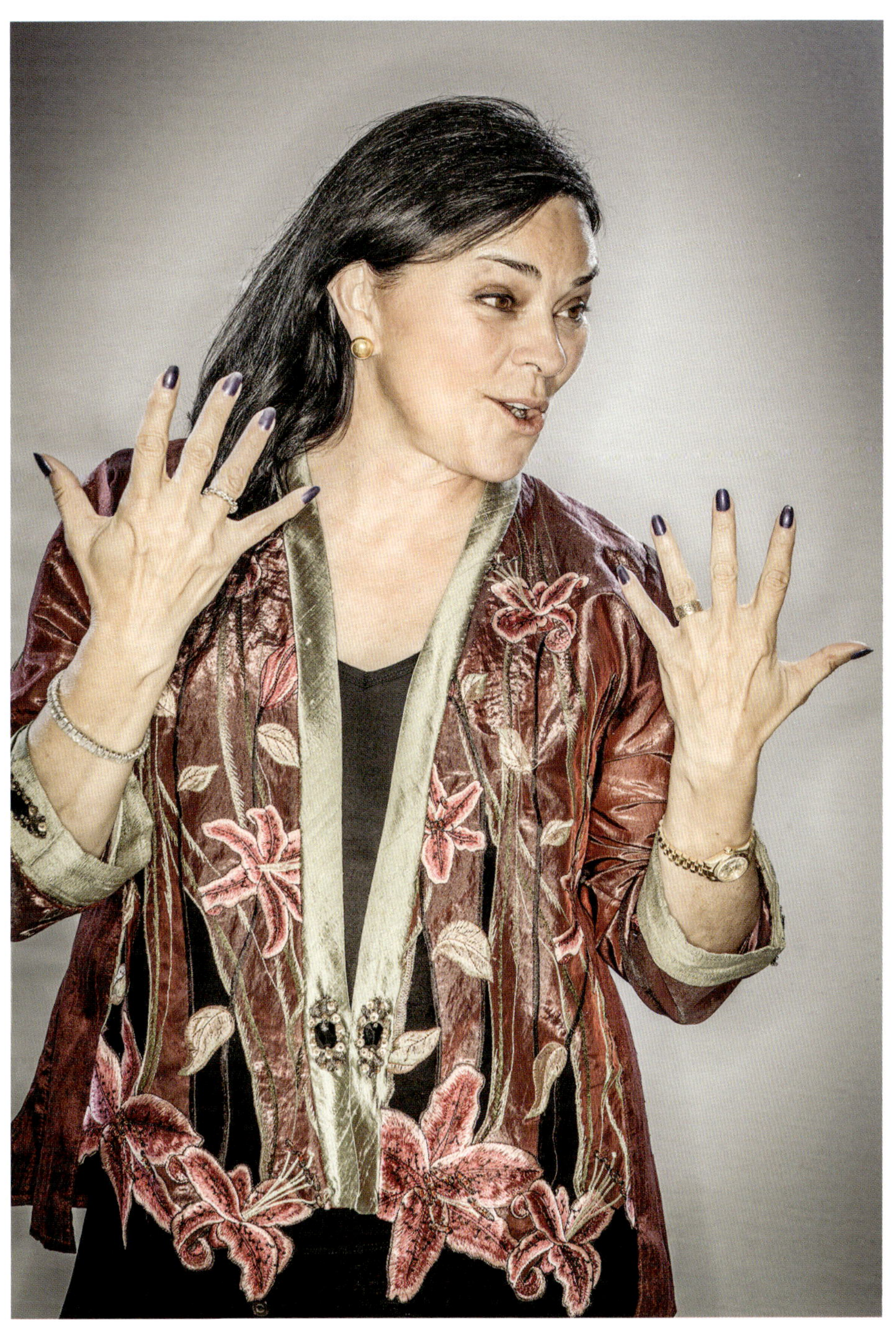

Neil, the man in black, is the literary equivalent of a rock God, prolific in novels, graphic novels and on Twitter. He attracts fans most authors can only dream of. I have been fortunate enough to photograph him a couple of times. The second time he asked, 'Why haven't you done a book of these portraits?'

One of Neil's creations is *The Sandman* series. I spotted some sand conveniently lying in the gardens. The sand was a bit damp so I spent a while trying to dry it in the blazing heat of the Scottish sun!

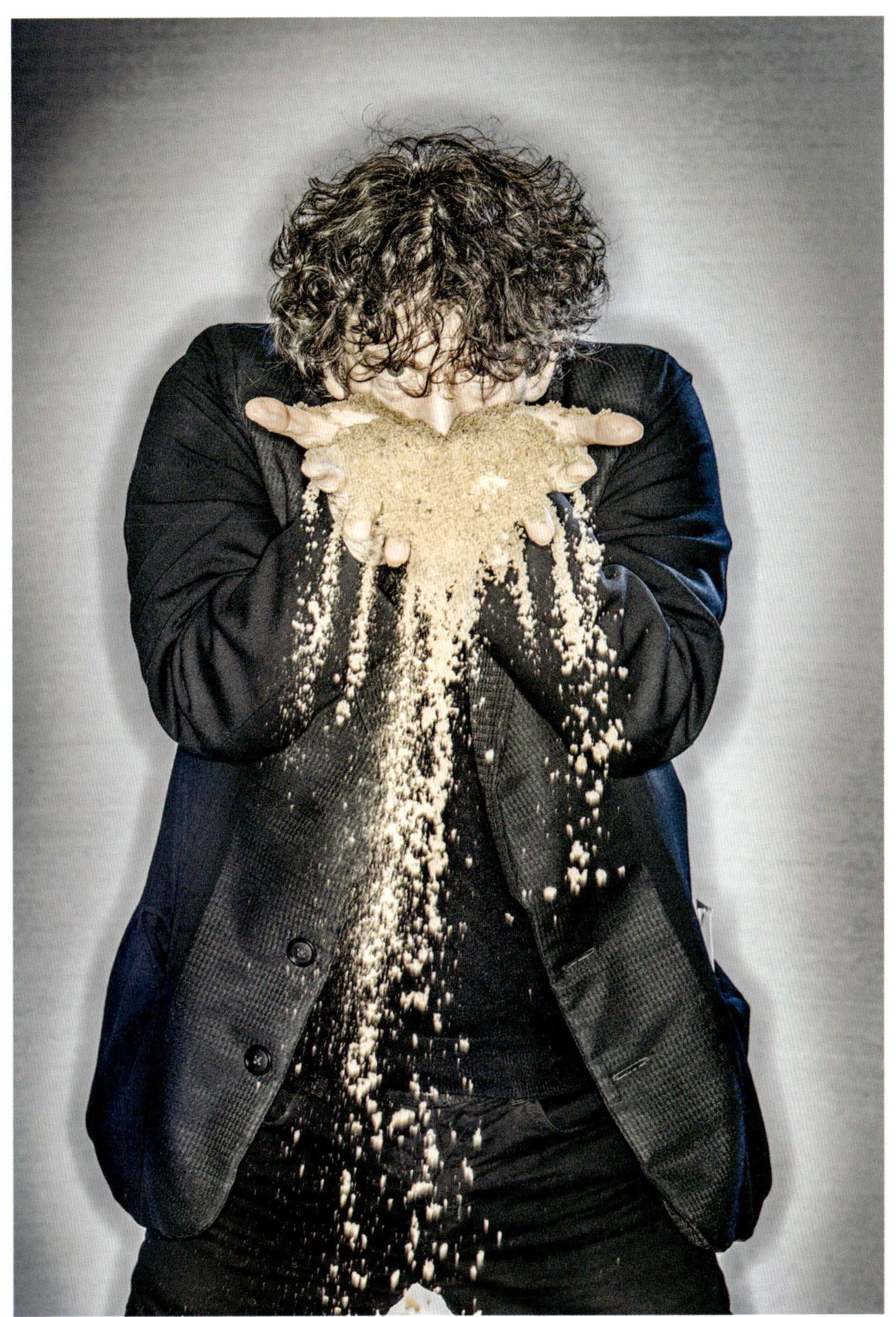

Janice Galloway was introduced to me by the writer and critic, Stuart Kelly. It progressed from a sober shoot to this. The lack of a specific brief affords the author and myself complete freedom to act and react to whichever 'Foreign Parts' a shoot may take us. We had a ball doing this.

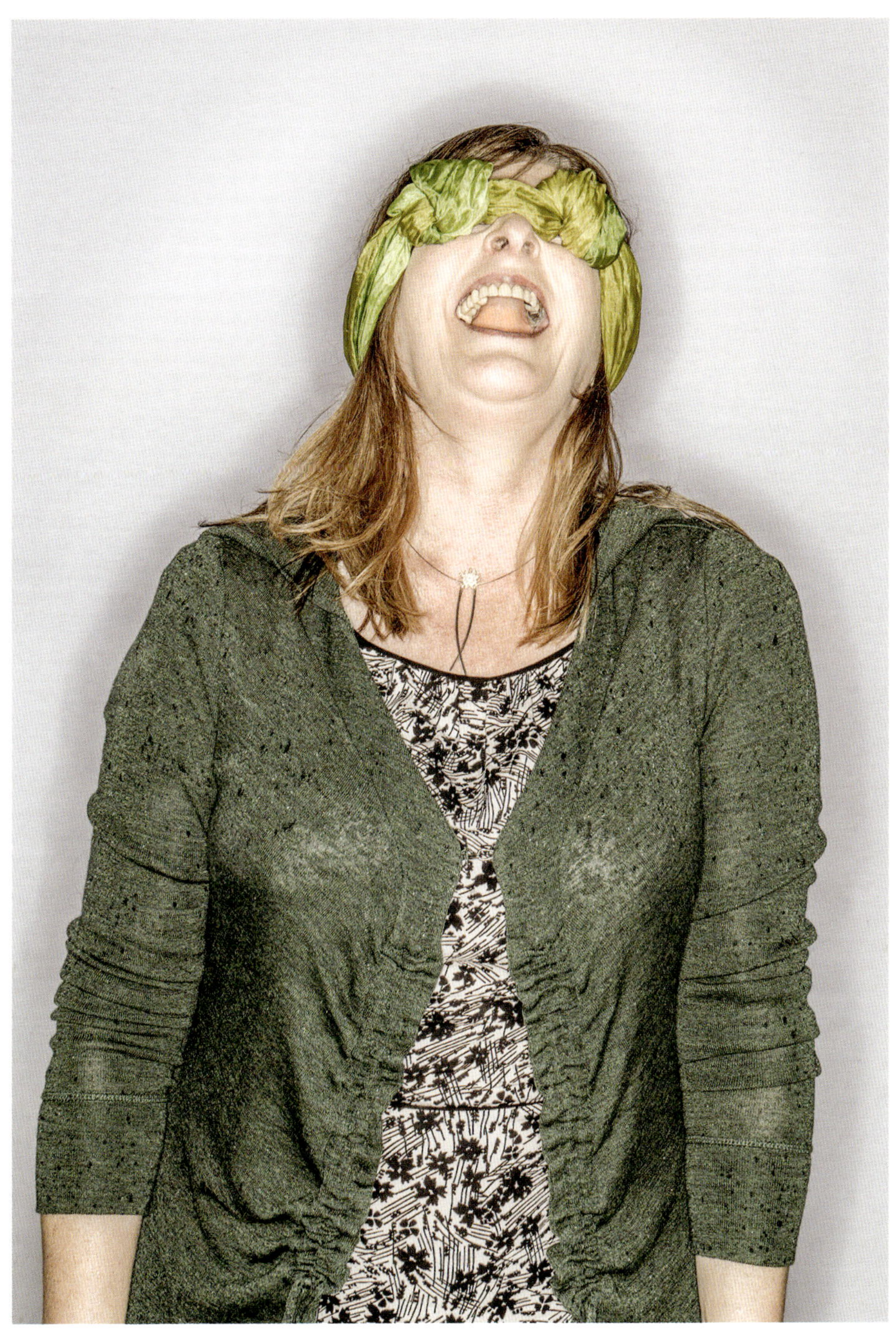

Author, comedian and presenter Dave Gorman, looking deliberately Gormless. I presented this idea to him and was fully prepared for a rebuffal but not only is that not in his nature, he was fully obliging. The eyes are all Dave's own work but sadly did not survive too long after this shoot.

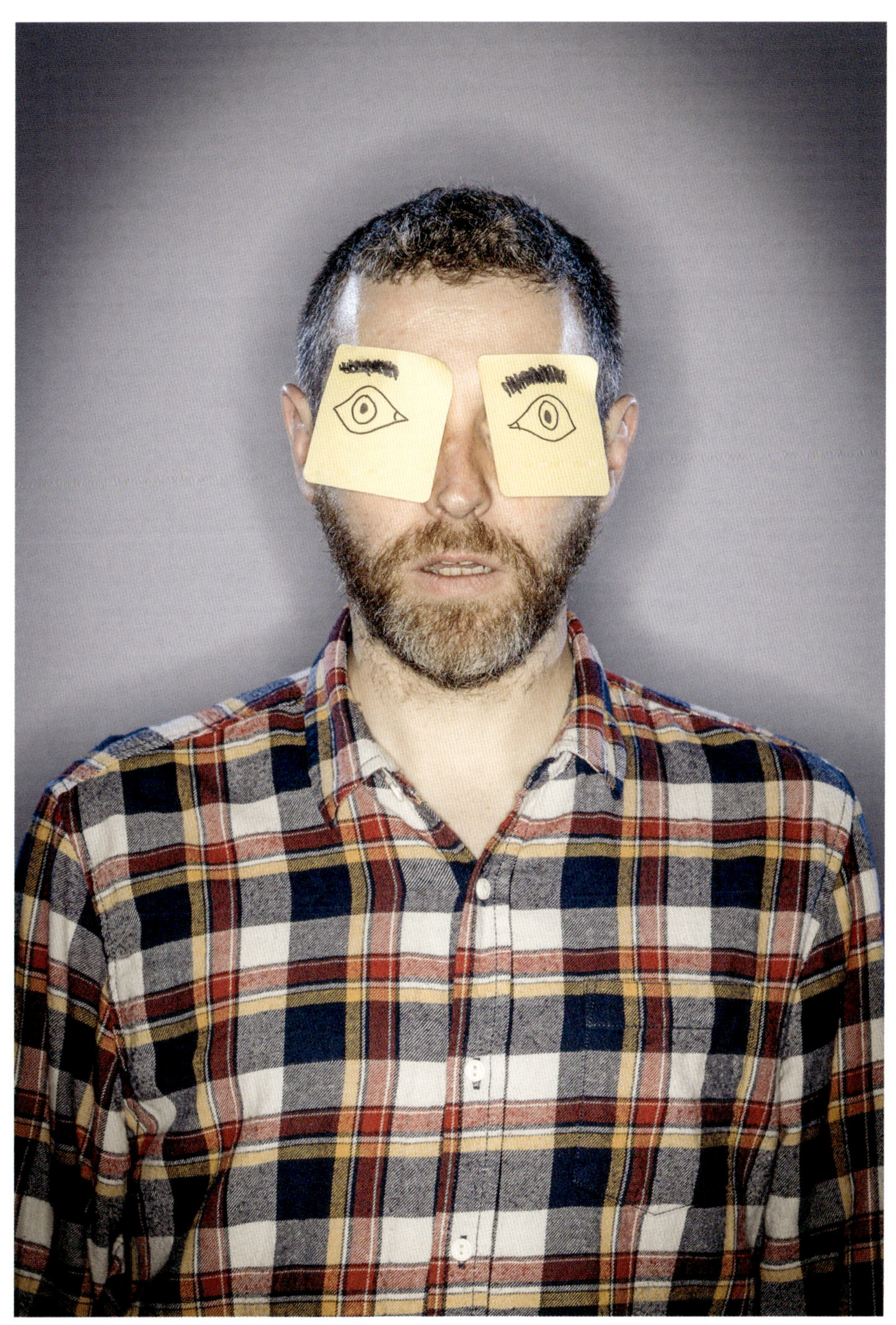

One of Scotland's most celebrated authors, I shot this, oblivious to his fame, notoriety and critical acclaim. His publicist came up to me and asked if I would like to shoot Alasdair. He had just finished a talk and signing and was sitting outside finishing a small whisky. 'Of course,' was my reply. Twenty minutes later along came this dishevelled individual who looked not so much like he had been dragged through a hedge as launched himself at it with reckless abandon. He stood there clutching his latest book and pointing at it.

'I don't want your book in shot,' I insisted, but he was adamant he had to have it, so that is what he is pointing to off frame. Sorry Alasdair.

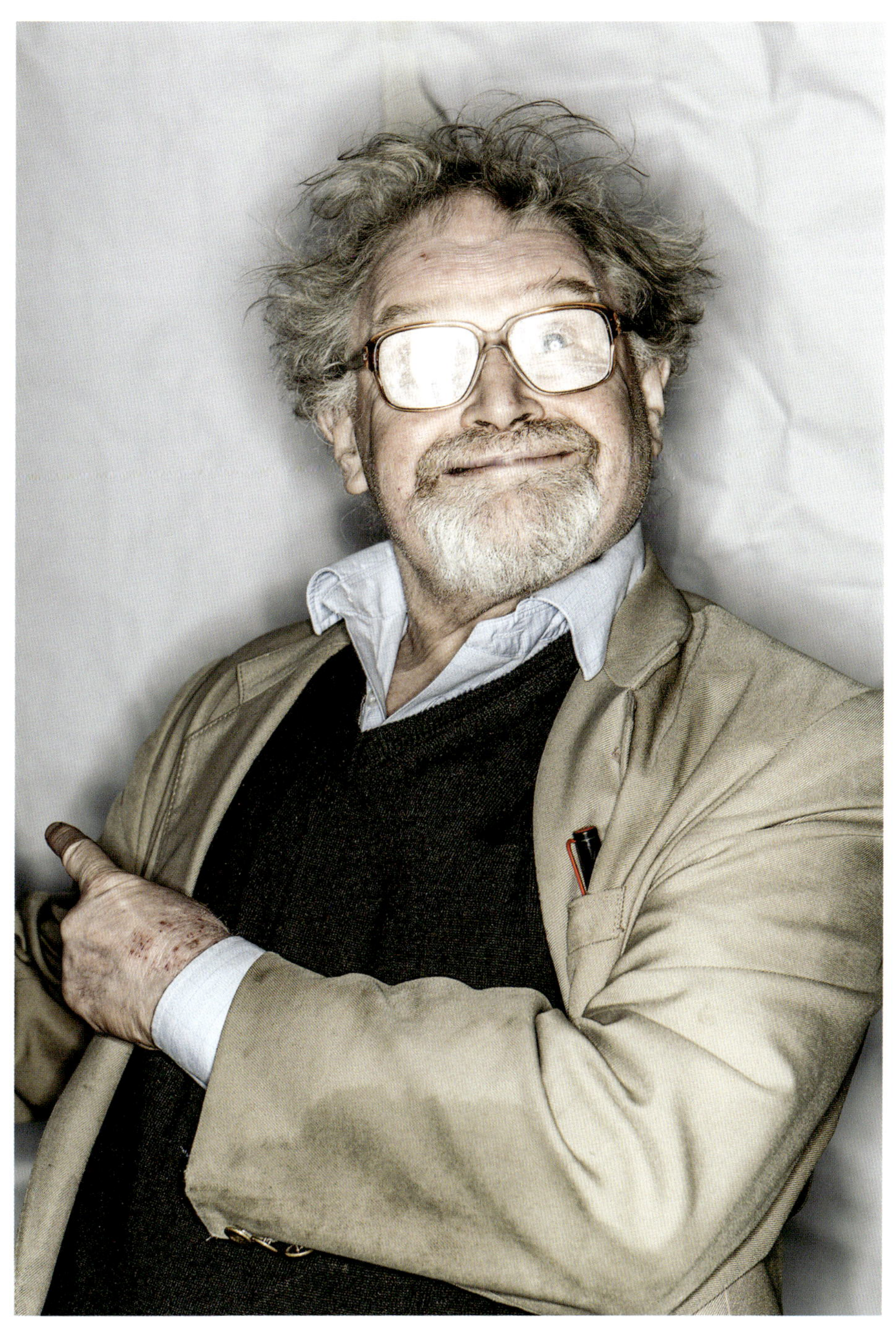

Bonnie wrote a book called *Entropy* which I mentioned whilst photographing her. 'Men always pick up on that book,' she said.

'Second law of thermodynamics,' I replied. 'Things move from a state of organisation to a state of chaos.'

. . . and so this picture is my interpretation of that law.

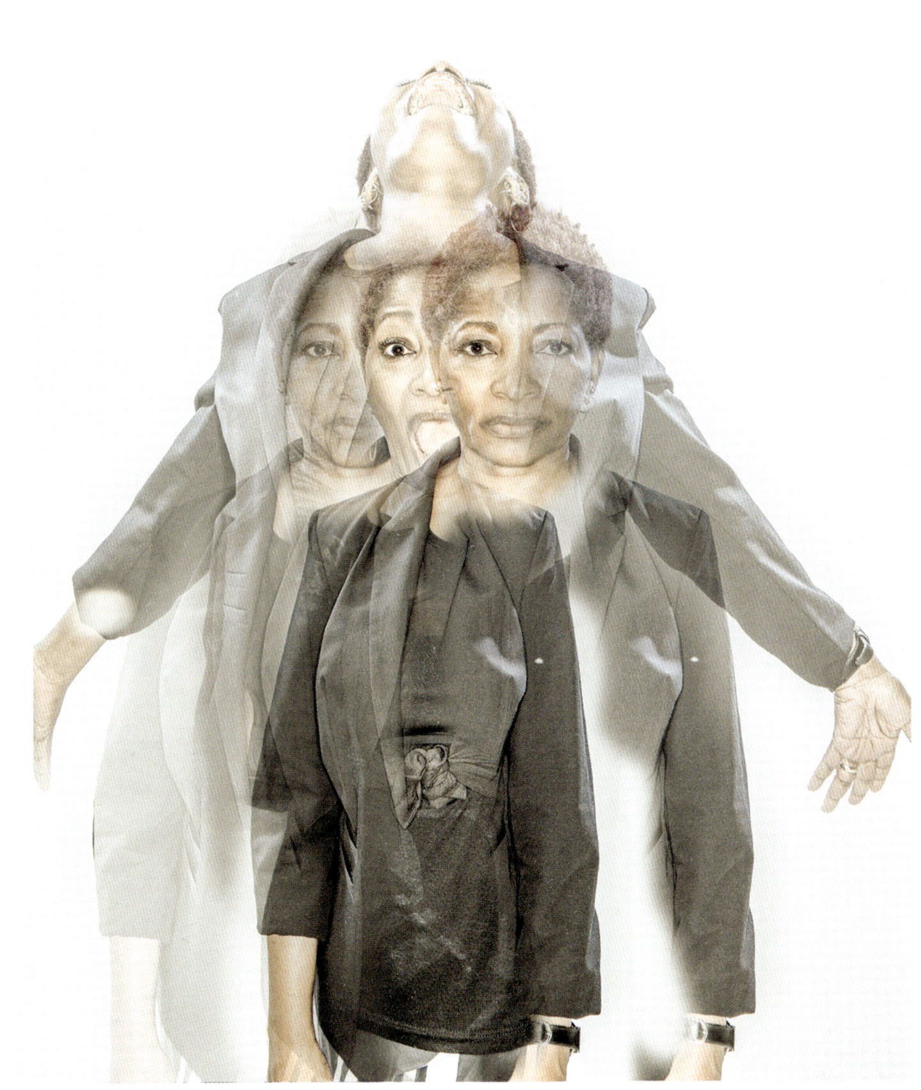

Nick, just prior to the shoot, struck by a flash of inspiration had sketched some ideas on his hand before he forgot them. I can empathise with this having lost any number of 'brilliant ideas' for want of pen and paper. You would never guess from his pen name or his real name, Nicholas Cornwall that he is the son of John Le Carré. He was a lovely guy full of energy and he also wore a hat therefore I am a big fan.

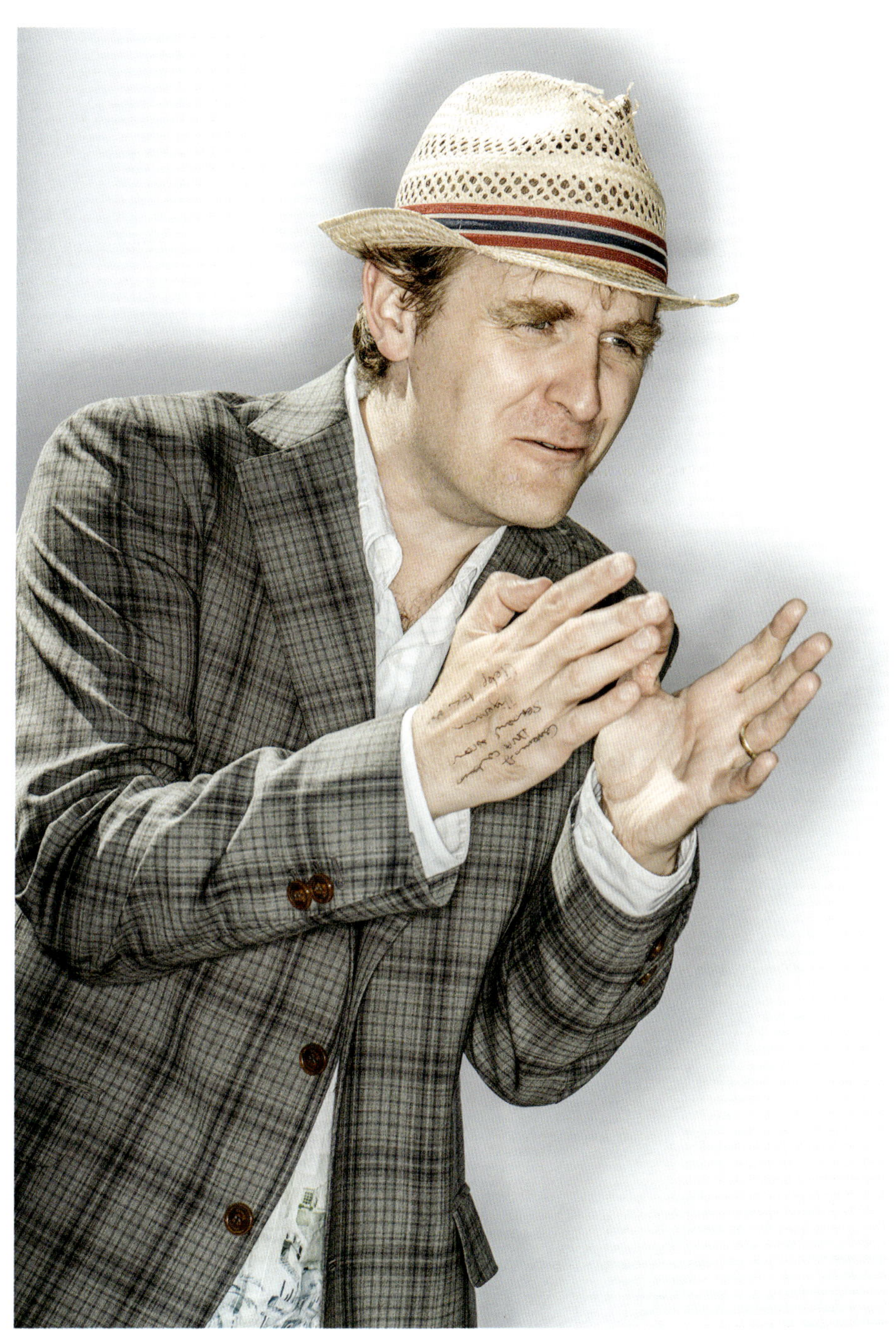

Seamus Heaney, Karl Miller and Andrew O'Hagan

'There's a horrible fallacy that exists in the popular discussion of fiction these days: the idea that a successful central character need be "likeable" or "sympathetic". It is surely more important that they be human, no?'

ANDREW O'HAGAN

I thought this quote from Andrew rung true to my approach to portraiture. A portrait to my mind should reflect humanity. Technicality is of secondary importance. Errors or imperfections are symptomatic of the human condition and thus an image where every little detail is intentionally perfected destroys the spontaneity and thus the humanity. I rarely begin with the end. A portrait is a development from the first frame to the last, albeit the time betwixt first and last can be painfully short.

Three giants of modern literature and sadly only one remains.

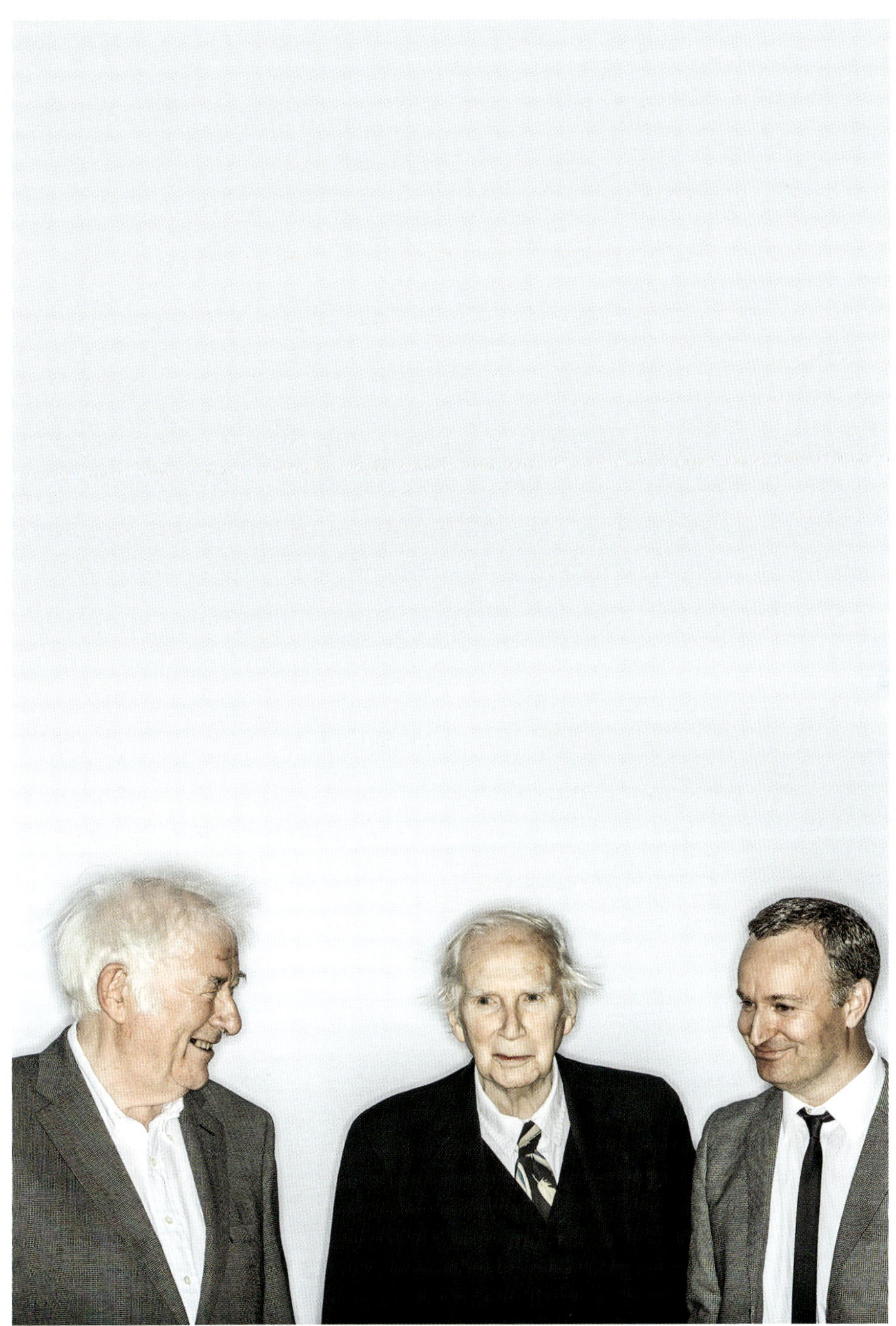

The agnostic bishop. Richard is a lovely guy. Strong on opinions but not opinionated. Well read, lyrical and a wonderful presenter too. He is a hard man to capture. I like the serene questioning gaze he has in this picture and the almost other-worldly quality of the image. He takes a more enlightened view of spirituality than many other writers and presenters.

'Truth is rarely simple and seldom obvious, which is why mature institutions recognise the importance of conflict and disagreement.'

RICHARD HOLLOWAY

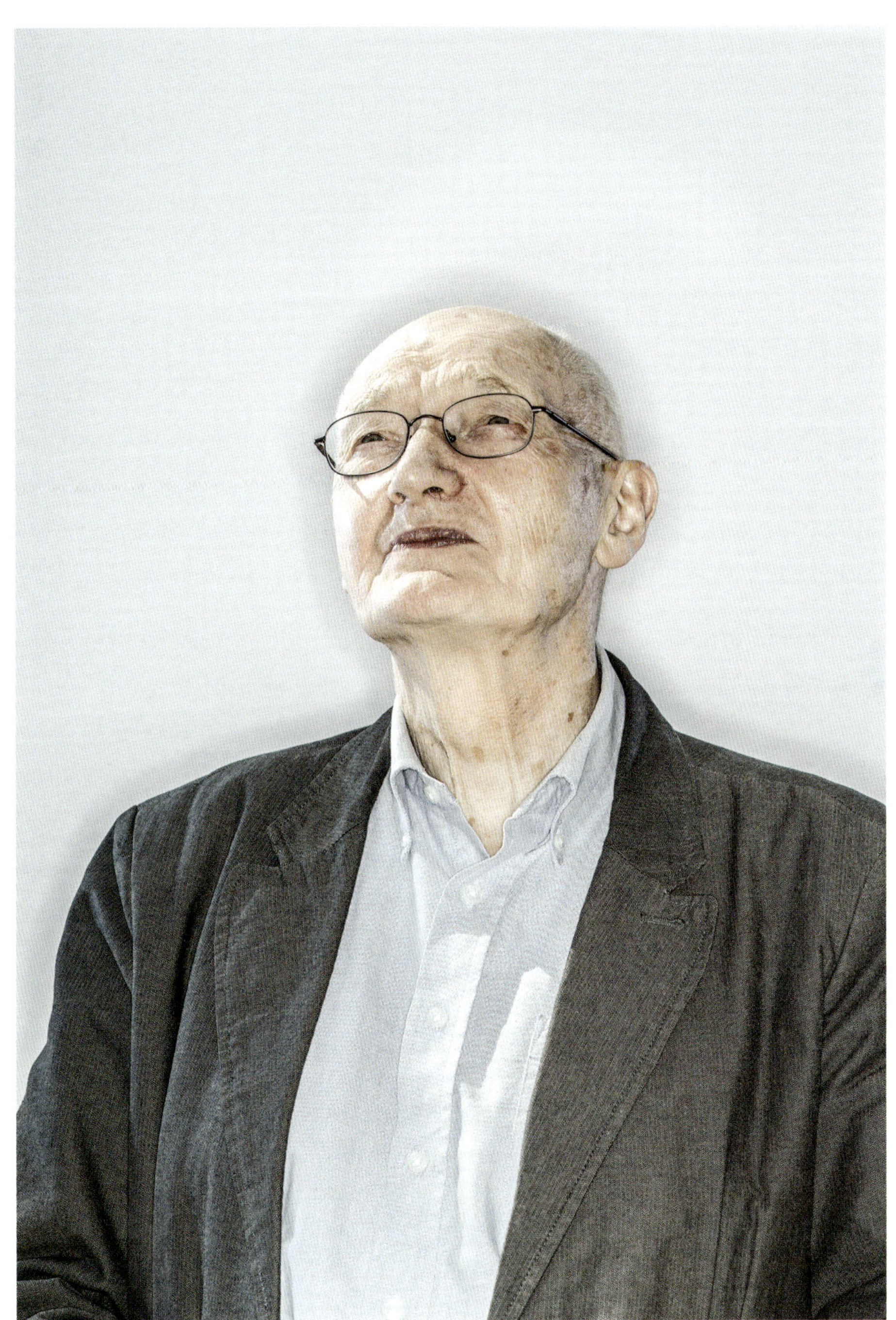

The first person I photographed for the very first Between The Lines Exhibition. Emmanuel is from Southern Sudan and whilst crossing the country to get to Ethiopia he was captured and forced to fight for the Sudanese Rebel Army.

Along with fellow soldiers he escaped eating whatever he could find to survive – snails and vultures. He was briefly adopted by aid worker Emma McCune but she died in a car crash and Emmanuel was later sent to England. He is a rap musician which may provide an outlet from the ravages of his earlier life and perhaps some solace. I realised, while conversing with Emmanuel that I wanted to portray the person behind the writing, the face between the lines, which a series of static, posed images would fail to do. It was the start of a journey.

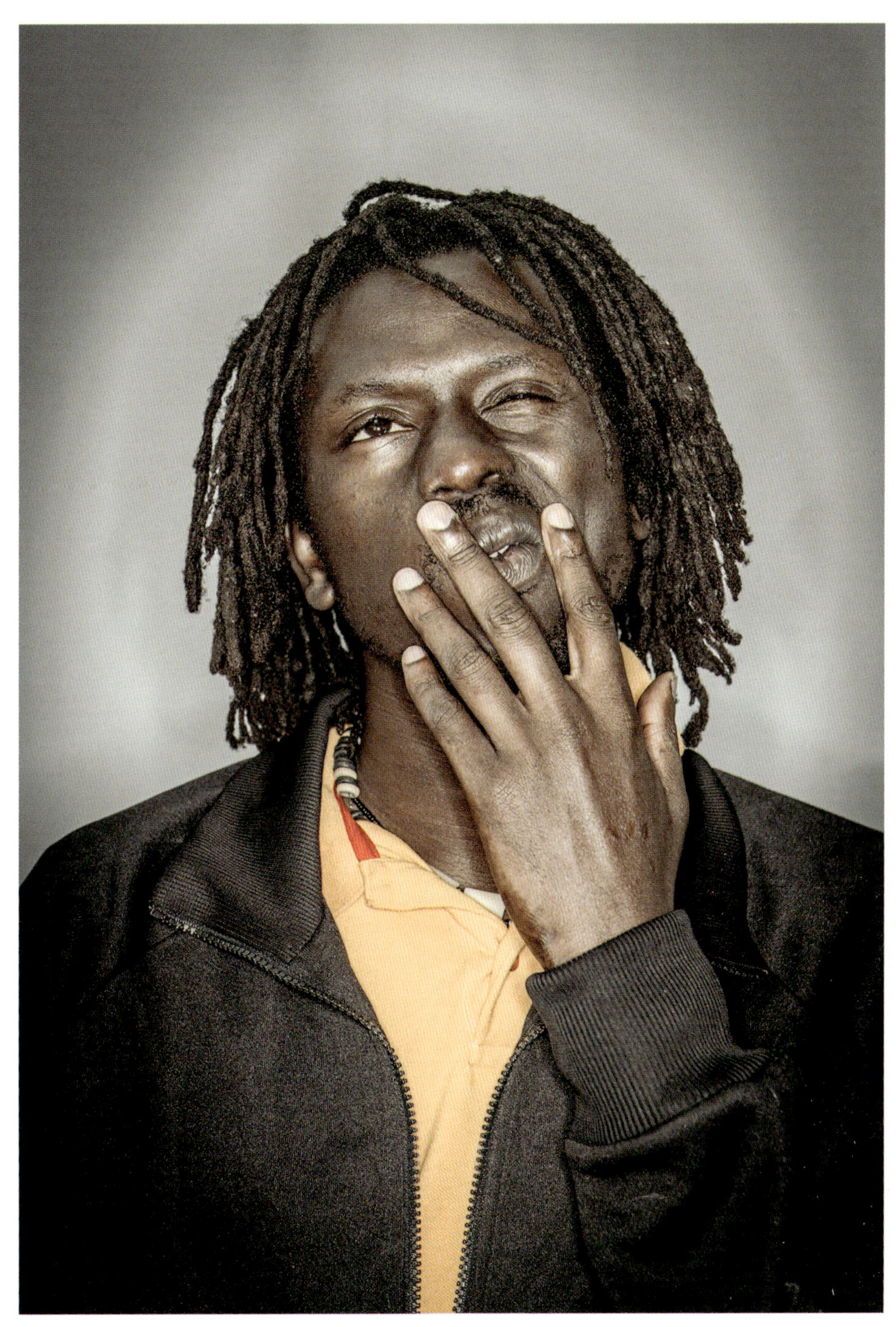

Gabriel Josipovici

This critically acclaimed author was a delight to listen to and photograph.
I felt we had solved the world's problems by the time we finished!

*'The only way to read is in the knowledge that there is an infinite
amount of time stretching ahead, and that if one wishes to taste
only a few sentences per day one is free to do so.'*

GABRIEL JOSIPOVICI

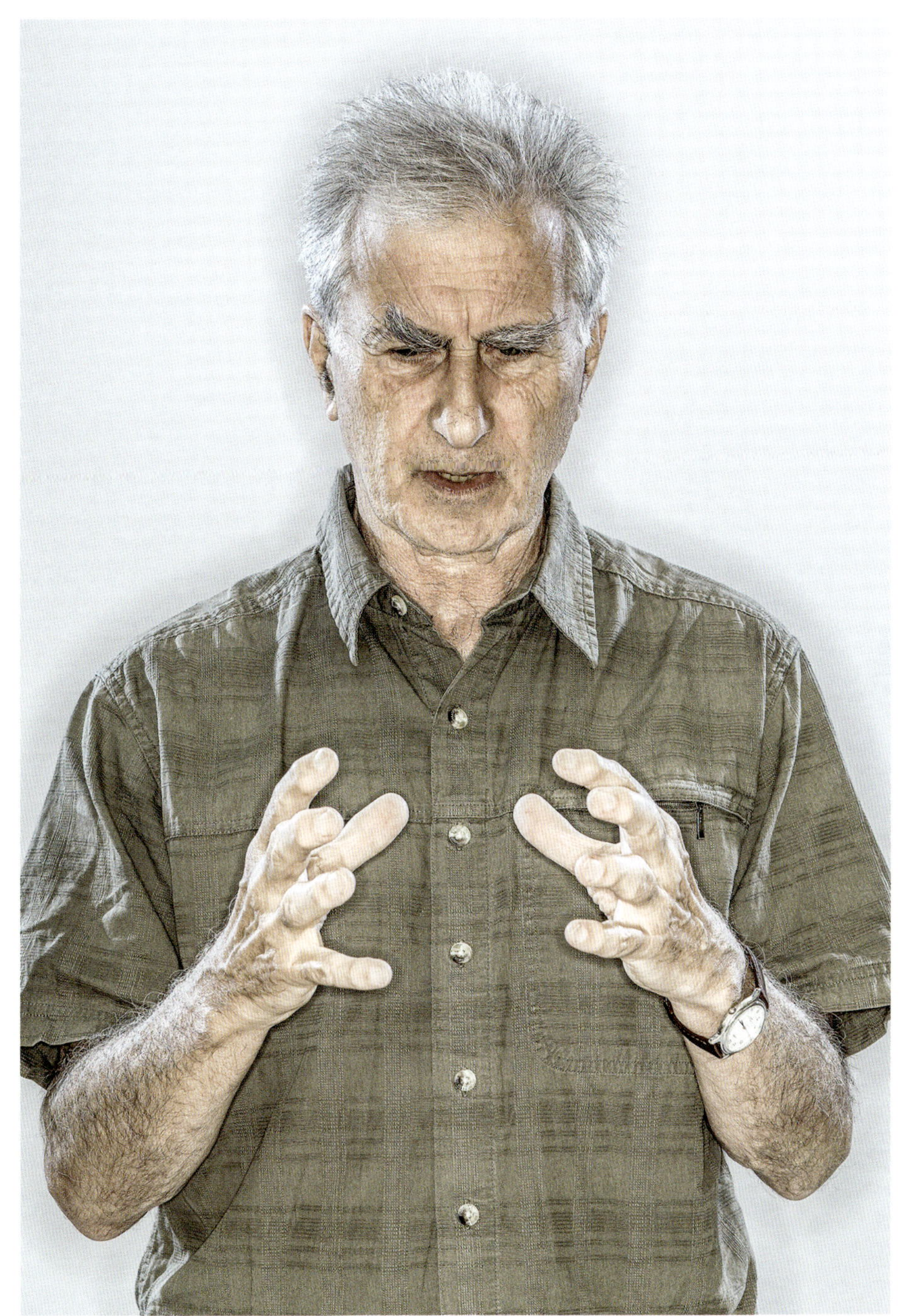

Alison hails from Dundee, a city with an increasingly literary reputation. I have it on good authority (I asked her!) that she used the initials A.L. in case her first book didn't do very well. It would provide a degree of anonymity from the baying mob who would have lined the streets to persecute her fragile, fragmented, feminine, frame! Fortunately she is now one of the country's most critically acclaimed novelists with a string of novels, short stories, TV and radio broadcasts and stand up appearances on her expansive CV. As a result she can walk tall even in Dundee. Alison is the only author I have photographed every year at The Edinburgh International Book Festival. There is something both poignant and humourous about her standing with Fragile across her mouth. I would say it was to represent the frailty of the written word but it also kept her quiet for a few minutes!

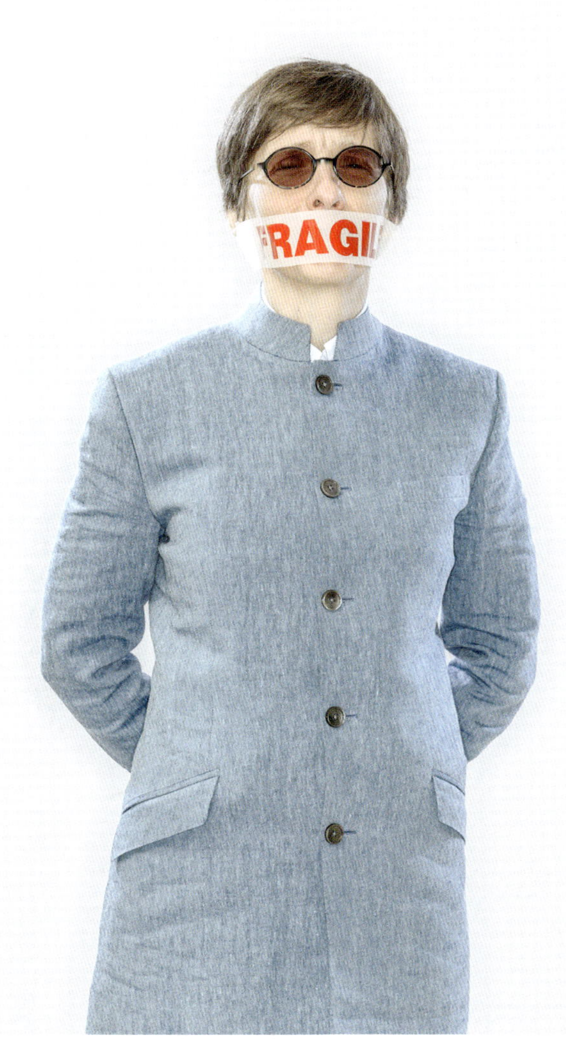
FRAGILE

German Jewish by birth but a British Citizen, Judith wrote *The Tiger who Came to Tea* and *When Hitler Stole Pink Rabbit*.

The former, a metaphor for troubled times when the Nazis were goose-stepping their way across Europe, the latter a semi-autobiographical book about escaping from Germany, her father being a marked man. He was a journalist, theatre critic and screenwriter. The Nazi's didn't much care for that nor his Jewish faith. That's the written word for you.

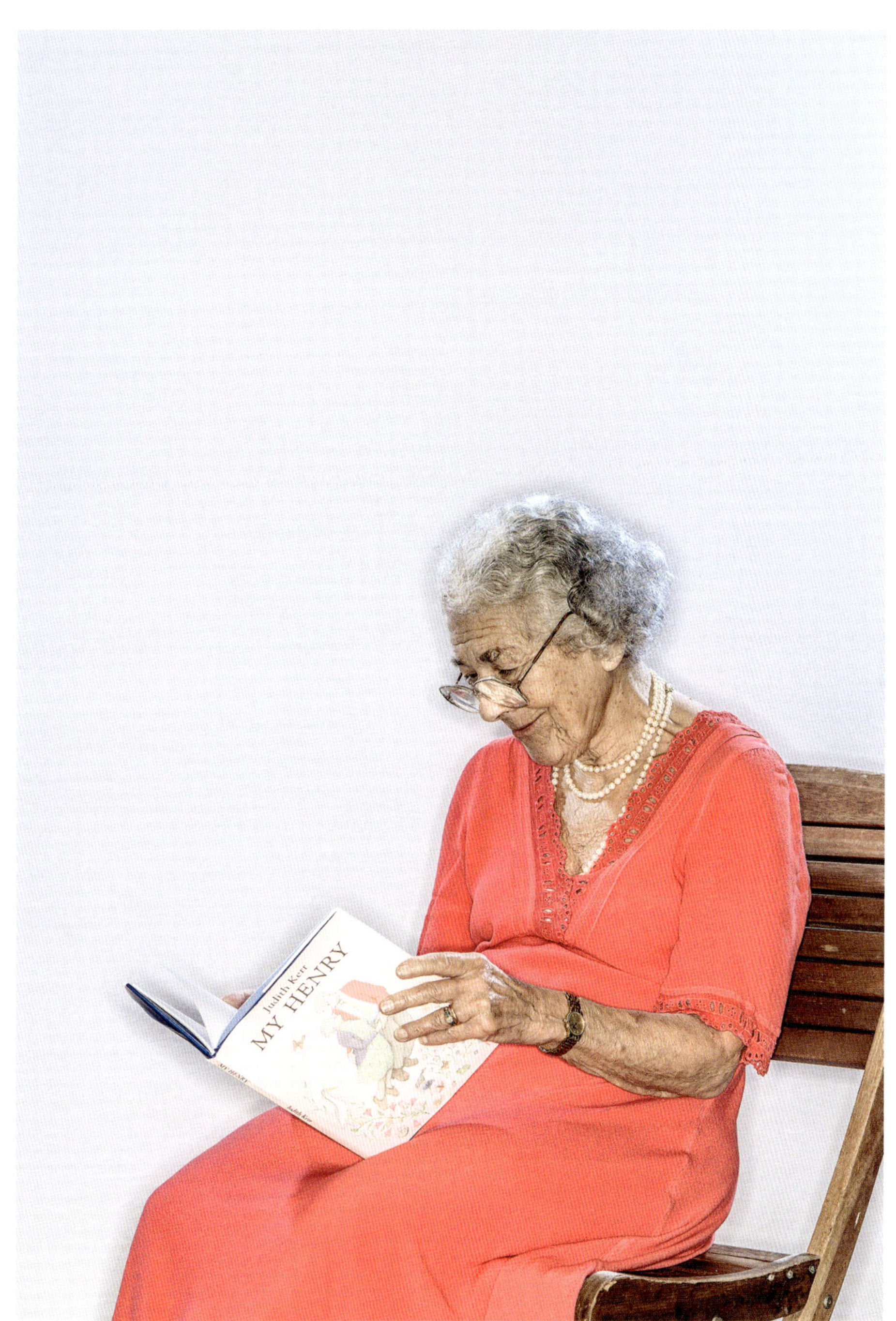

Norwegian Karl Ove Knausgaard came to prominence with the release of his autobiographical books and the somewhat controversial title of the first one, *Min Kamp* which is the Norwegian equivalent of the notorious, *Mein Kampf* written by one A. Hitler.

Handsome, gnarly with faded blue eyes to match his faded blue denim, his face and demeanour told stories in themselves.

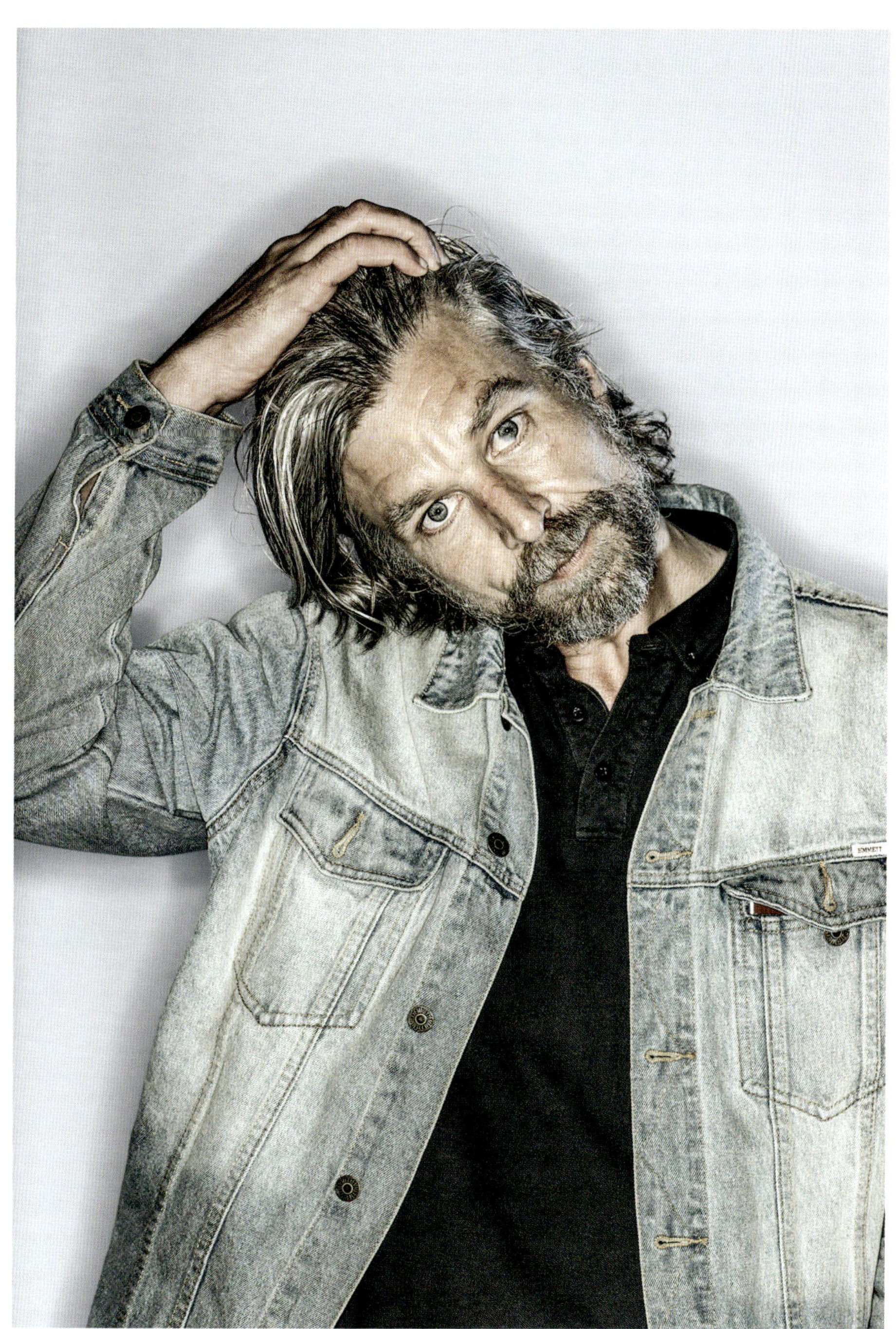

Hanif Kureishi CBE is amongst the fifty greatest writers since 1945. So says, not me, but *The Times*, not that I don't say it either! He has won so many awards I put it to him he was just showing off!

This picture was not staged. Mid-way through the shoot he rubbed his eyes and I suspect he knew I would take a picture at that moment – visualising a scene or character for a new screenplay perhaps?

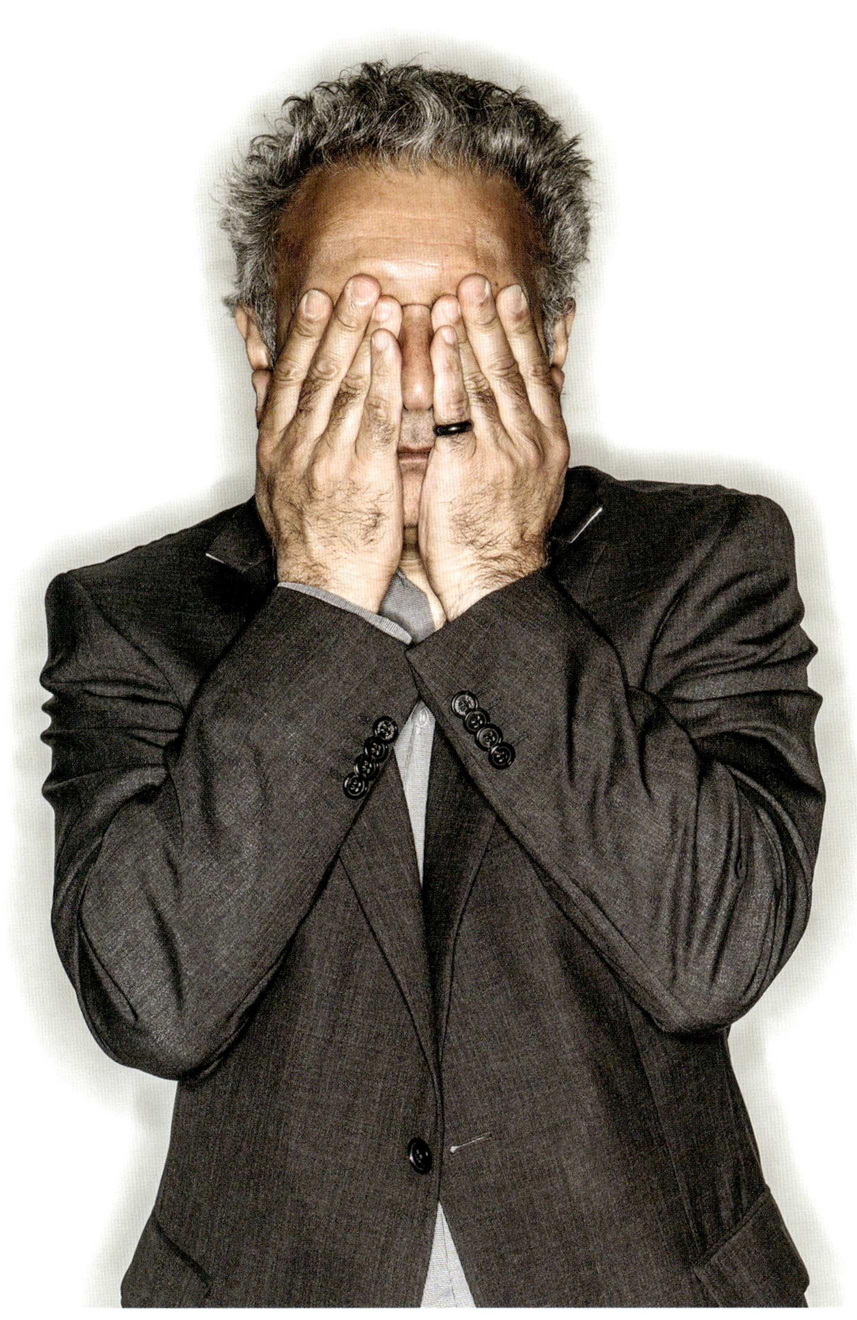

American Agony Aunt Irma Kurtz. I e-mailed Irma and asked about using her picture in the book. Without hesitation she said, 'Yes, call me.' I called and she was flustered. 'What's up?' She had been called in to do a talk about sex and didn't have enough time to prepare.

Irma is a striking woman and just shy of eighty. I'd have knocked twenty years off that.

To steal one of Nora Ephron's, *When Harry Met Sally* lines,

'I'll have what she's having.'

I'll bet she has heard some stuff in her forty years of being the 'Godmother of all Agony Aunts'. I love the energy in this picture.

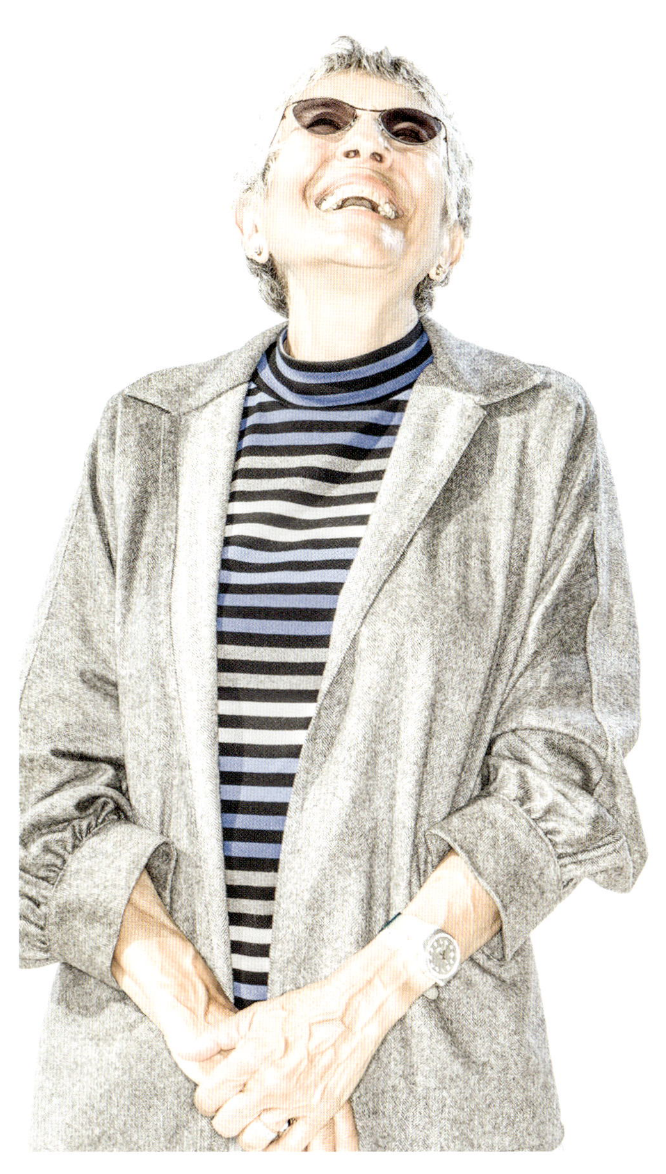

Talking of energy, Phyllida Law gave an impromptu performance of South African dancing having recently been there. South Africa may be a way from Glasgow where Phyllida was born. Perhaps she honed her dancing skills in the famous Barrowlands Ballroom. I wonder if any article ever doesn't mention her famous daughter. At the time of this shoot I was oblivious, I'd be a terrible Papparazzi, so I won't mention it suffice to say, two stunning and talented women.

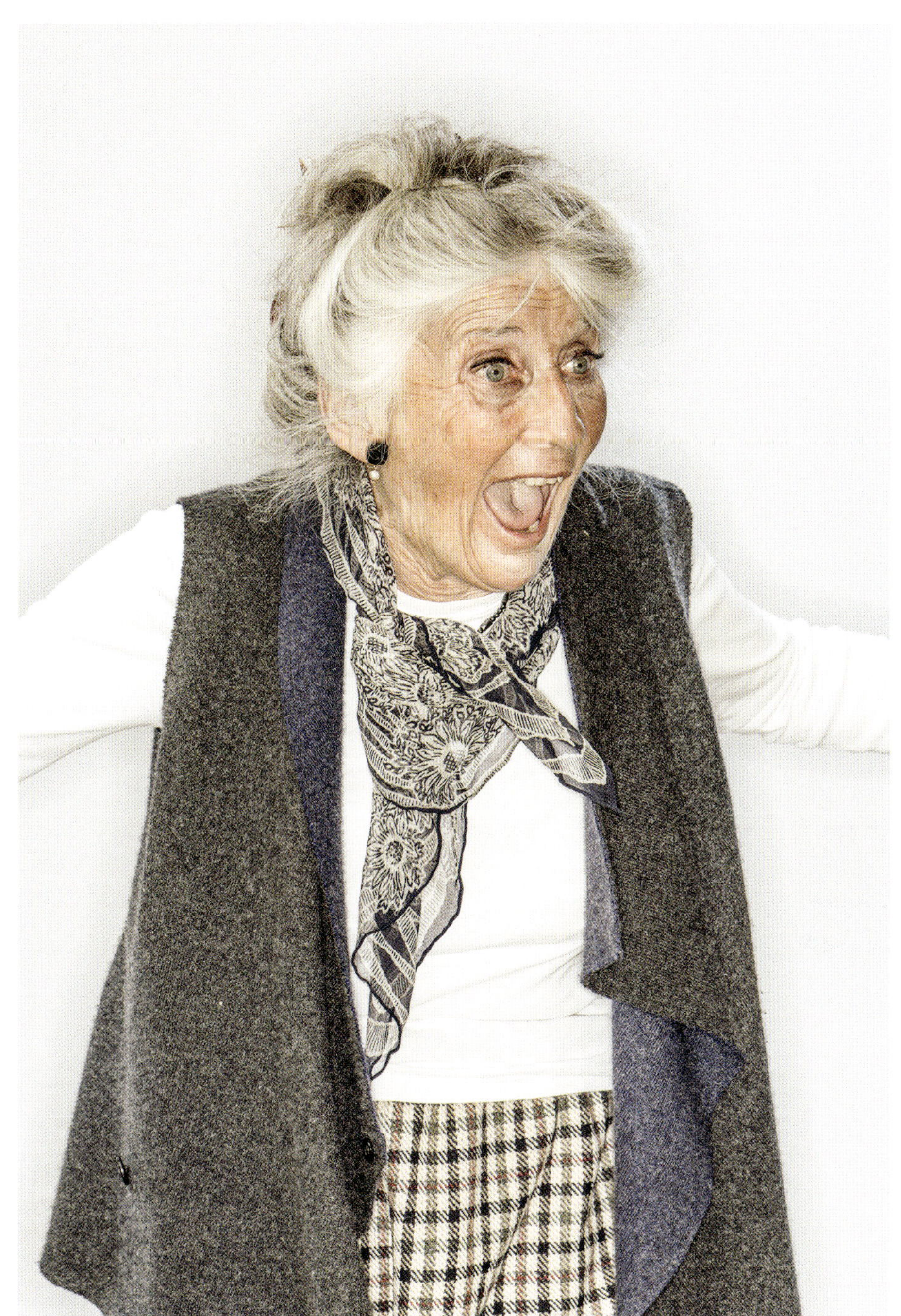

'You're a photographic Love God. And I adore you!'
KATHY LETTE

The firey, feisty and fabulously feminine Kathy Lette.

Try these on for size.

'I think therefore I'm divorced.'

'No wife ever shot a husband while he was vacuuming.'

'Ironic how you can't get kids out of their beds in the morning but you can't get them into their beds at night.'

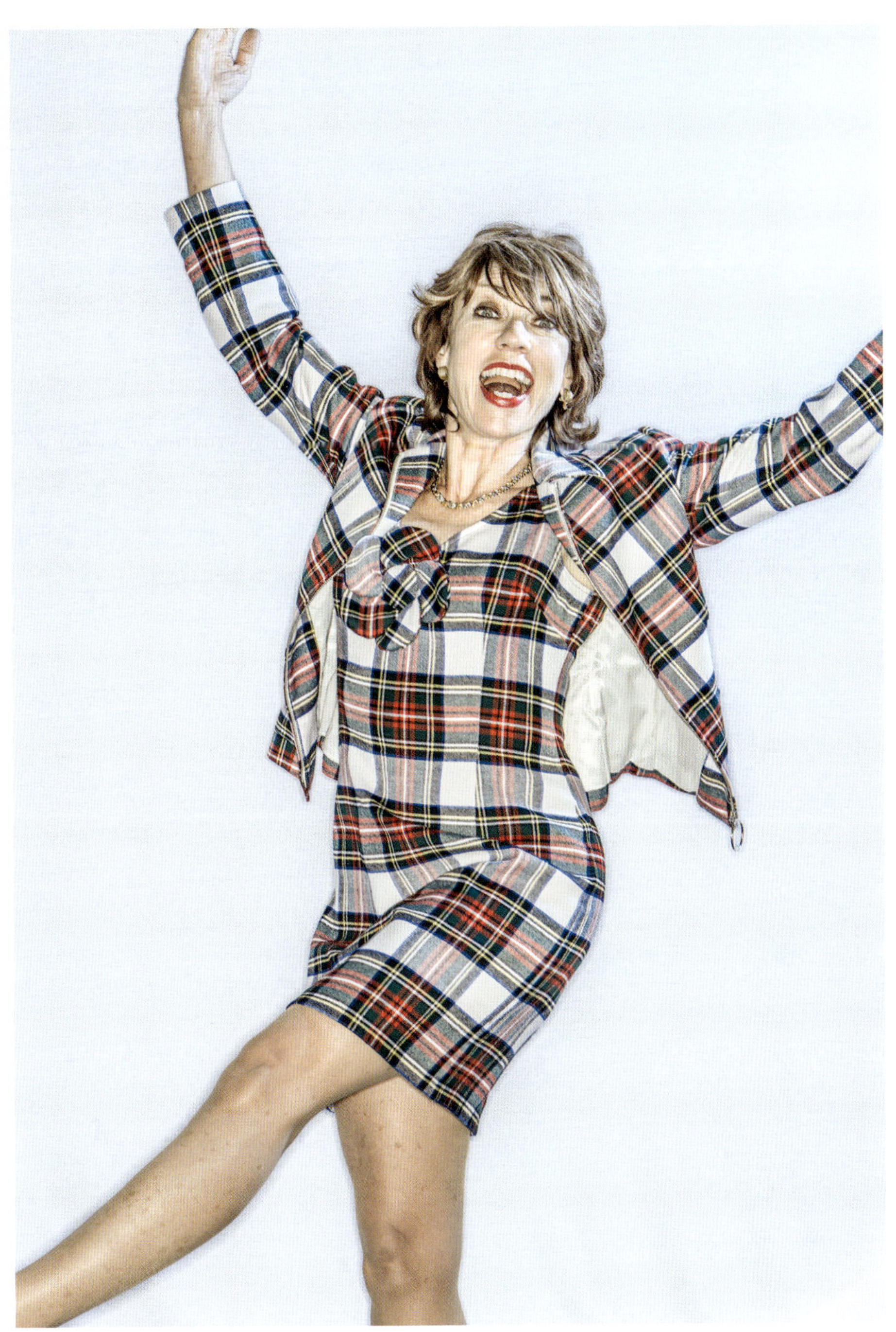

Author of a *Siberian Education* based on real life experiences in a Siberian prison. Those tattoos all refer to various gang symbols. It has subsequently been claimed the book is not, as many thought, based on real life experiences but is instead largely fictional. The tattoos were real though.

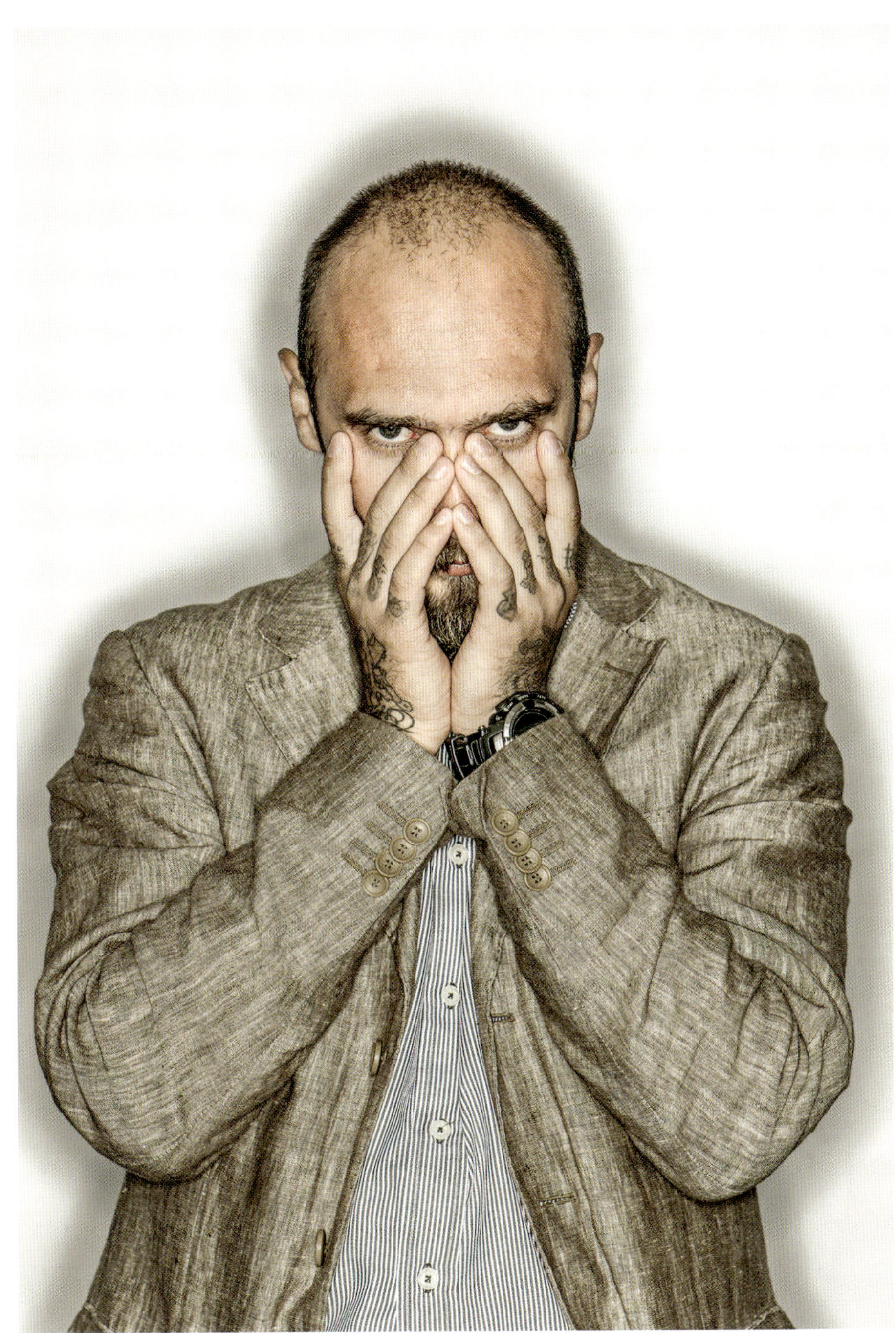

John Lloyd and Jon Canter

John Lloyd producer of Blackadder and QI, and novelist and scripwriter Jon Canter continue the *Meaning of Liff* book originally co-written with Douglas Adams who is now hitch hiking his way around the heavens. I had a chat with the two Jo(h)ns which didn't disappoint. Witty with a silent 't'.

'Gradgery (n.) The insistence by elderly ladies who have fallen asleep in their armchairs that they were never asleep in the first place.'

'Letchworth – The Door charge at a lap dancing club.'

'Dunstable – Ex Police man.'

'Dover – Ex Diver.'

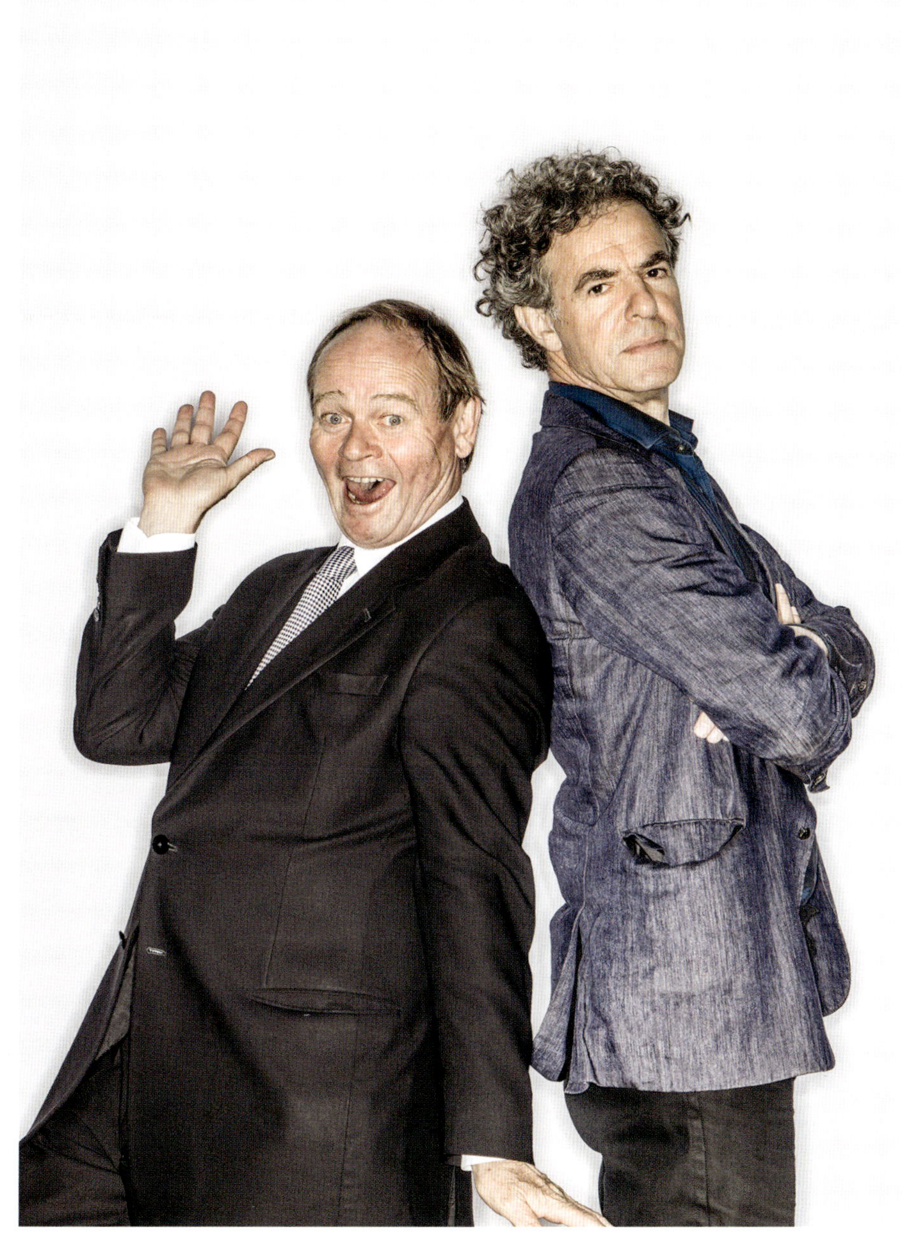

Adam turned up to the shoot clutching a glass of water. He was about to go in front of his audience. One of his books is called, *Instruction Manual for Swallowing* so after a few frames I persuaded him to clutch the plastic cup between his teeth and tilt the glass of water over his head. Two, maybe three frames. Adam, somewhat damper than when we first met seemed unperturbed.

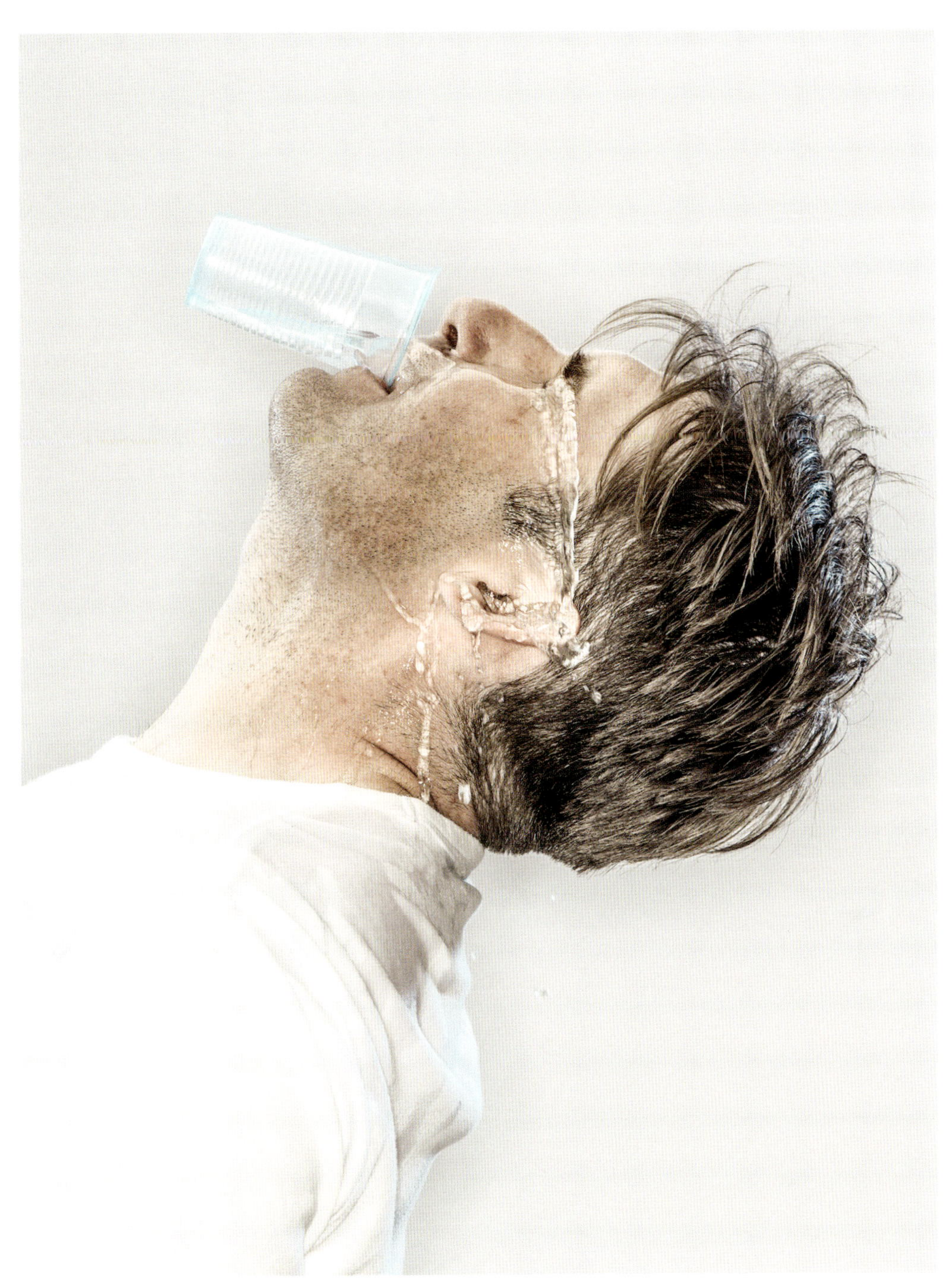

Benjamin Markovits

A former basketball player, Benjamin had written about Lord Byron and I managed to capture him in a Byronesque pose; alternatively I may just have told him one of my very poor jokes. I cropped the photograph to highlight the loftiness appropriate to a basketball playing scholar of Byron.

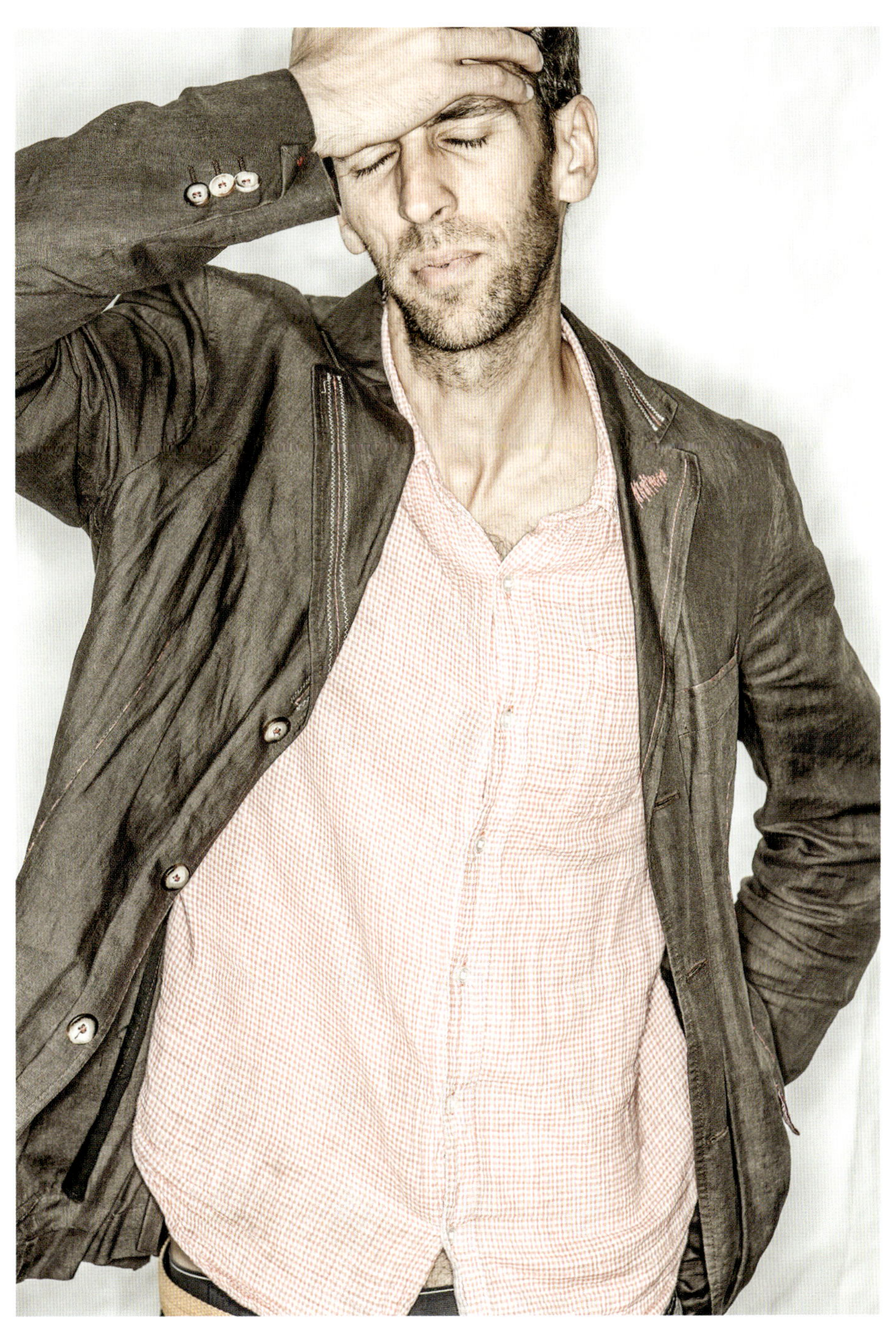

George is the man behind the *Game of Thrones* phenomenon. Being such a cultural afficionado when I saw his name, I thought it was George Martin, the producer of The Beatles! Little did I know. A man in high demand. Off stage crowds of people were waiting to get close to the great man and were it not for the fact he is metaphorically chauffeured between various media, he would come across as very ordinary, albeit with a less than ordinary waistcoat.

When I read of the complex interwoven plots of the books, interweaving a mesh of images seemed entirely appropriate.

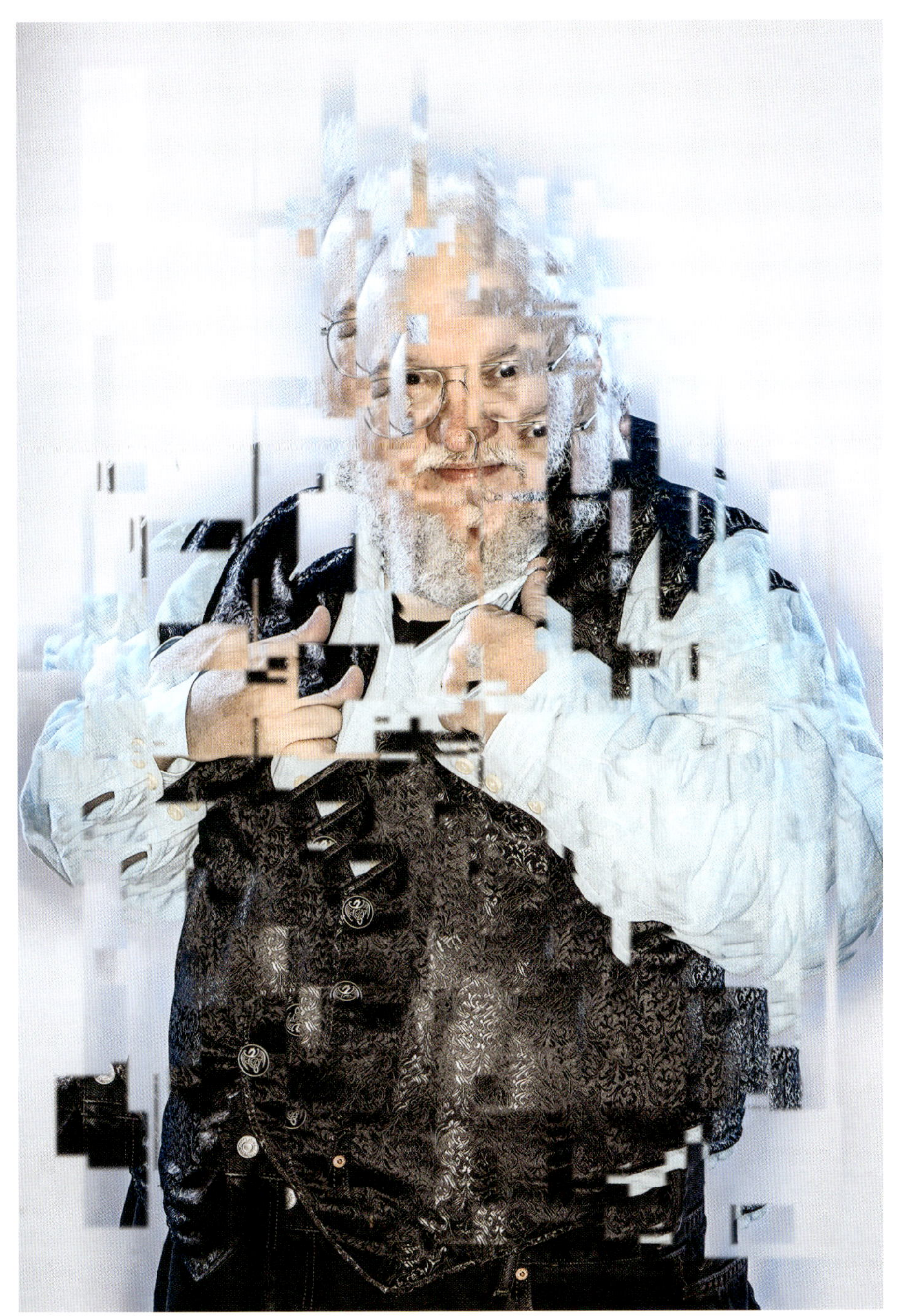

Professor Smith is a writer who shot to prominence following a successful academic career in Medical Law. Alexander's *The No. 1 Ladies Detective Agency* series propelled him into the public eye and now must be one of the most recognisable writers of his generation with a fabulous back catalogue of both books and attire. In this picture he seems to be clutching an imaginary glass of wine. Wishful thinking perhaps.

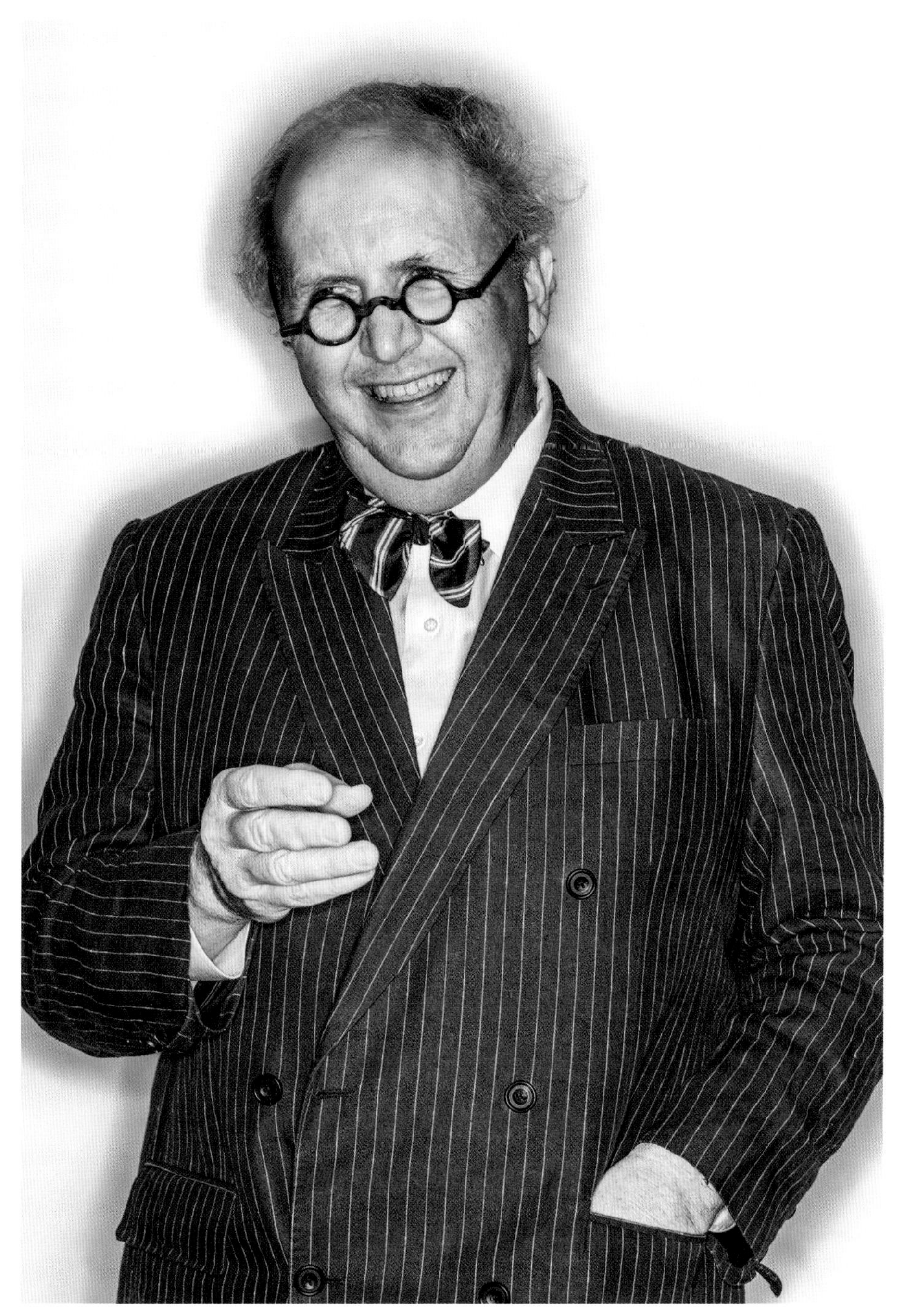

I have photographed crime diva Val several times and never know what to expect. I mean that in a good way. (Once she had a parrot on her shoulder.) This was the very first frame from this shoot and a few months later it was projected above her as she received an honorary doctorate from Dundee University.

'It's great to have a photograph that shows joy, not like the usual author's photographs'

VAL McDERMID

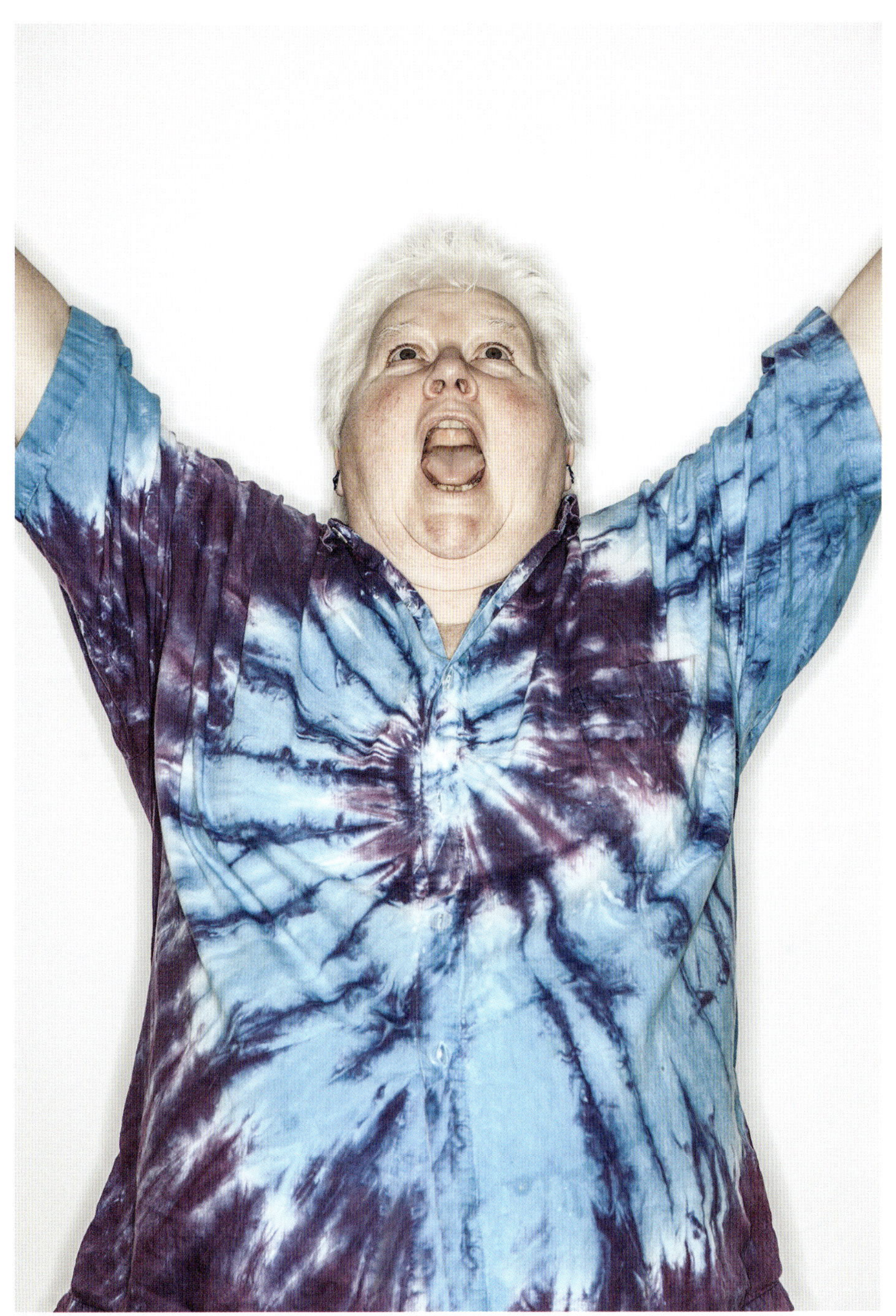

Ian McEwan

IAN McEWAN

'Literary heavyweight knocks out photographer with a "cutting" quip.'

Ian wrote a book called *In Between the Sheets* which is almost what the series of exhibitions was to be called but it may have given the wrong impression.

I like Ian, we had a great chat afterwards and no offence was taken.

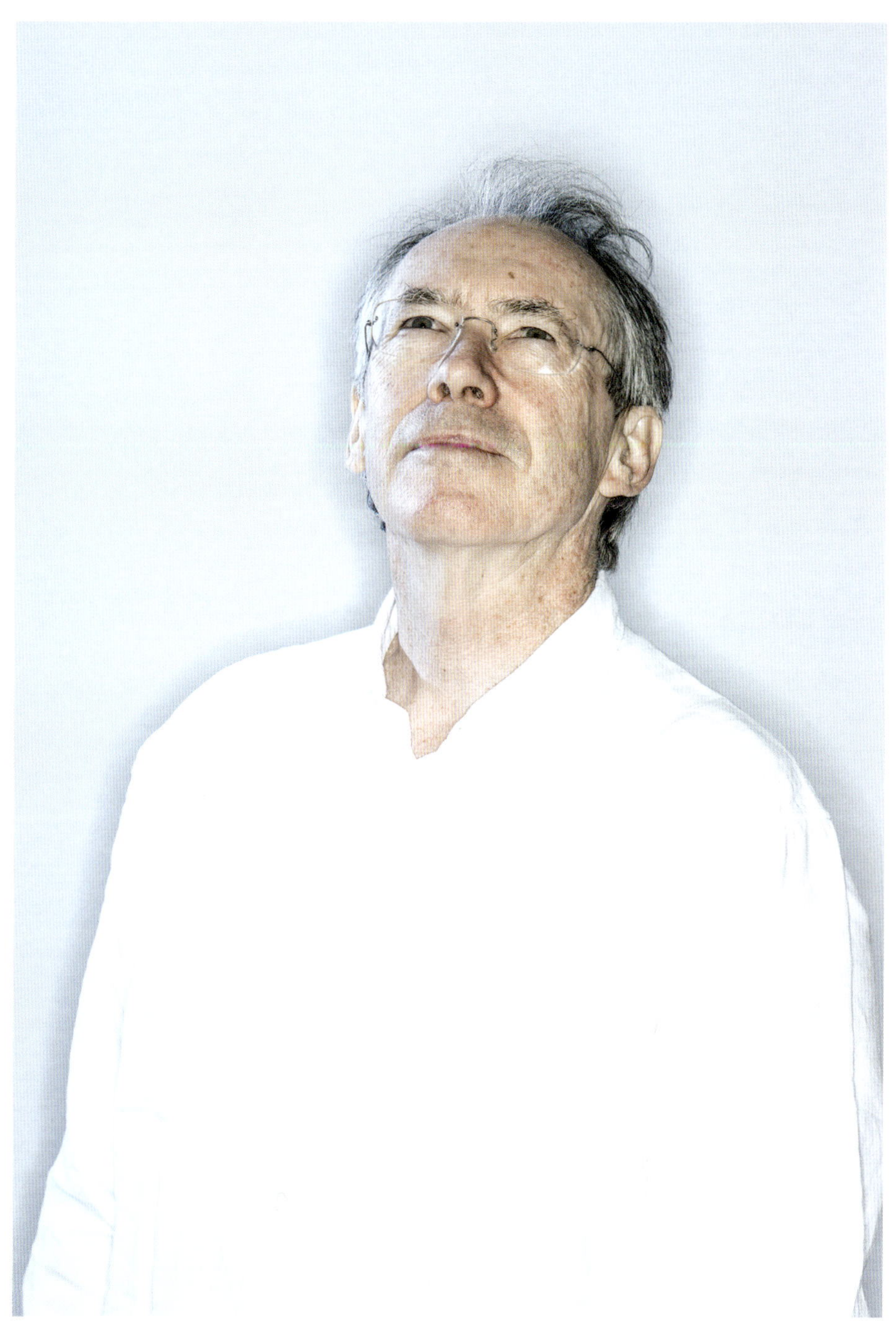

Tartan Noir writer with Clark Cable looks, William McIlvanney's books are as gritty and characterful as his face.

'Writing is a way of sharing our humanity.'

WILLIAM McILVANNEY

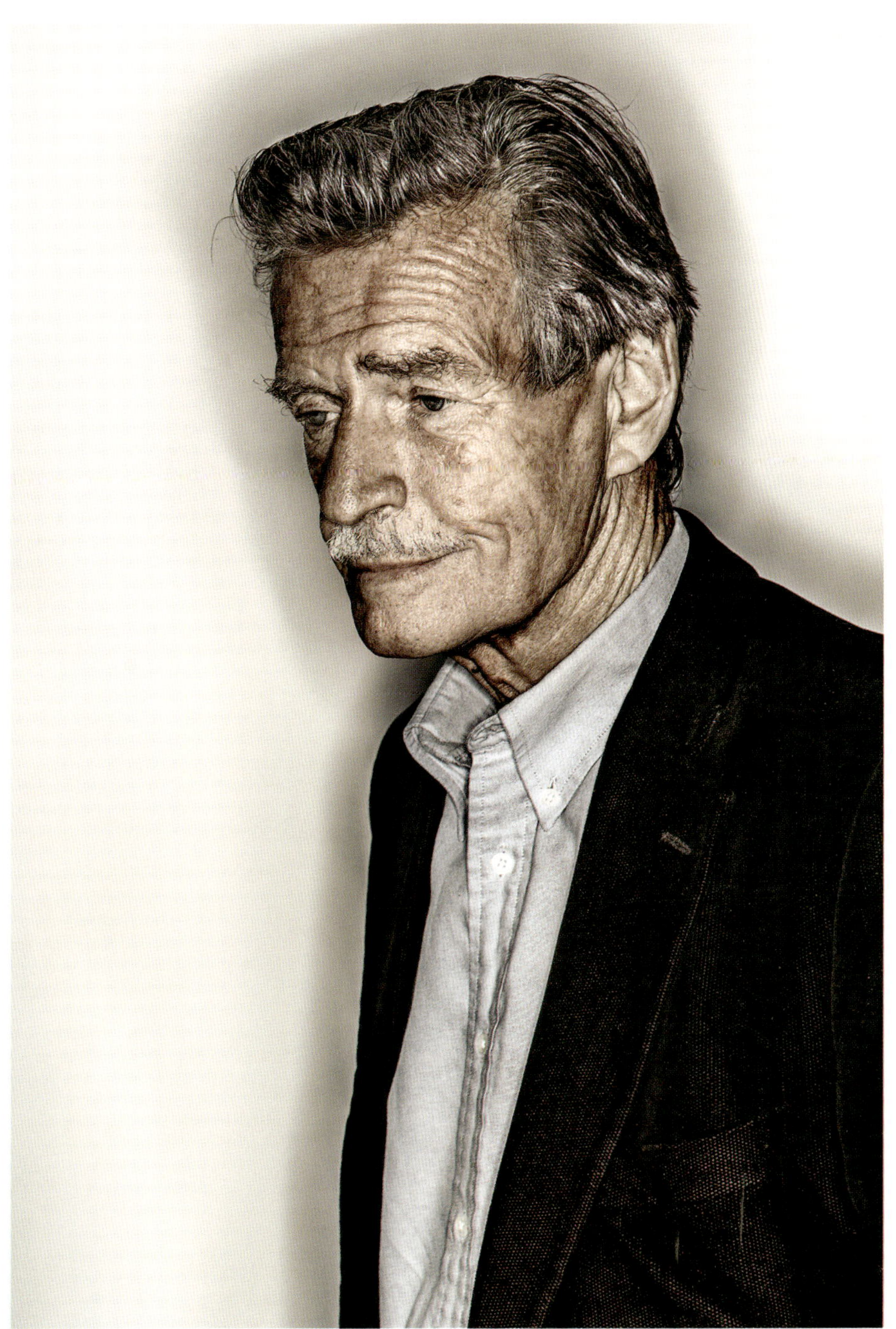

Children's author Jonathan Meres wanted something abNORMal! So I asked a colleague to throw a jug of water over him!

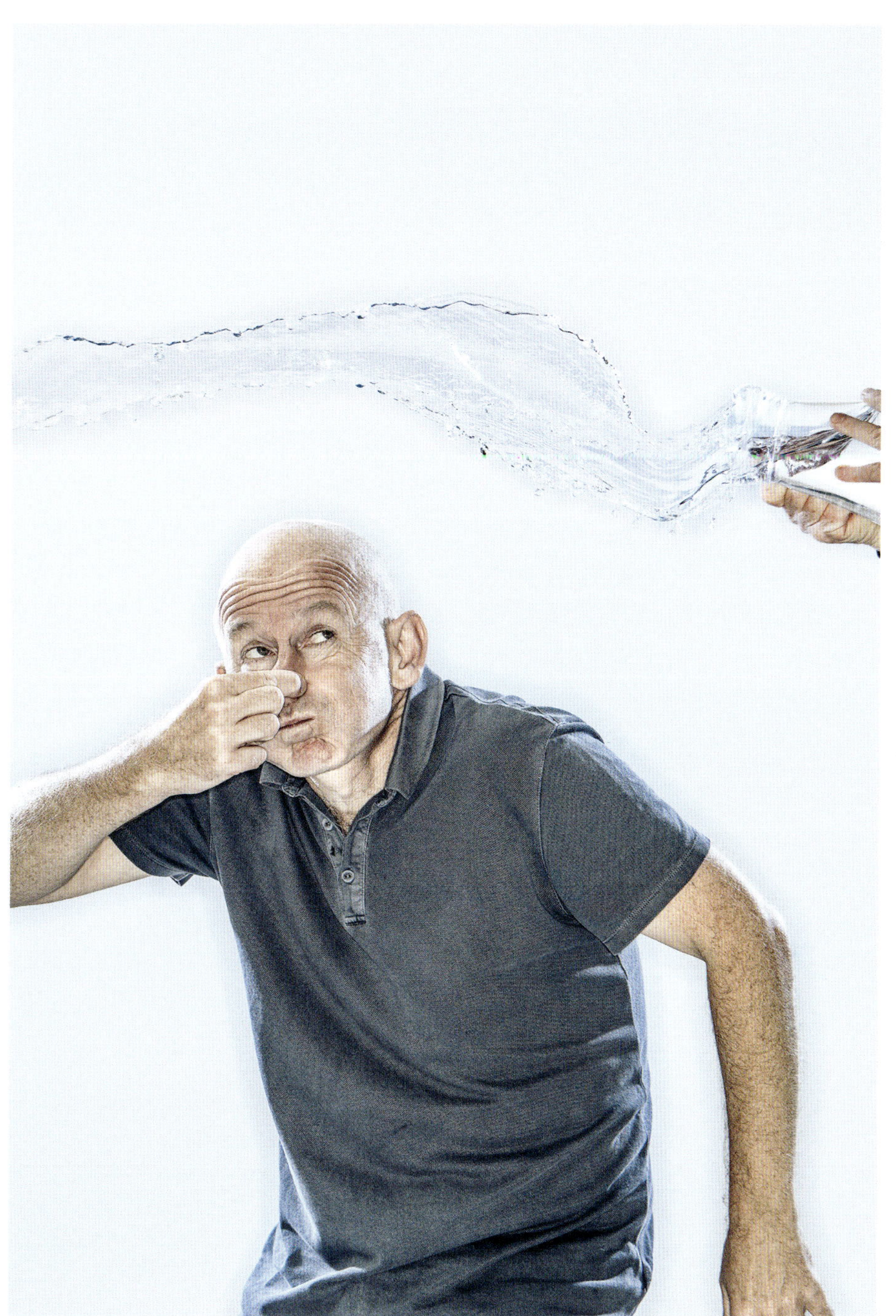

Boston abider, Ben Mezrich has written a collection of stories that almost have to be true lest they would seem too fantastical. Heists, hoaxes and hokum several of which have made the silver screen. Most famously, *The Accidental Billionaires* became the Oscar winning film *The Social Network*. He also wrote a book called *Sex on The Moon* which has very little to do with sex and more to do with the protagonists reinvention of his character into a daring but doomed criminal.

I chose this as the inspiration for this image.

'Your picture of me is the best I've ever had done. I call it my "rock-an-roll" portrait – it's the closest I'll ever come to looking like a genuine rock star.'

BEN MEZRICH

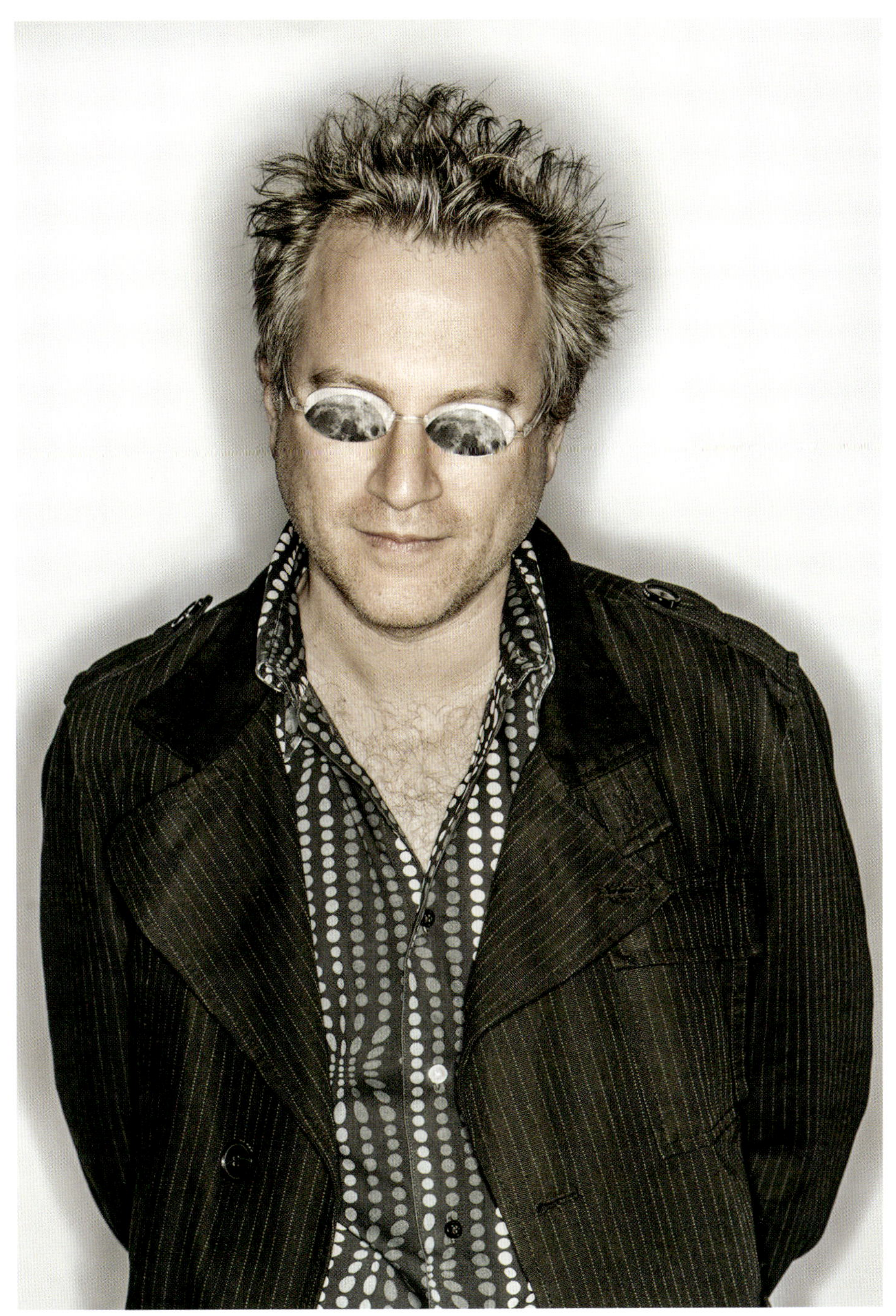

Science Fiction author China Miéville. China cuts an extraordinarily striking and handsome figure, adorned with tentacled earrings. Photographically this is one of my more posed works. The result, a slightly disconcerting image, 'Like some alien parasite,' Alison Flood, *The Guardian*.

When on display in the exhibition China confessed he had walked by several times, furtively snatching glances of the portrait but had been too embarrassed to stop and stare perhaps worried he was caught like Narcissus admiring his own reflection.

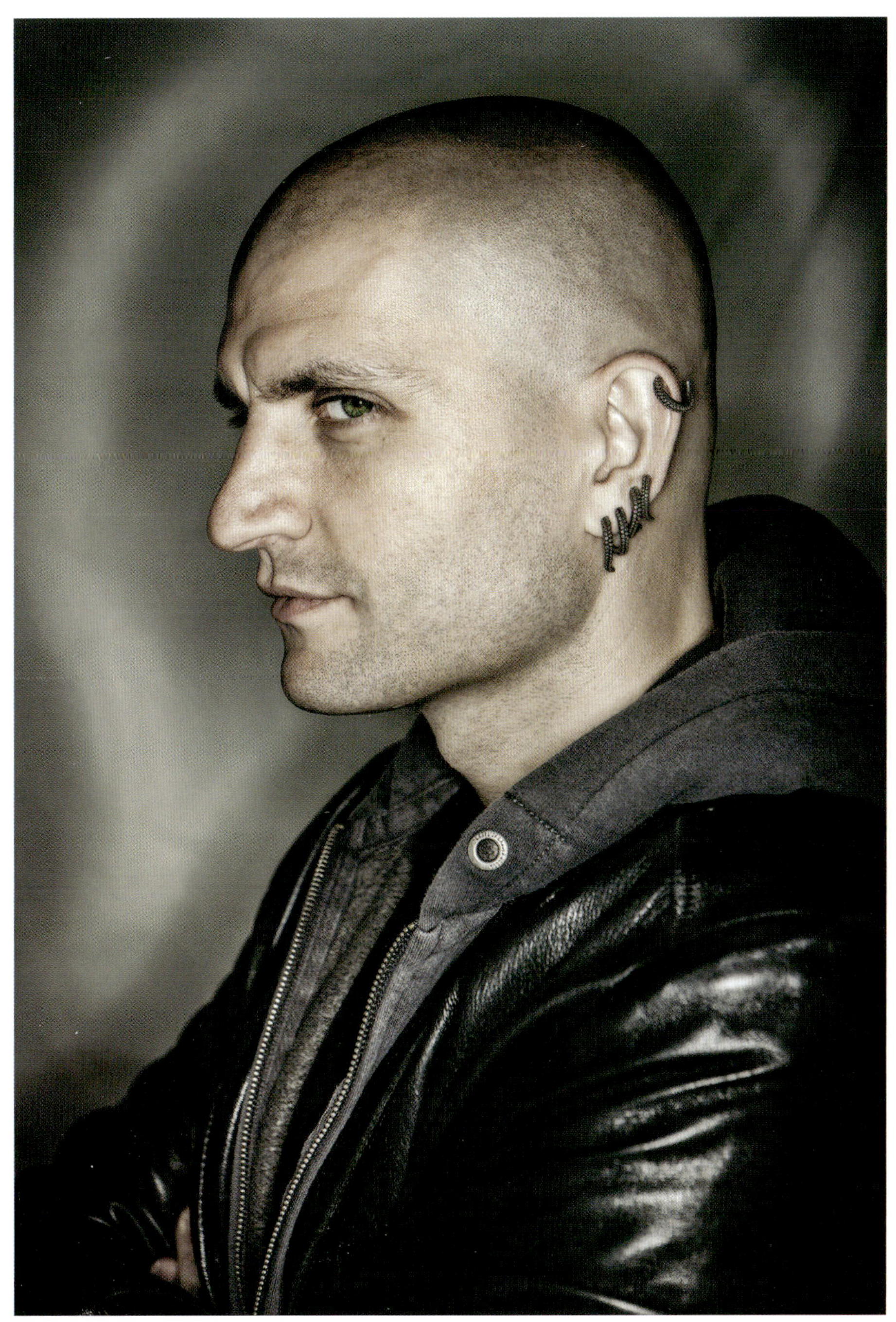

Denise Mina is a striking woman, a crime writer with a killer fashion sense. I have been lucky to photograph Denise a couple of times. This is her 'yeti jacket', her words not mine. I also wanted to show Denise's hair style and a profile seemed to be the natural choice but her unconventional stance seems like a question mark against the typical studio portrait.

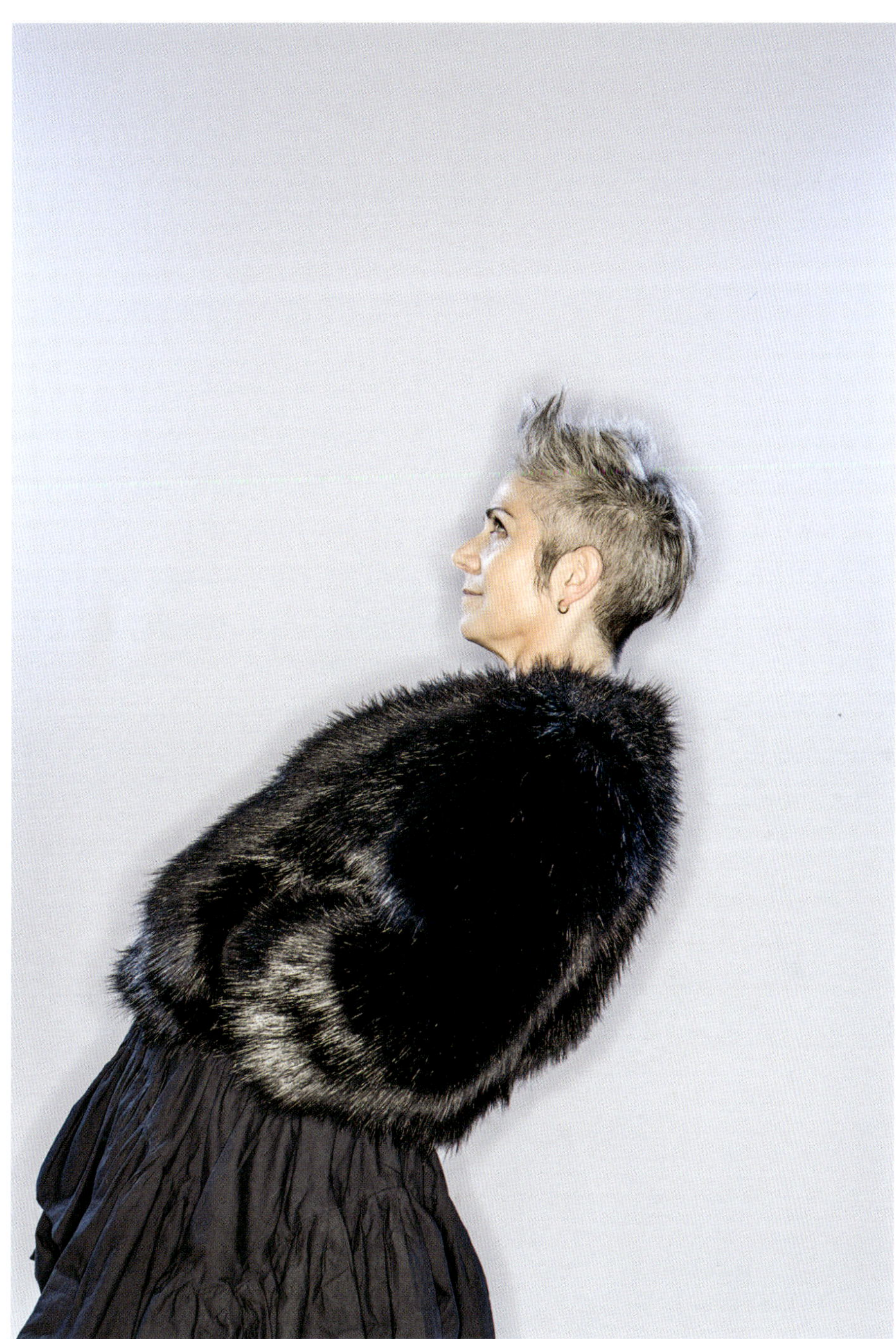

Nicola arrived slightly reticent about having her picture taken. Authors sometimes look at the images on display and wonder what they have to do when in truth they don't *have* to do anything. No-one is forced to be someone they are not. Within a few frames Nicola was well on her way to becoming a superhero! I have no idea how this came about but in the course of a conversation, ideas spring up and I run with them . . . sometimes they relate to the author's book, other times not. Perhaps it was her confession that she did daily exercises.

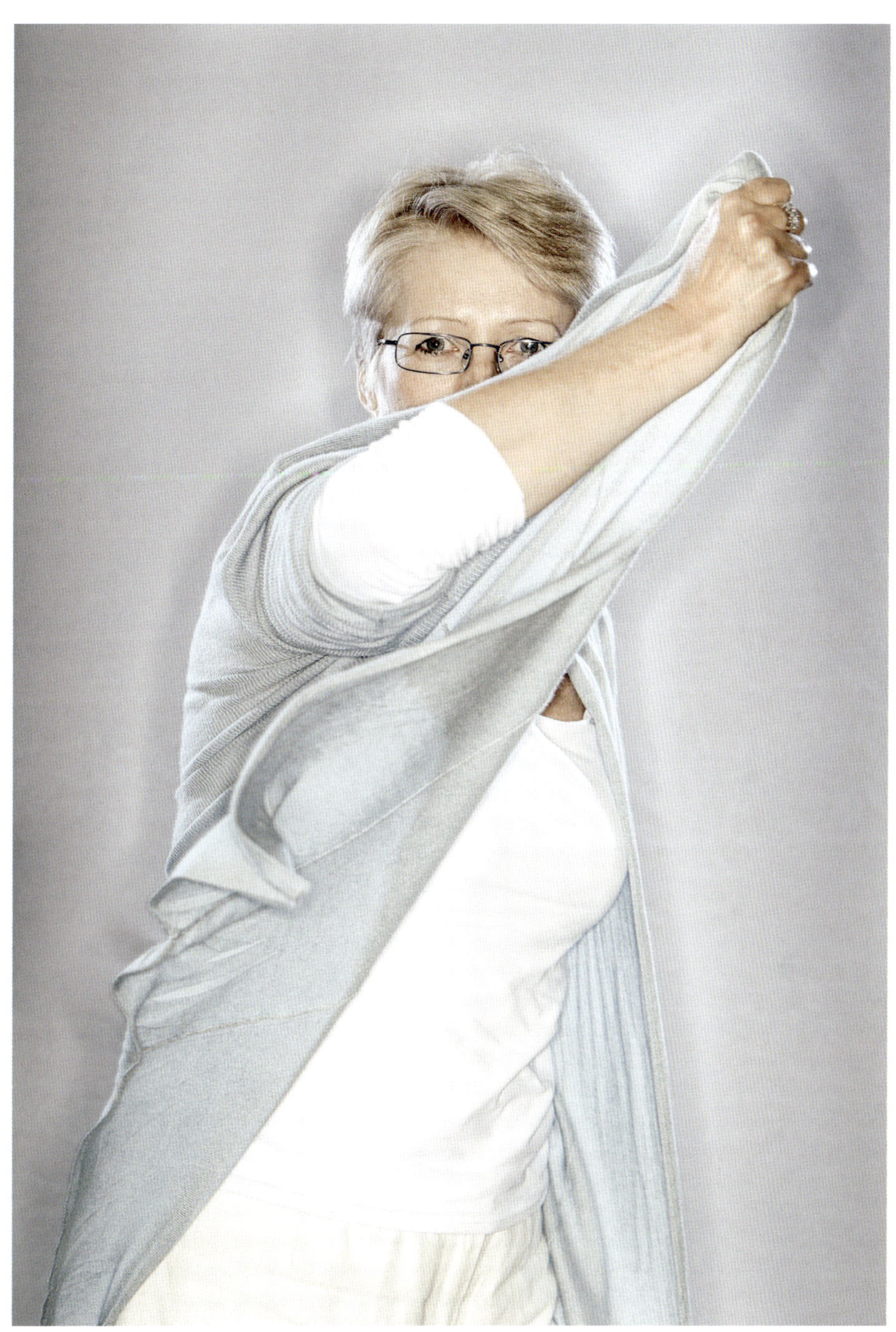

Kate and crow. Kate is huge, not physically despite the oversized brothel creeper shoes she wears. Huge, having written a succession of best sellers.

The crow I could not resist having in the photograph although it took some persuasion to agree! We tried bread, peanuts, chocolate but it could not have been less interested. I asked Kate to hold her jacket together to reflect the black of the crow. As a result a mysterious looking Dr Doolittle meets The Birds.

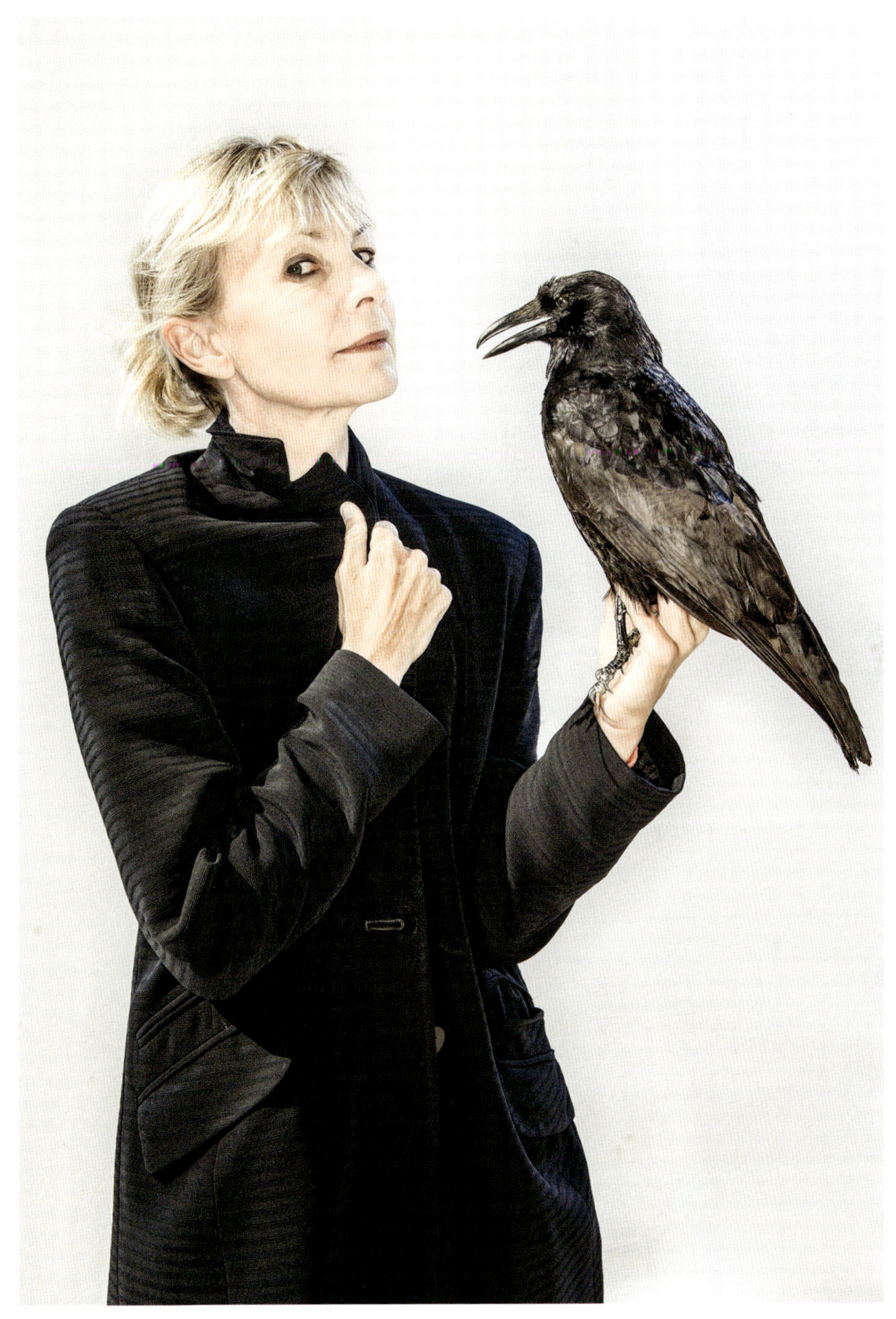

Irish born, New York resident, Paul Muldoon is an acclaimed poet. Winner of the Pulitzer Prize plus piles of other awards and like so many people of his level, very unassuming.

The *Times Literary Supplement* describing him as 'the most significant English-language poet born since the second World War.' Ah well, you know what they say, 'give a dog a bad name and he'll live up to it!'

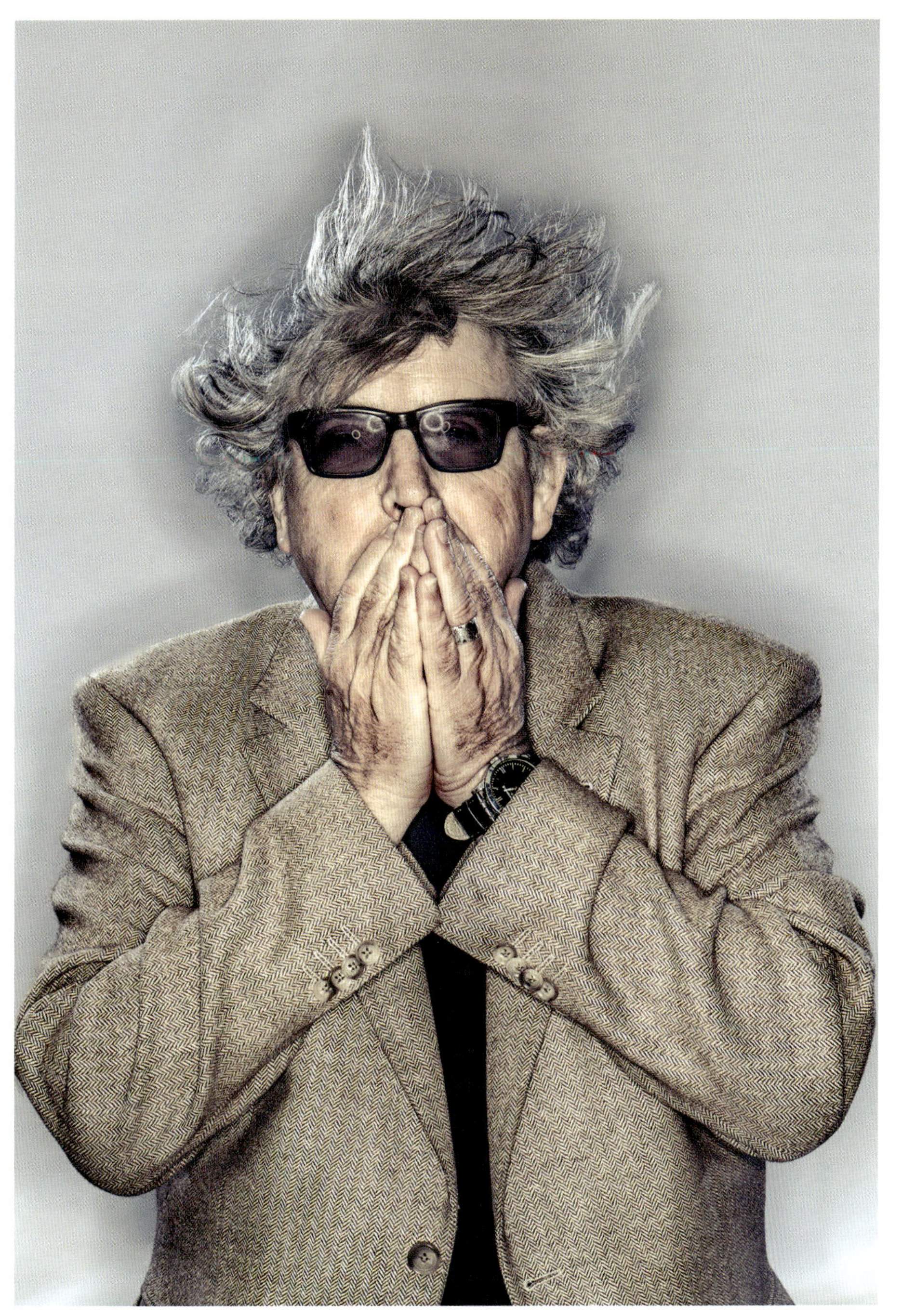

Former Norwegian footballer, rock star and financial analyst, Jo Nesbo has done rather well in the literary field too with a series of bestselling *Harry Hole* novels. I am a fan of anyone who has an alliterative name! Jo wore a T-shirt with a picture of his footballing hero Zico but I prefer Zinedine Zidane!

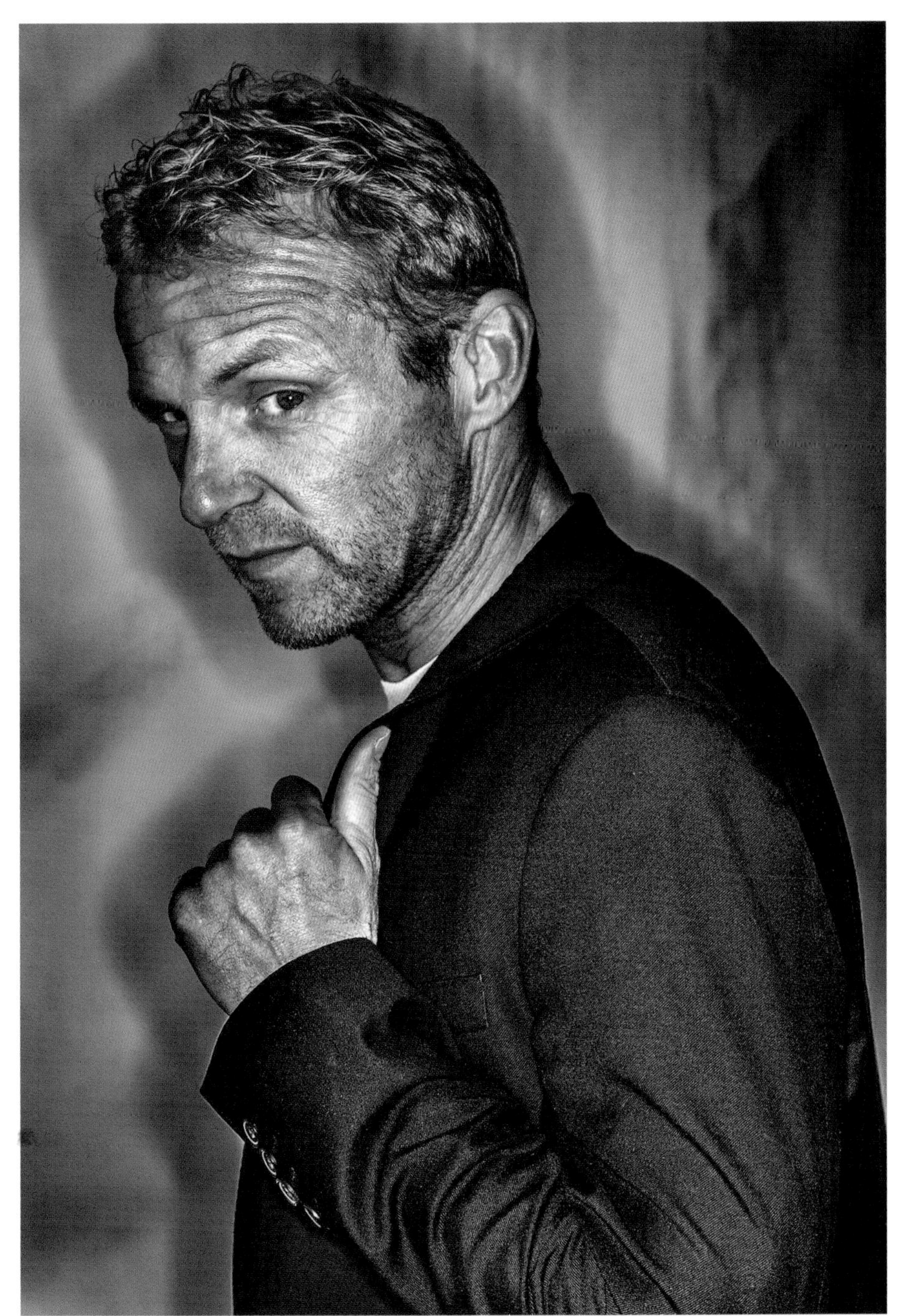

Patrick had a cold sore which when he pointed it out became an immediate focus for deliberate attention. I had brought along a 'Nessie' hat from one of the tourist shops to photograph the 'Patrick Ness Monster', which I thought was tantamount to genius! Patrick did not, resolutely refusing to wear it. Katie Green however loved it and insisted on wearing it. In the words of George Bernard Shaw, 'You Never Can Tell'. Patrick, amongst many others, wrote *A Monster Calls* which is now a major film starring Liam Neeson and Felicity Jones.

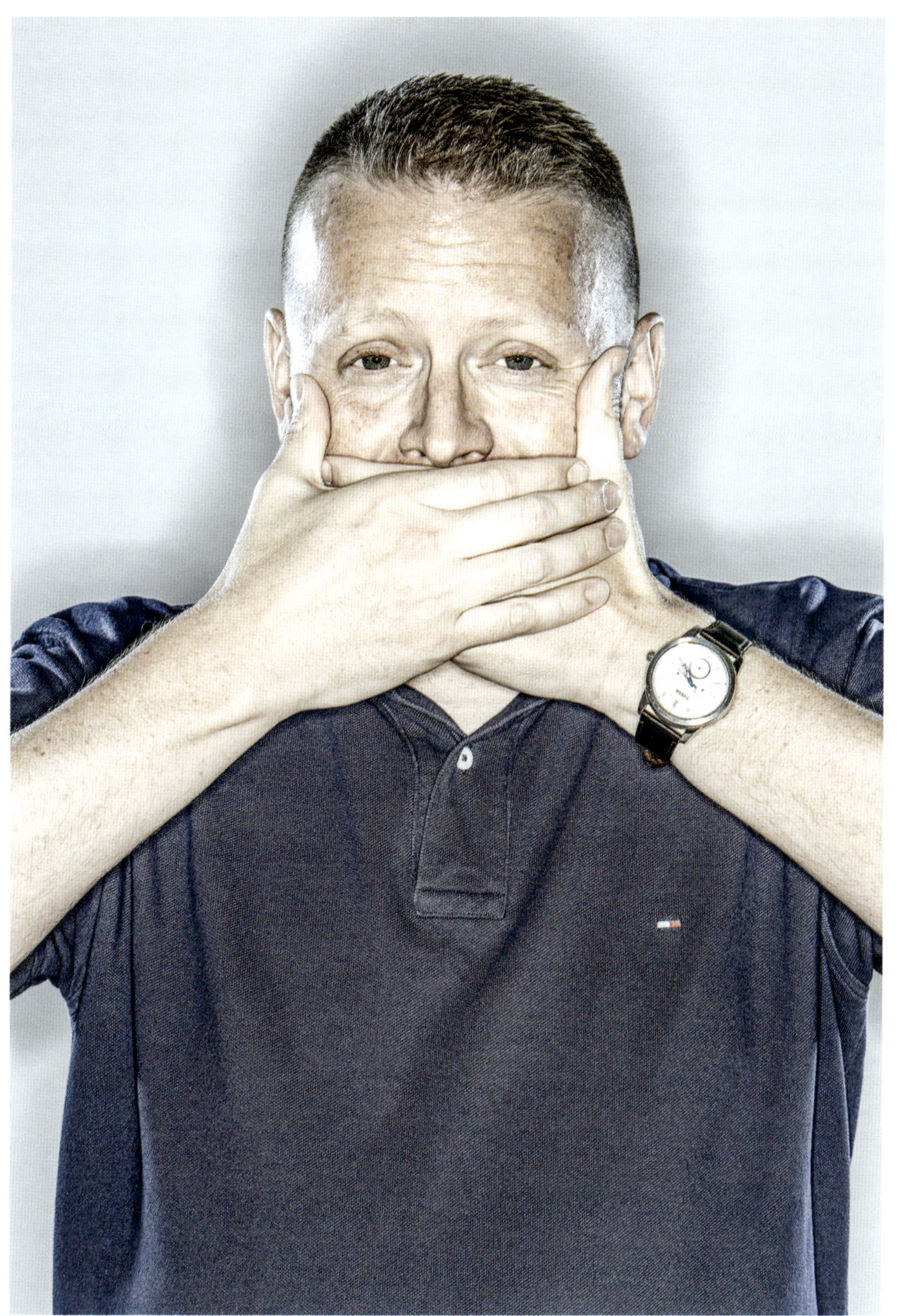

Booker prize winner Ben looked at the pictures after I had shot them. 'That's the one' he declared, 'that's the one to use.' I agreed . . . and so I did!

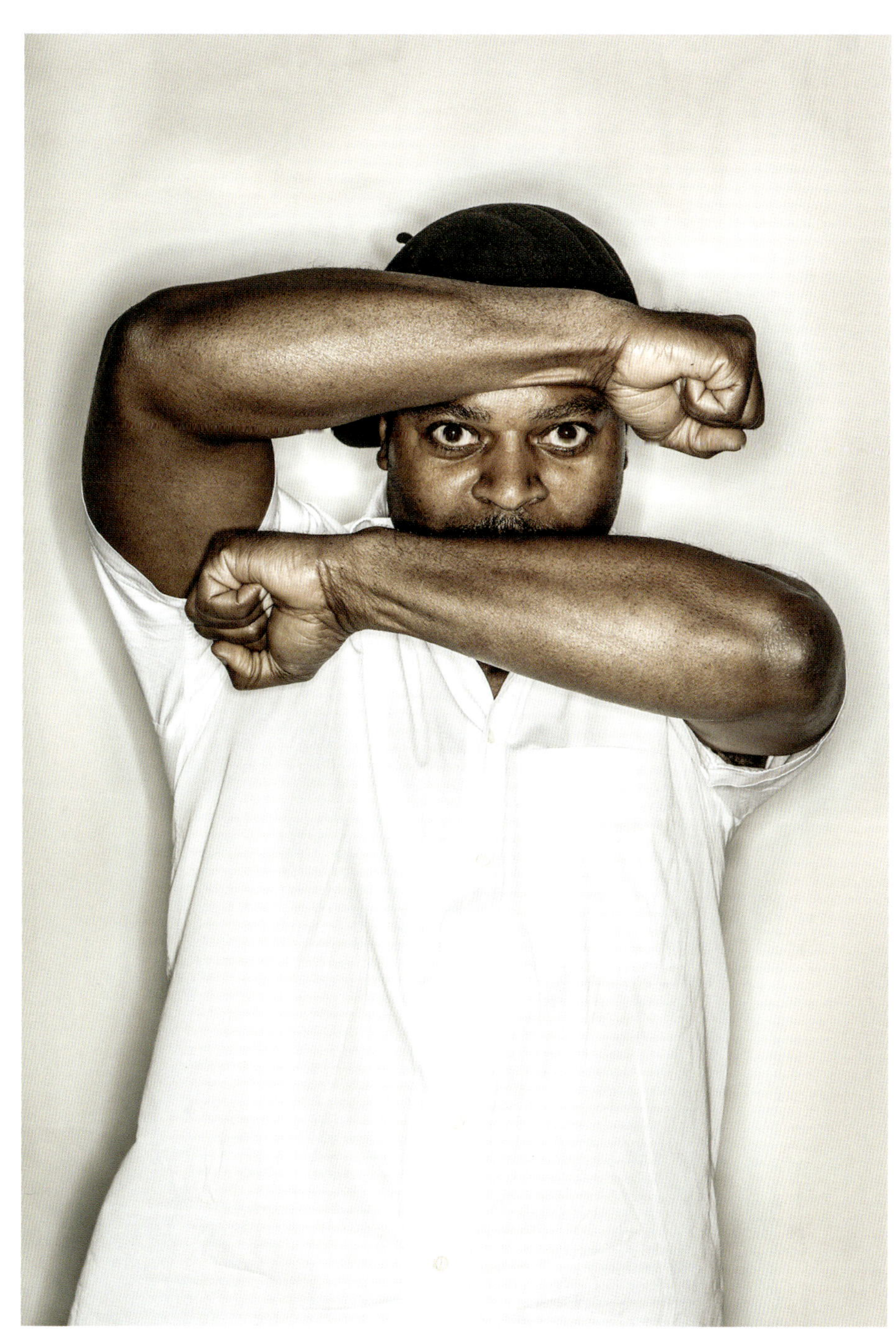

American Pulitzer prize winning poet Sharon Olds. A woman who expresses herself visually as well as through her poetry. She had a hypnotic quality to her. The pictures were full of character. She exudes a beautiful confidence.

'I was a late bloomer. But anyone who blooms at all is very lucky.'

SHARON OLDS

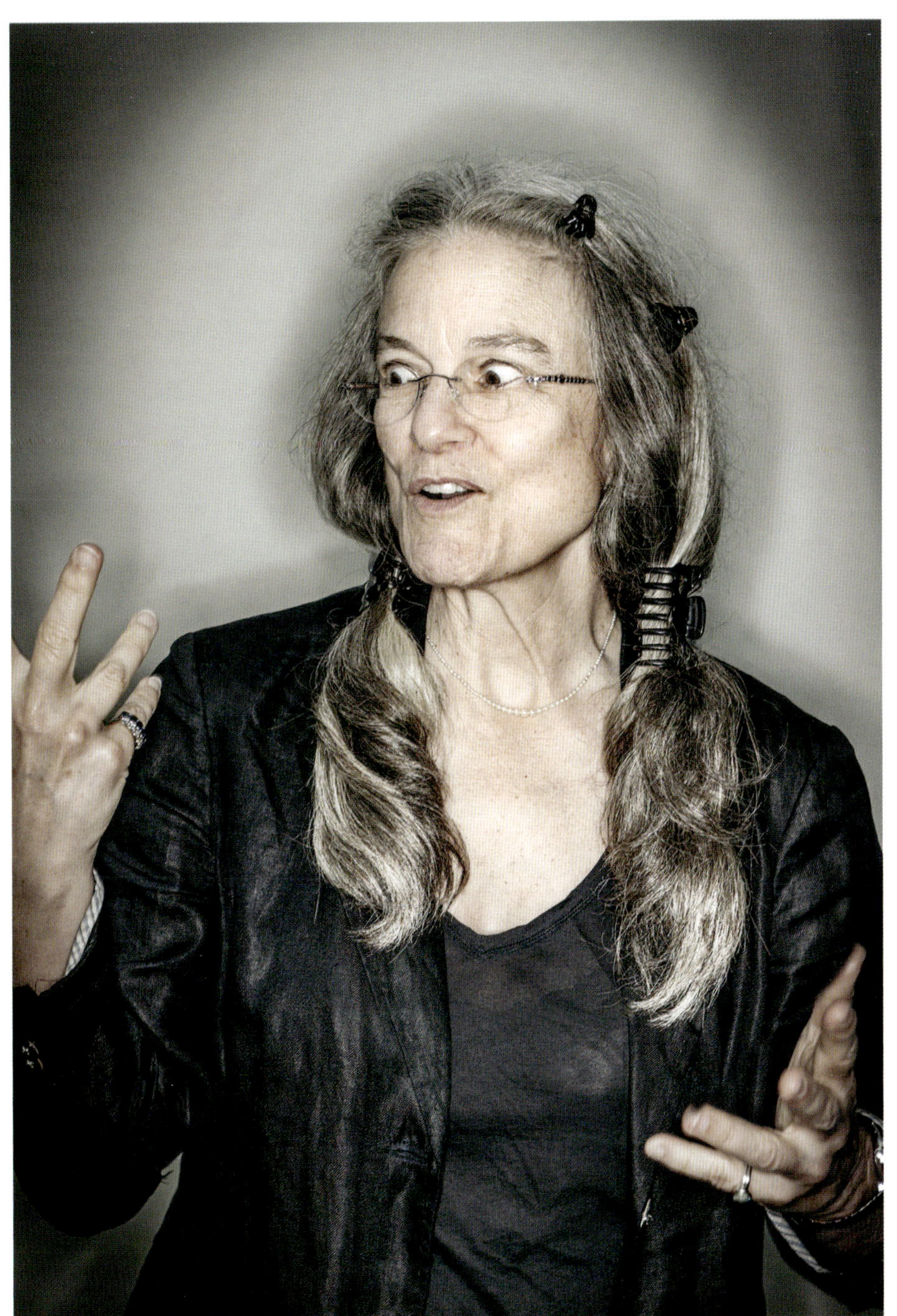

Does Michael need an introduction?

Given the number of people peering into my en plein air studio and the occasional flash and background chatter from authors and public alike, clearly not. Iconic comedian, presenter, actor and author.

*'I saw novelists as being admirable people and I thought . . .
I thought . . . maybe, one day, I could be one of them.'*
MICHAEL PALIN

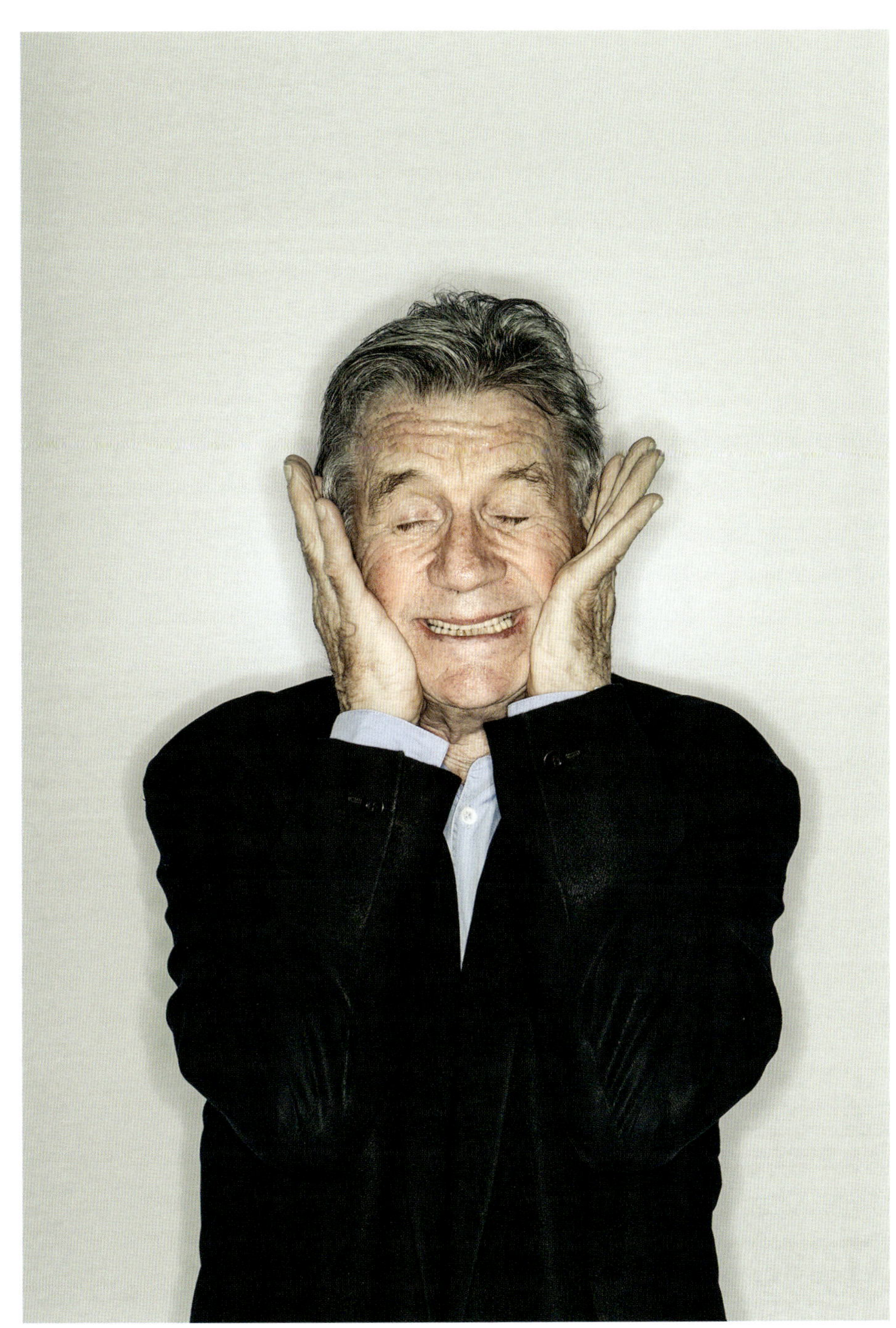

Author of *The Damned United*. Football is a subject I know little about and frequently have to bluff my way through: I was caught out when photographing a well known rock star and Manchester City fan who asked which team I supported, then asked who their manager was; 'Brian' was my answer because I had remembered David's book all about Brian Clough.

His glasses reminded me of an old fashioned TV and his gaze that of an ardent football fan watching Match of the Day.

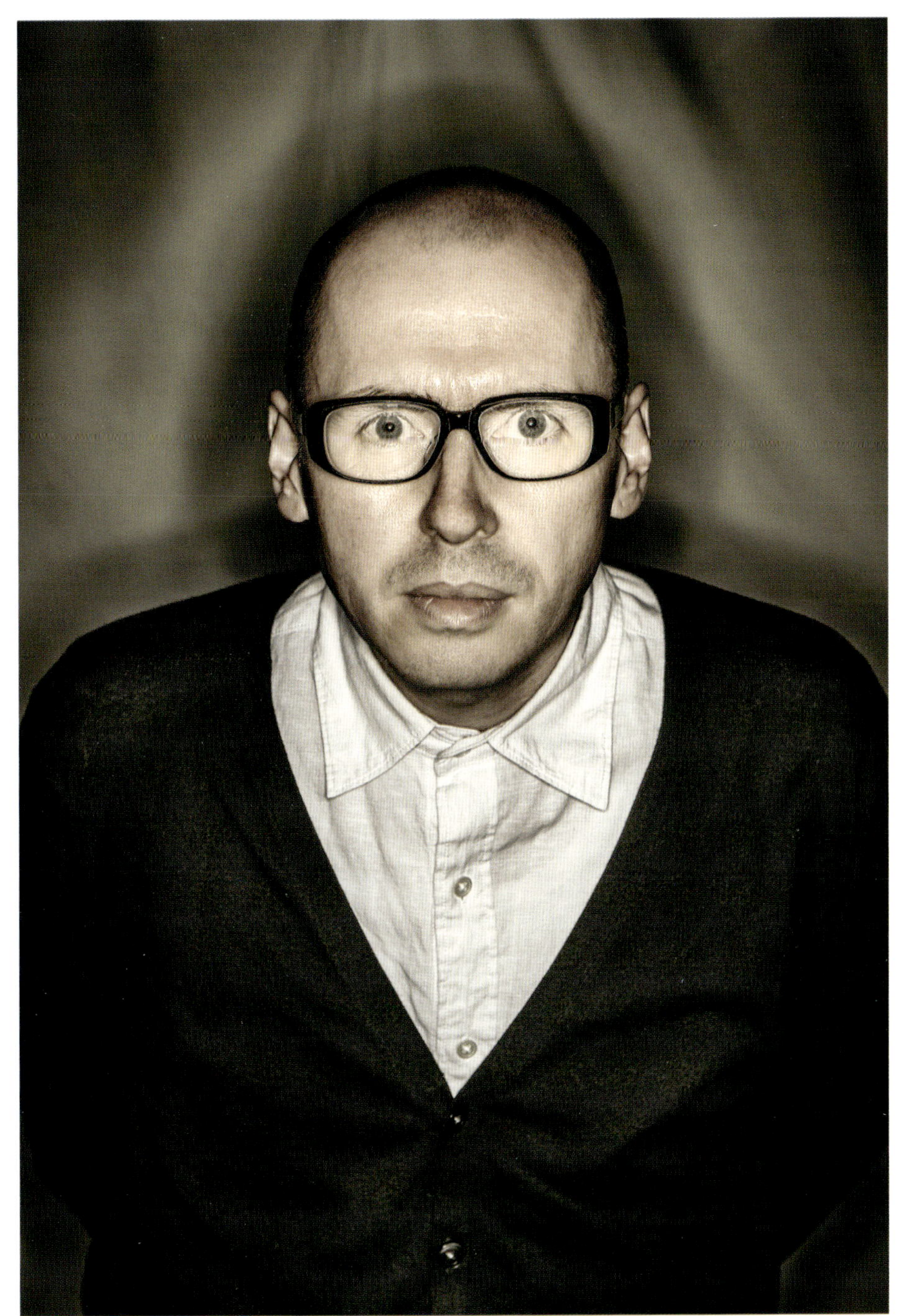

DBC stands for Dirty But Clean. Jetlagged from an early age having been bundled across the world from Australia to the US then England, back to Australia, back to England, then back to the US, before heading for Mexico. Experience gleaned and thrust upon him along the way no doubt good grounding for a writer.

Cigarette in hand, a wink to camera, wind-blown hair and a political statement to boot, Pierre himself is an inspiration for a character in a novel.

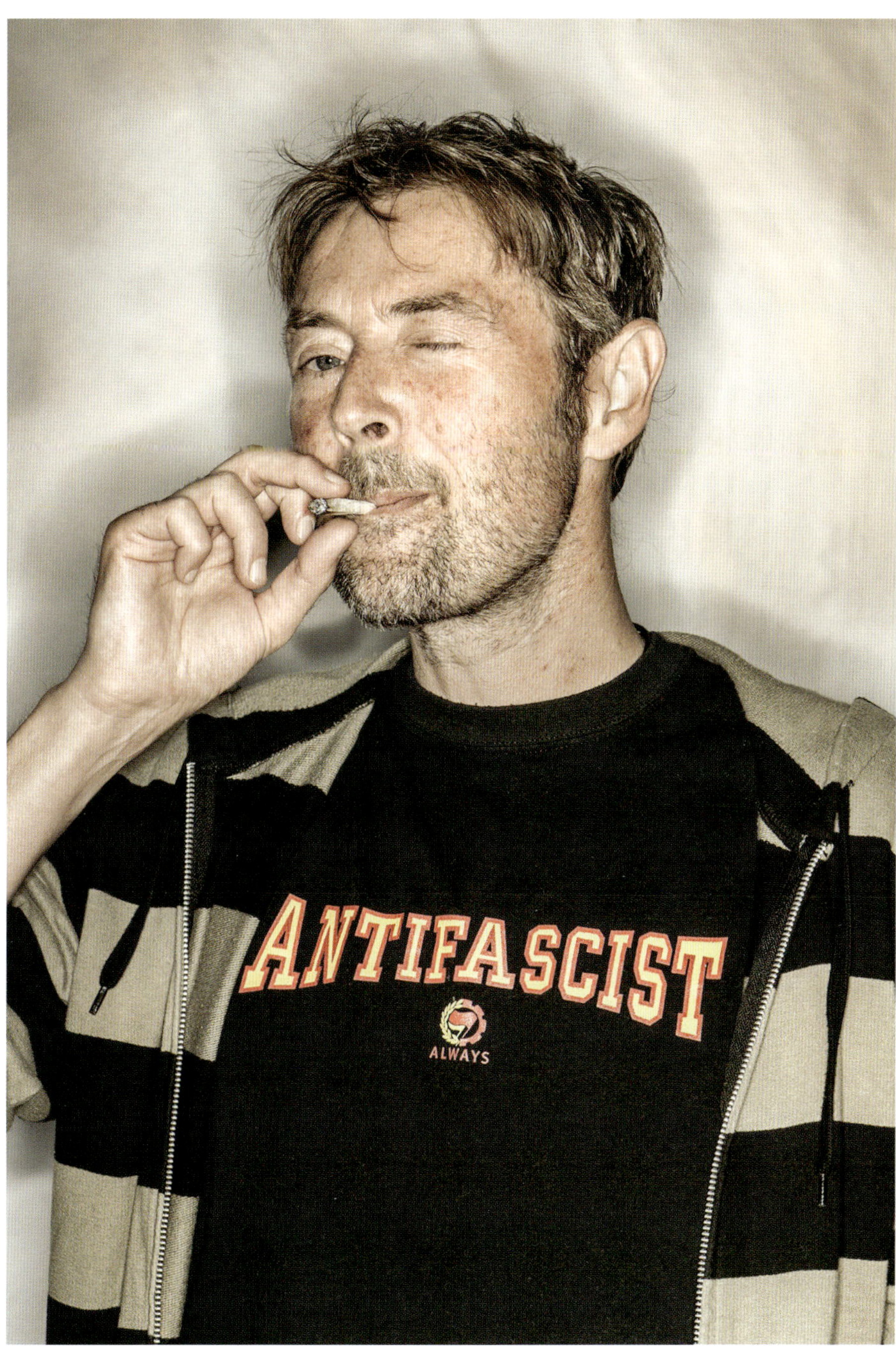

ANTIFASCIST
ALWAYS

Philip Pullman's trilogy *His Dark Materials* has been a radio broadcast, a theatre production and a film. He has written a host of other books many of which seem multigenerational. I questioned him about the controversy he has attracted and his reply was simple, 'I would rather people just read the books.' Doubtless much of the criticism was from people who hadn't. So much so that on the back of his book, *The Good Man Jesus and the Scoundrel Christ* is written 'THIS IS A STORY'.

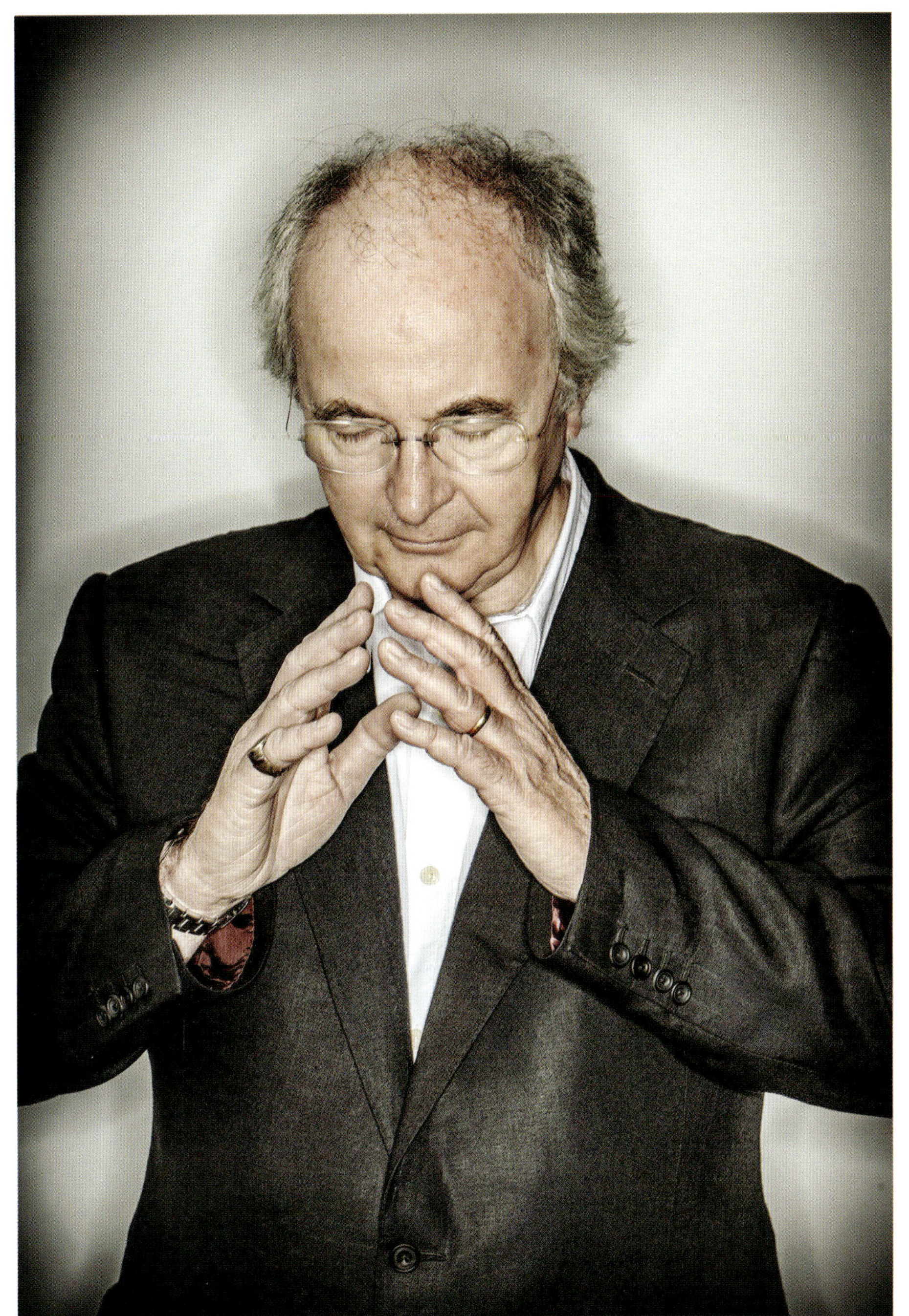

David Rain

David may be considered an unlikely Australian but that is only by the stereotypical views of Australians. That said he has lived for many of his days in the UK. I am always fascinated by what makes people tick and David grew up in a house with no television, a communist father from the outback and has dual Australian and British citizenship. I like the simplicity of this image. David was unsure about the glasses but I told him they were so outrageous he had to wear them.

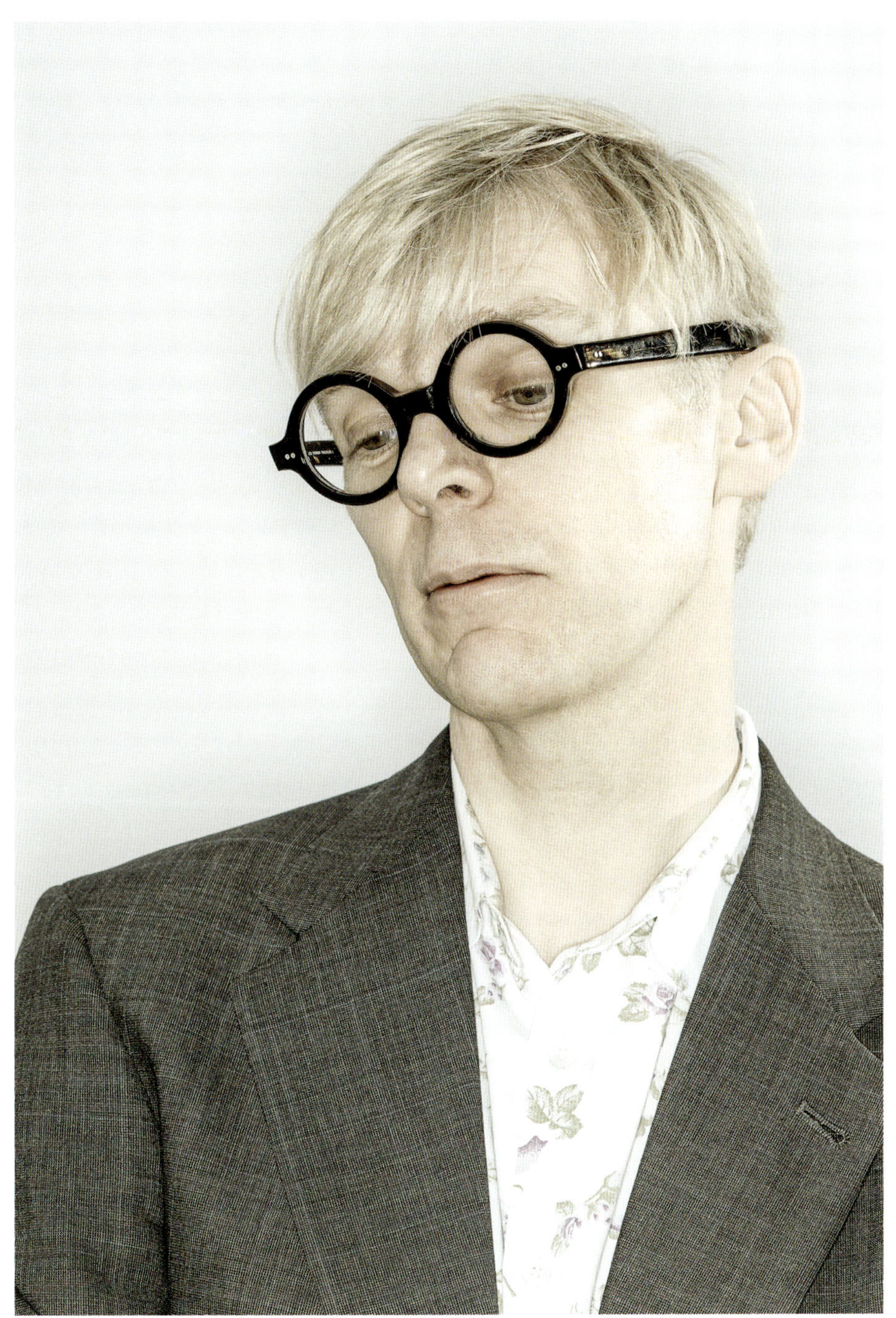

Britain's most successful crime writer. My previous photograph of Ian produced quite a strong image so I knew I had to come up with something equally eye catching. I was using a paper backdrop and it had begun to get a bit ragged in the rain so I asked Ian to tear a hole and put his head through. It was inspired by Jack Nicholson in *The Shining*. I shot a few frames and eventually Ian just burst through the whole sheet. This was one of the earlier photographs and adding the text was an afterthought. I went to the bookshop, grabbed a couple of Ian's books and shot a few pages. Without looking at the text I chose one and superimposed it onto the blank sheet of paper. The next day someone pointed out to me the line in the text that read, 'You're not exactly a poster boy yourself.'

Pure chance.

mention once that you were in the police. That's how I got your number …'

'What's happened?' Fox repeated, aware that both Naysmith and Kaye were now listening.

'Jude's had a bit of an accident …'

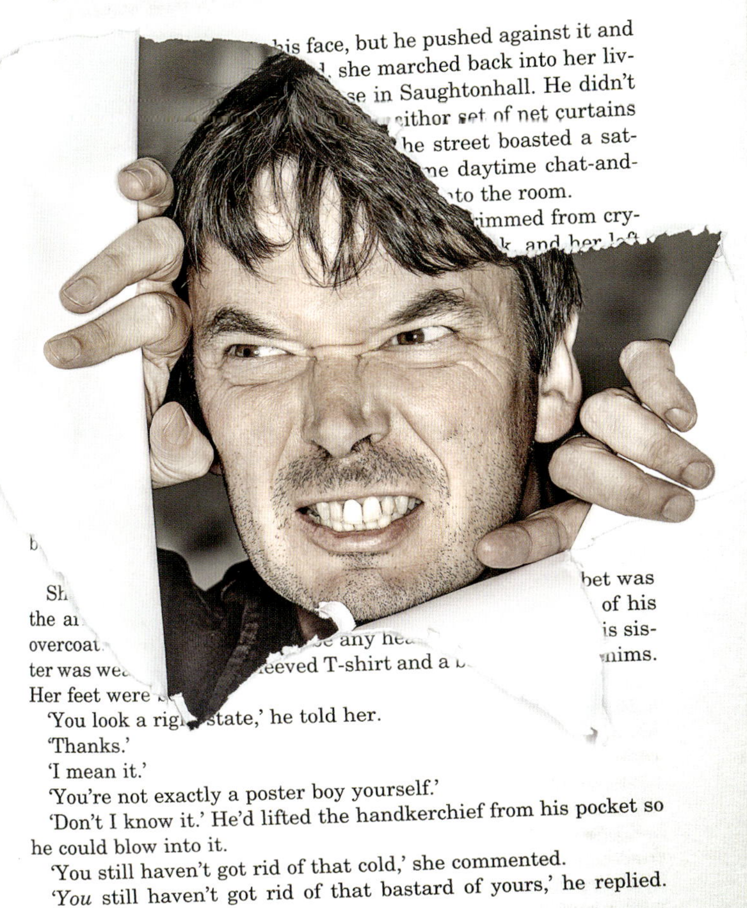

'You look a right state,' he told her.

'Thanks.'

'I mean it.'

'You're not exactly a poster boy yourself.'

'Don't I know it.' He'd lifted the handkerchief from his pocket so he could blow into it.

'You still haven't got rid of that cold,' she commented.

'*You* still haven't got rid of that bastard of yours,' he replied.

'Where is he?'

A man who came to prominence in the UK in the 80s with *Not the Nine O'Clock News* and has been there, or thereabouts ever since. Some noises off had said to tread carefully as he could be a livewire with a short fuse but as is usually the case I could have said anything I wanted and probably did. I discretely placed a copy of his book near the cameras, like a peace offering, in case, having done numerous interviews, having his picture taken was not his number one priority. Griff, as it transpired, was a delight. I am not sure whether having a copy of his book nearby made any difference but he was a charming, erudite man.

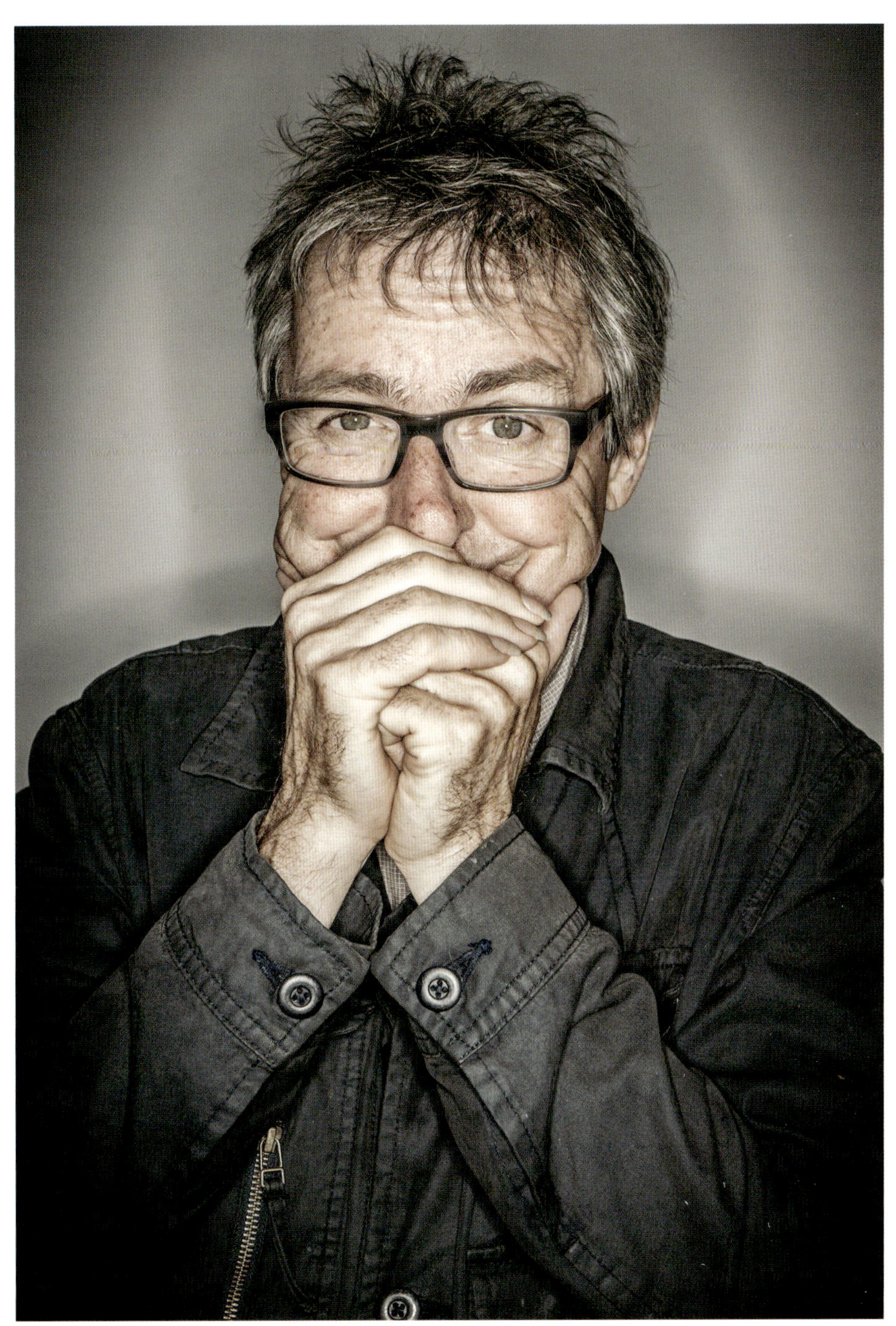

Nile Rodgers, musician, producer and writer came to prominence in the 70s with his band Chic. His career has subsequently been super-charged, collaborating with a variety of artists including Pharrel Williams and Daft Punk.

Having also produced David Bowie, Madonna, Duran Duran etc, I anticipated Nile would have an entourage with him. I was wrong. Nile arrived. No entourage. No ego just a man with a lot of stories and a guitar, oh and dreadlocks. I often gravitate towards some kind of anonymity in pictures, so after a few frames I suggested Nile hold his dreadlocks across his face which led to this picture.

An active Twitter user Nile's battle with cancer is no secret, he has a youthful energy and exuberance and is more in demand than ever so I am grateful I got to spend some time with him and listen to some of the tales.

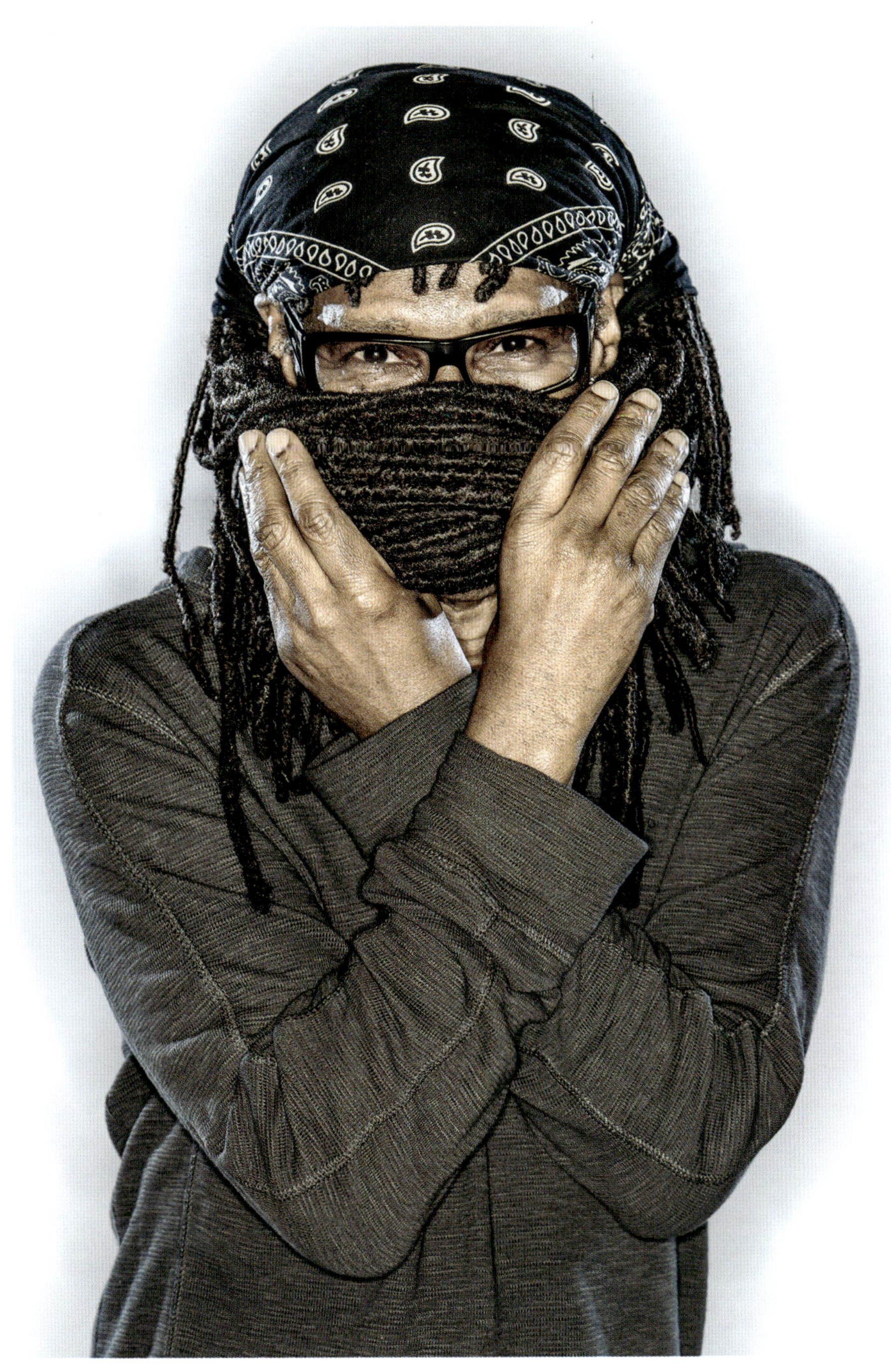

I read Jon's biography before meeting him and saw he had been at the same university as me, in the same faculty and at the same time so immediately we had something to talk about. He turned up with a pint of beer in hand so in the first few frames that is what he was holding.

Jon wrote *The Men Who Stare at Goats* which became a film with Ewan McGregor and George Clooney. I didn't have a goat but did have a rubber duck. This was one of these photographs where chance played a part because this picture was used on the cover of his subsequent novel *The Psychopath Test*.

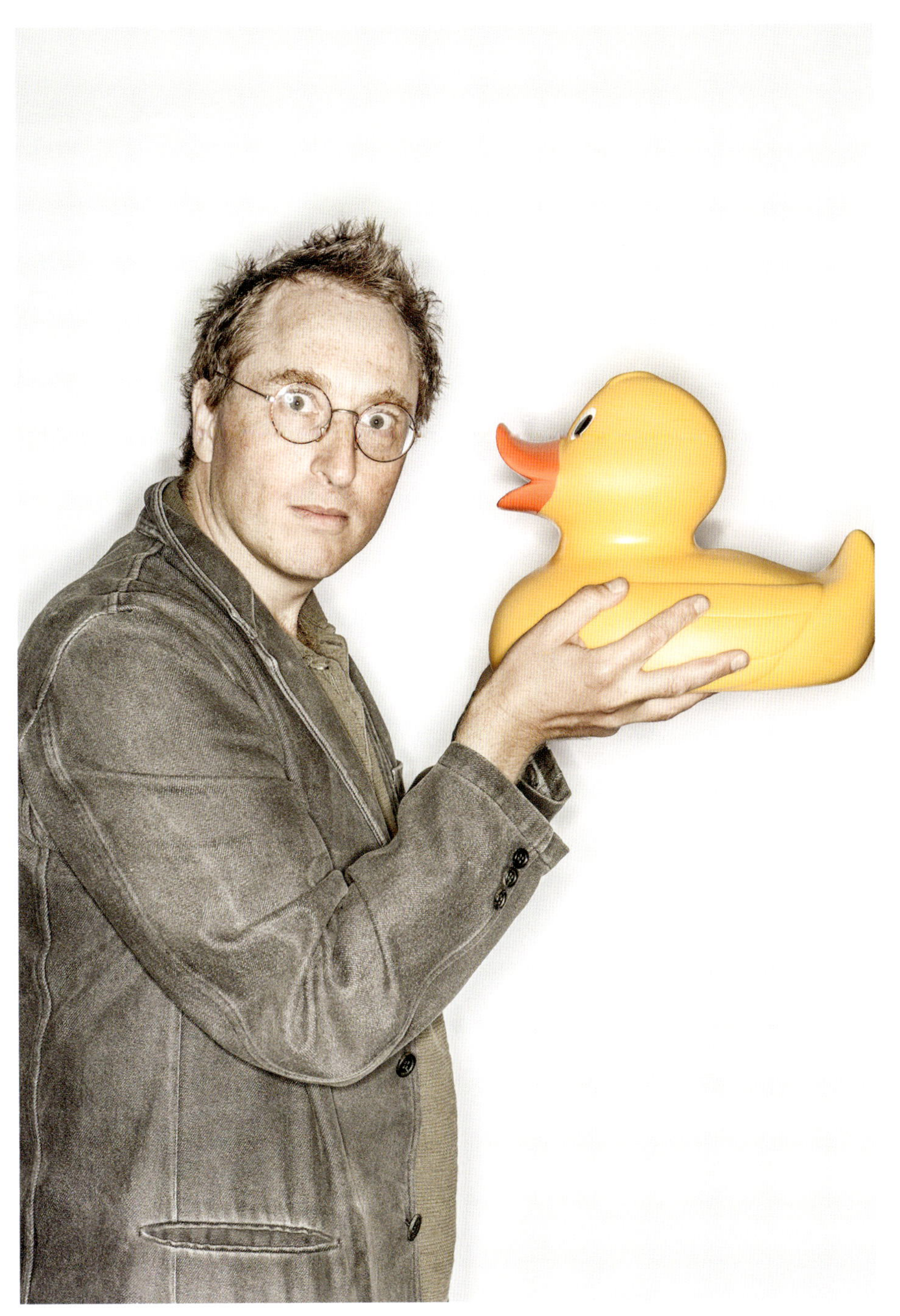

Another author whose portrait hangs in the National Portrait Gallery in London. Poet, performer, presenter Michael was like a coiled spring. Wind him up, stand back and shoot. I am sure he has his cup of tea moments but not here.

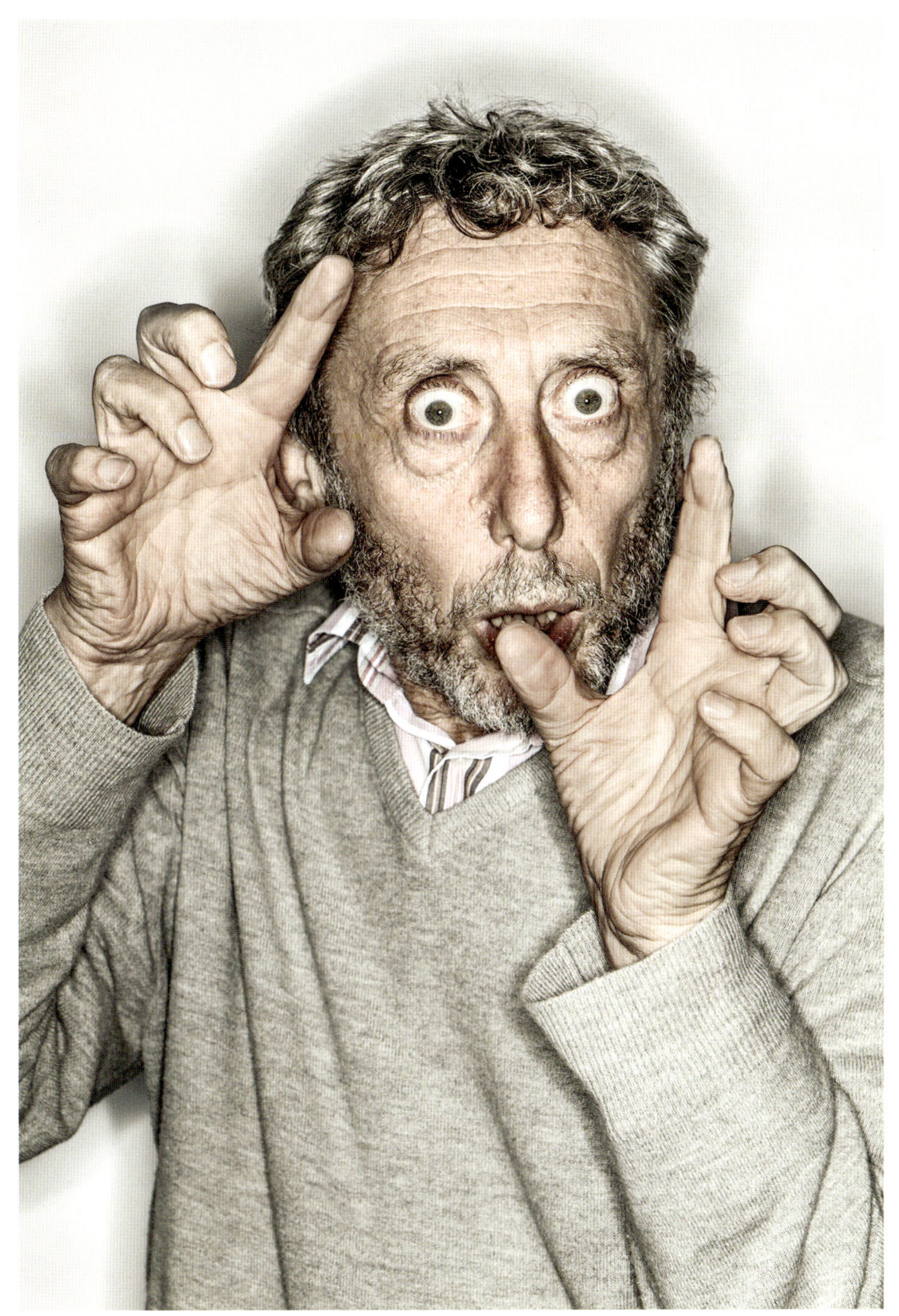

'There shall be a photographer in my next book and he shall be evil'

So Meg told me after she saw her portrait the next day.

If I like it, it's going up! That said very often people like the photographs of other people and not themselves. It's an interesting dichotomy.

I'd hate to be a nice photographer.

After all, the baddies get all the best lines . . .

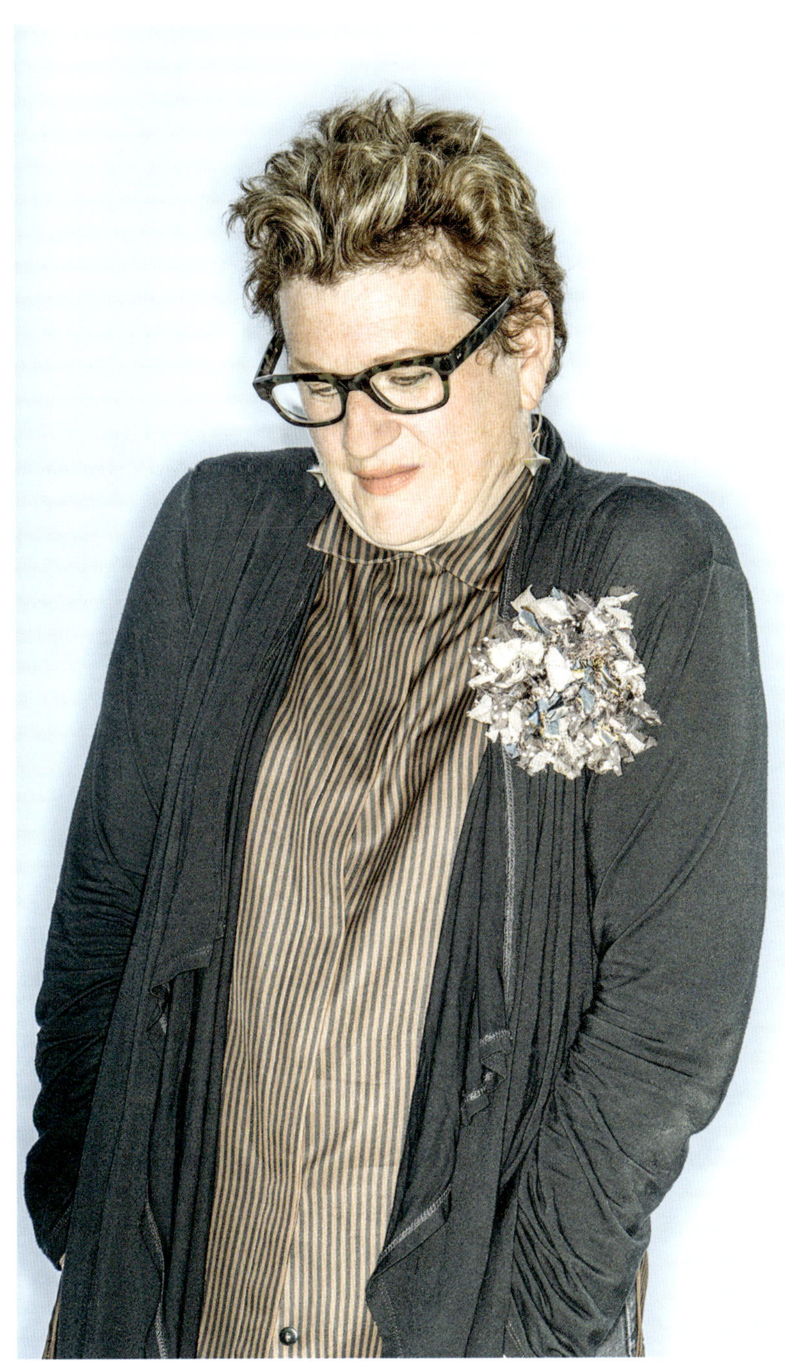

Son of the former Archbishop of Canterbury, his *Grantchester Mystery* novels having been received to great acclaim.

James turned up and completely took me by surprise. I have photographed James twice and this is one of the more subdued pictures. The first time he turned his glasses upside town and started smoking a pen. I am often ask me how I get the expressions and authors to do things. In the case of James he saw my pictures and completely got it.

'I try to write novels that are entertaining and yet serious at the same time. I've always been interested in how the comic and the profound can combine'.

JAMES RUNCIE

I am not sure whether I captured that in this picture but there are elements of solemnity combined with the bizarre: that T-shirt and tie!

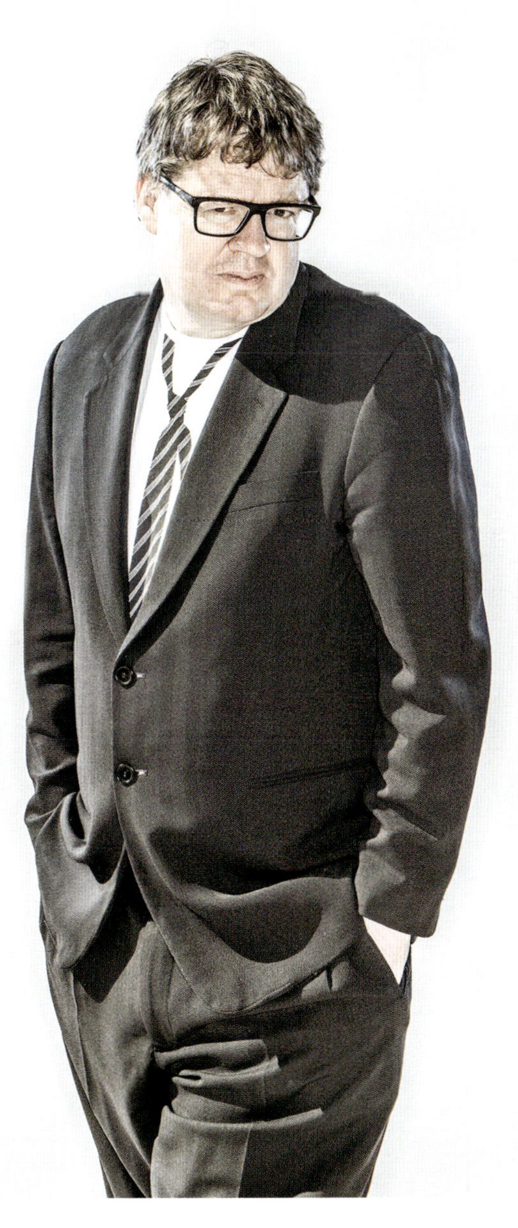

Say 'Salman Rushdie' and what's the first thing that comes to mind? In my case it is the Wizard of Oz as Salman has written a book about the film which may seem odd except the first story he ever wrote aged ten was called *Over the Rainbow*.

> *'Only under extreme pressure can we change into that which it is in our most profound nature to become'* . . .
>
> SALMAN RUSHDIE, *The Ground Beneath Her Feet*

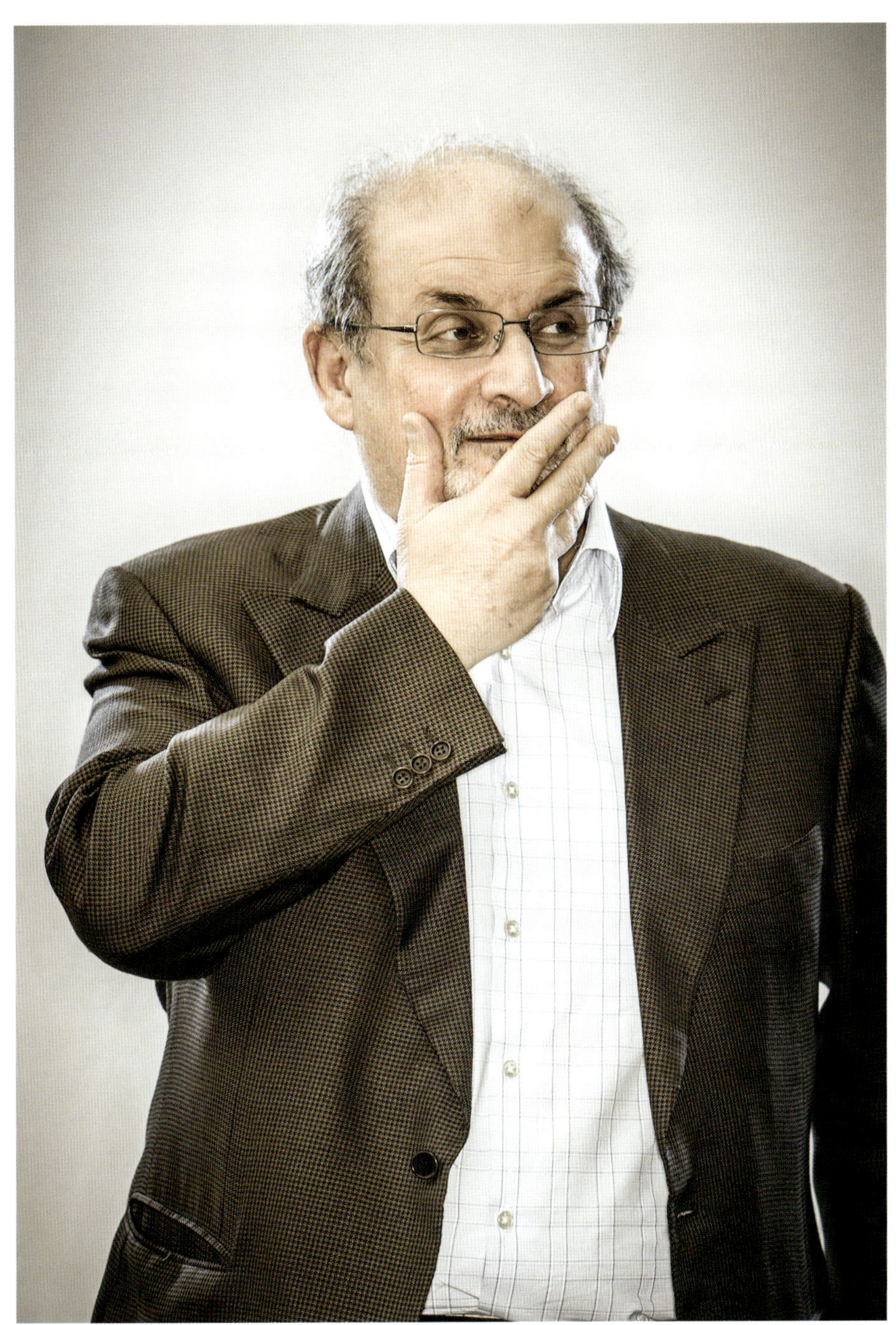

I can't remember if this was partly inspired by one of Marcus' books *The Ghosts of Heaven* or *She is not Invisible*. Either way Marcus' scarf provided an anonimity suitable for either.

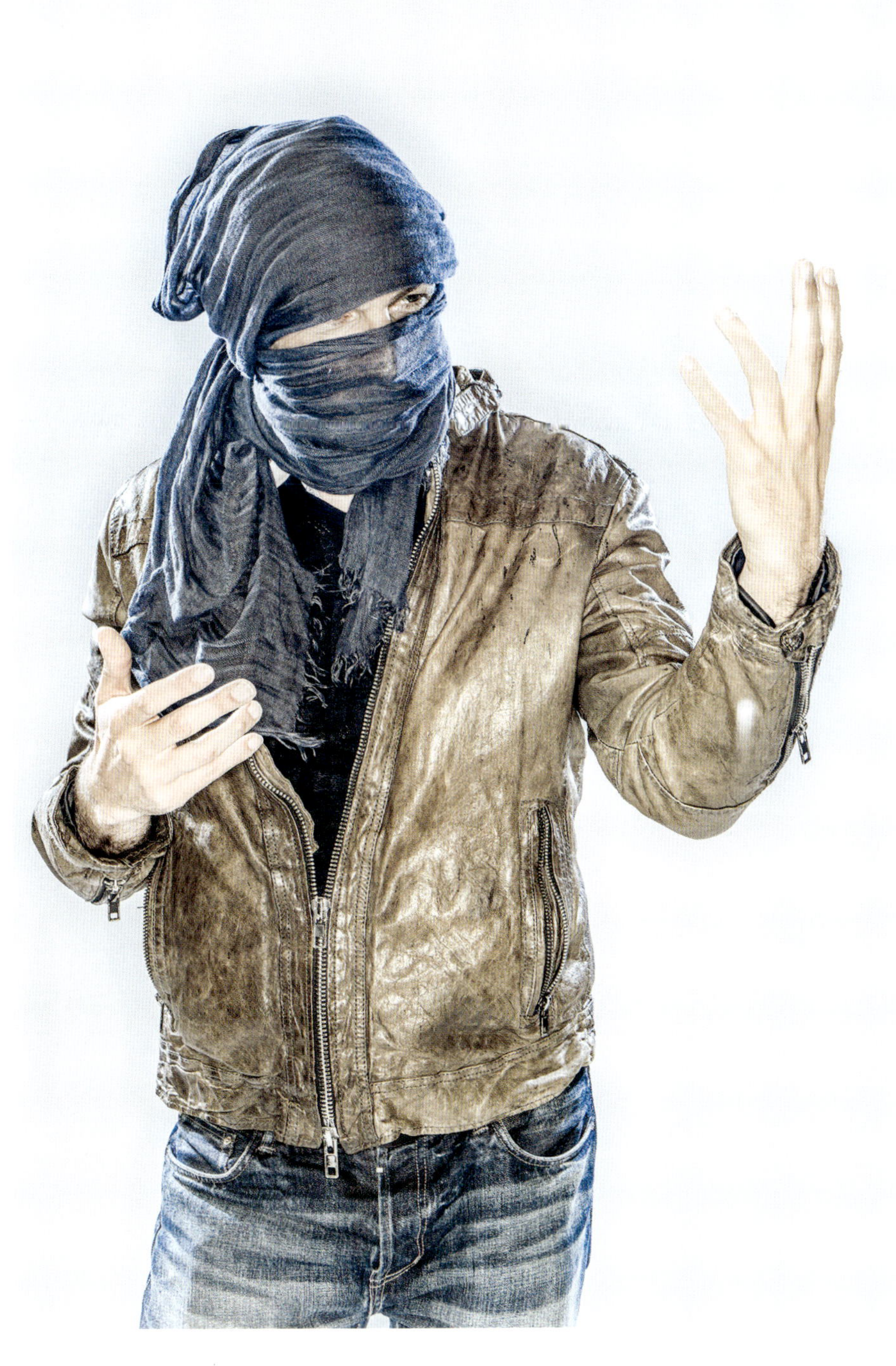

Will Self and Maglorian

Maglorian, now that's a name you want to shout out in a park. Very little danger anyone else's dog will come running. Will was late for his event and against Edinburgh Book Festival rules also brought his dog. It all made for a frantic photoshoot and a ubiquitous image.

'Whatever respect photography may once have deserved is now superfluous in view of its own superfluity.'

WILL SELF

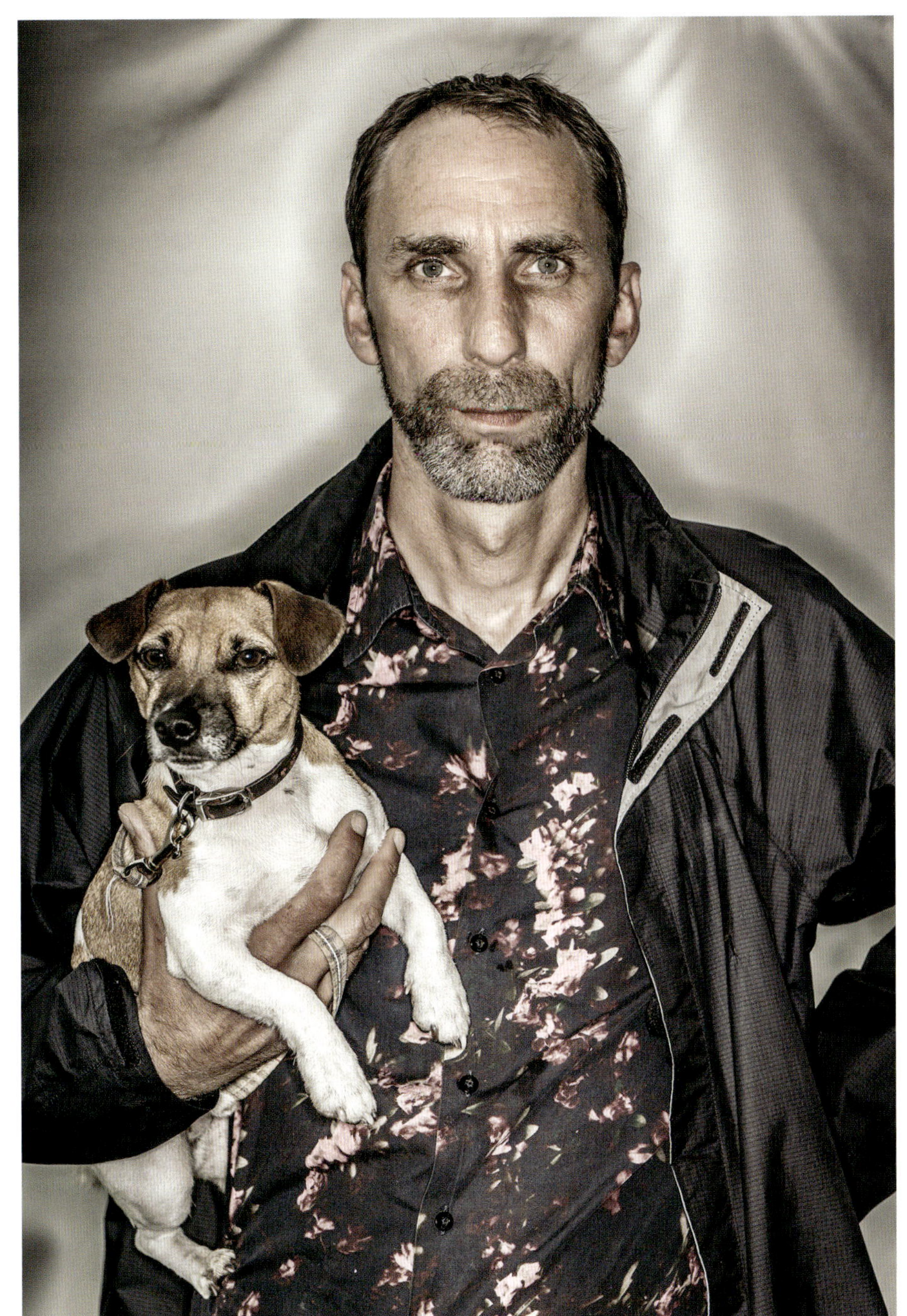

Sara came to me with this concept. I don't make a habit of asking female writers to strip off in a public arena! I did have to shoot this early, before the public were on site. Although I am in a private area reserved for press and authors, the public can see in. That said things did over-run and a quick holding up of a back cloth was called for to protect my modesty, Sara couldn't have cared less! The make up artist was Sara's daughter. One of the days I was glad it didn't rain.

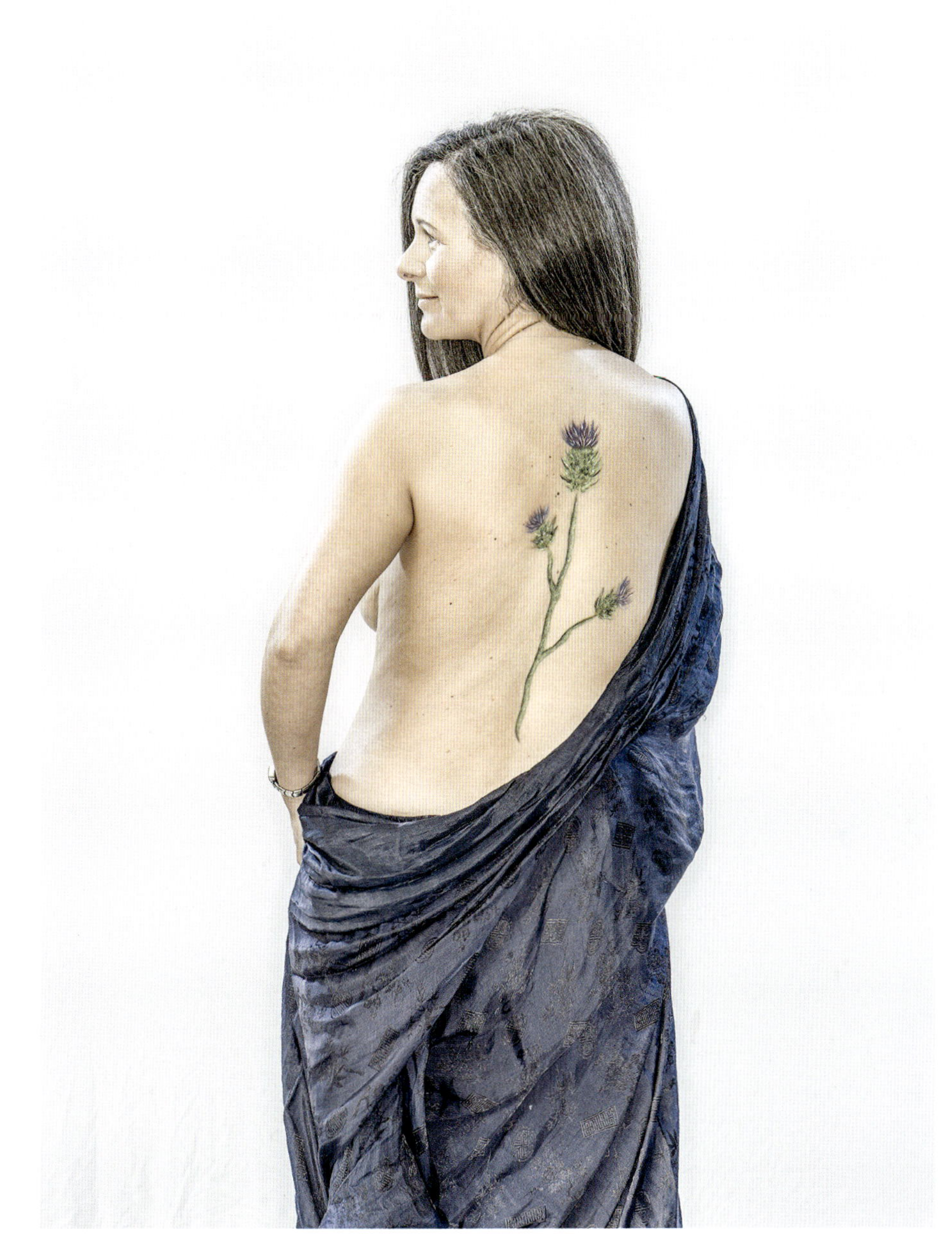

Crime novelist John Gordon Sinclair. A man used to being in front of the camera, John agreed to this idea as having previously had Mark Billingham shoot himself, I thought I would continue with the murderous theme. Thankfully health and safety were not about although it had to be taken quickly, not for fear of suffocation but because when breathing inside the bag, it kept steaming up. By holding his hands up he was able to pull the bag against his face to enable a clearer shot. He is more handsome than he appears here but it was great fun to do.

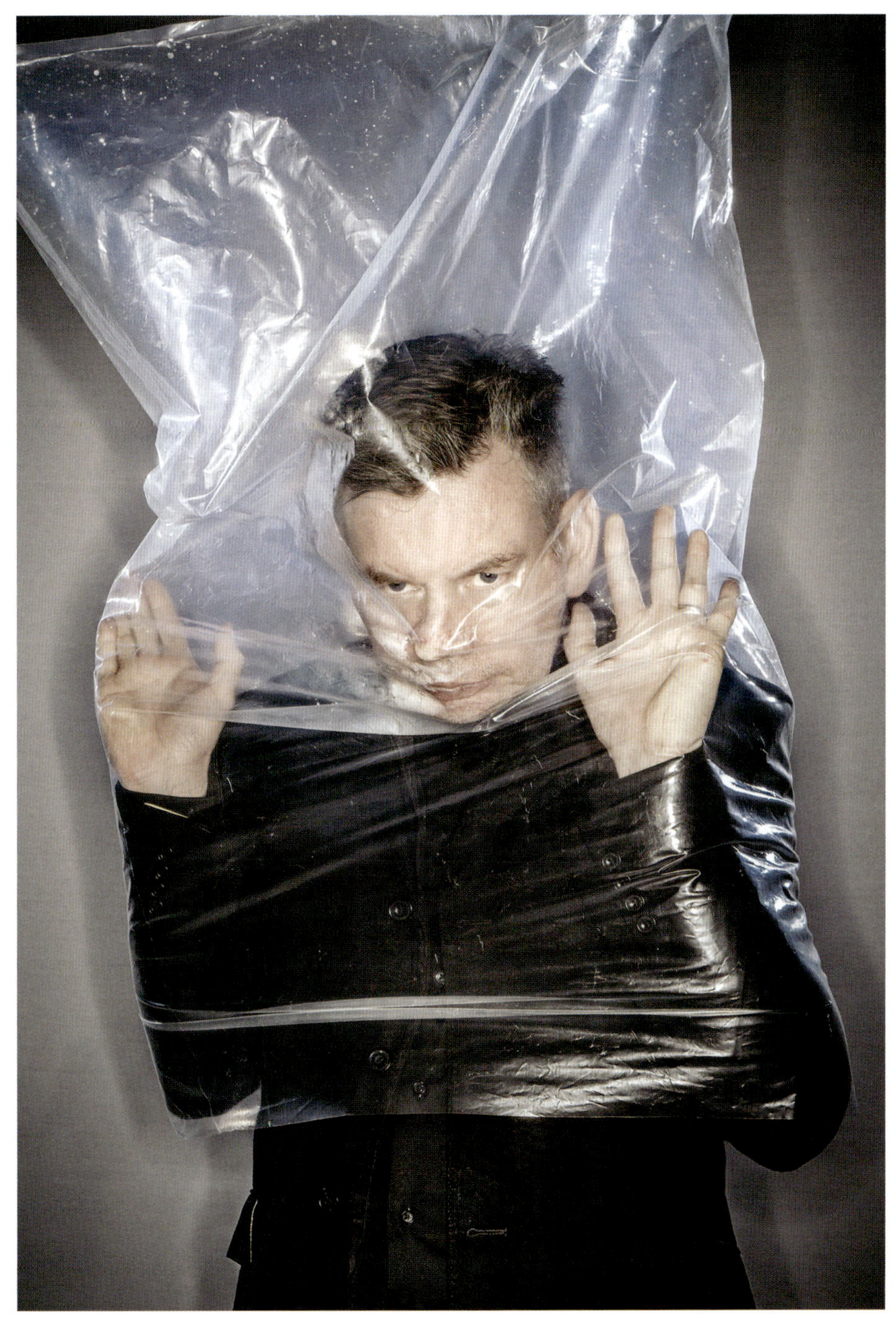

Icelandic. I feel that could say it all. There is something of the Bjork in all things that emanate from Iceland, at least that is my experience of all the authors I have photographed from this part of the world. Sjon has collaborated with the aforementioned singer but comes very much with his own voice from the land of fire and ice and apparently dapper dressers.

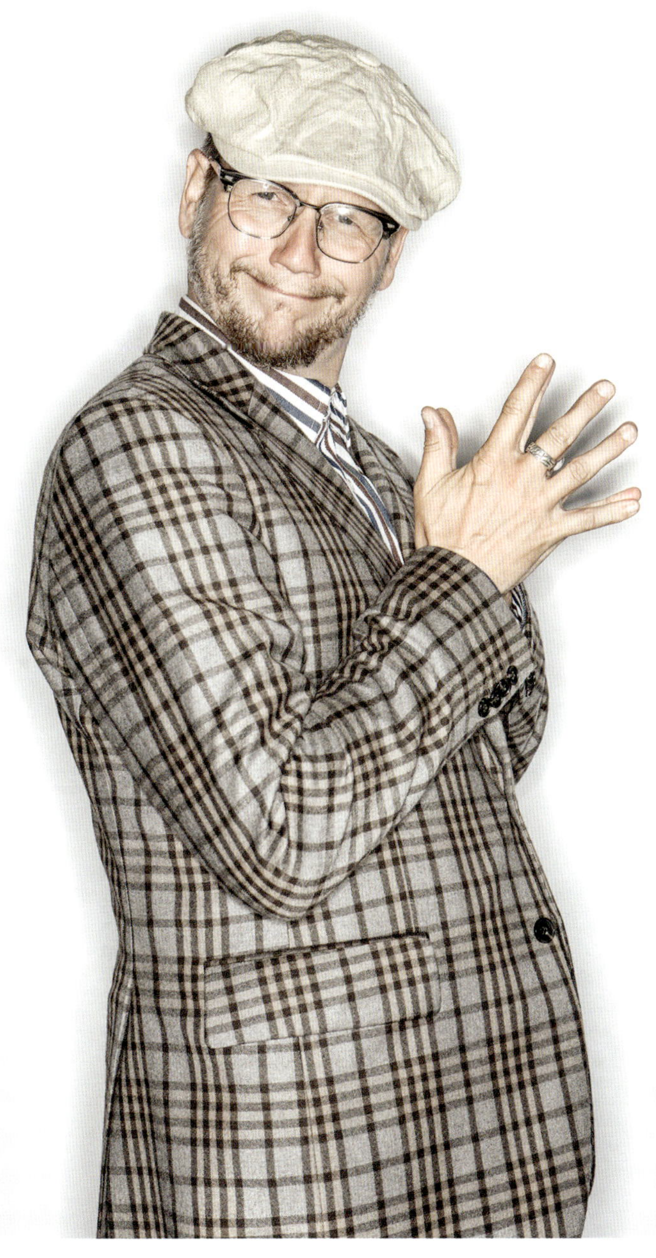

Ali hardly writes a book without it being at the very least shortlisted for a major prize.

Recently awarded a CBE and the Bailey Prize for her time shifting novel, *How to be Both*.

> *'Books mean all possibilities. They mean moving out of yourself, losing yourself, dying of thirst and living to your full. They mean everything.'*
> ALI SMITH

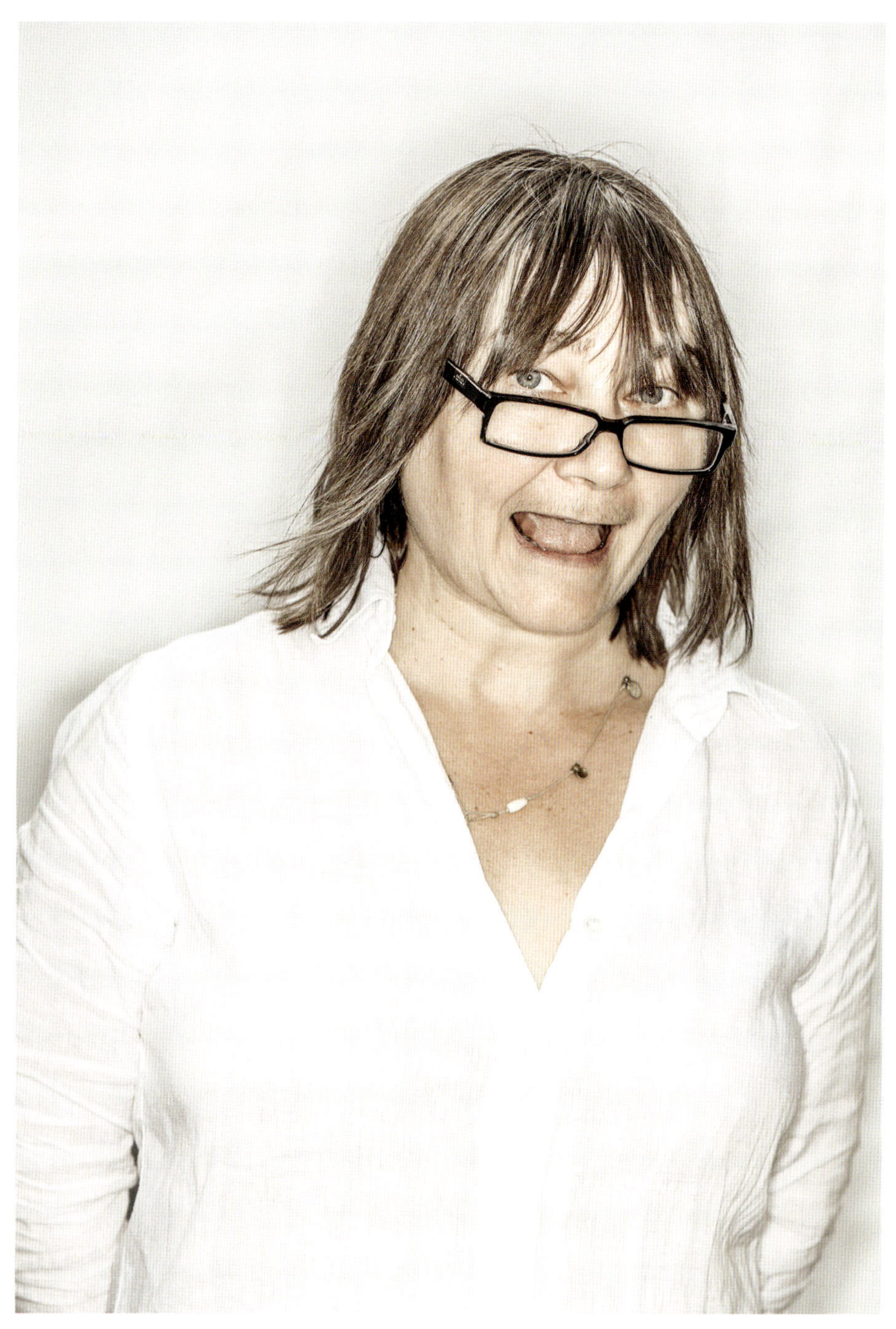

Neal is a science 'fictionesque' author. He lives in Seattle home also to Starbucks, which sounds equally sci-fi in its own way, although perhaps more Buck Rogers than Neal's 'cyberpunk' literary style.

Knowing that, the photograph looks planned, when in fact it was completely by chance. I took the first picture of Neal and he looked at the flash and immediately said,

'Oh that's too bright. I don't think I can look at that.'

'Just cover your eyes then,' I replied, which he did. I took another picture.

'Better?'

He looked through between his hands. Flash.

'Oh sorry.'

It wasn't until I was looking at the pictures on screen I realised it was this alienesque, Cyclops that I had to use.

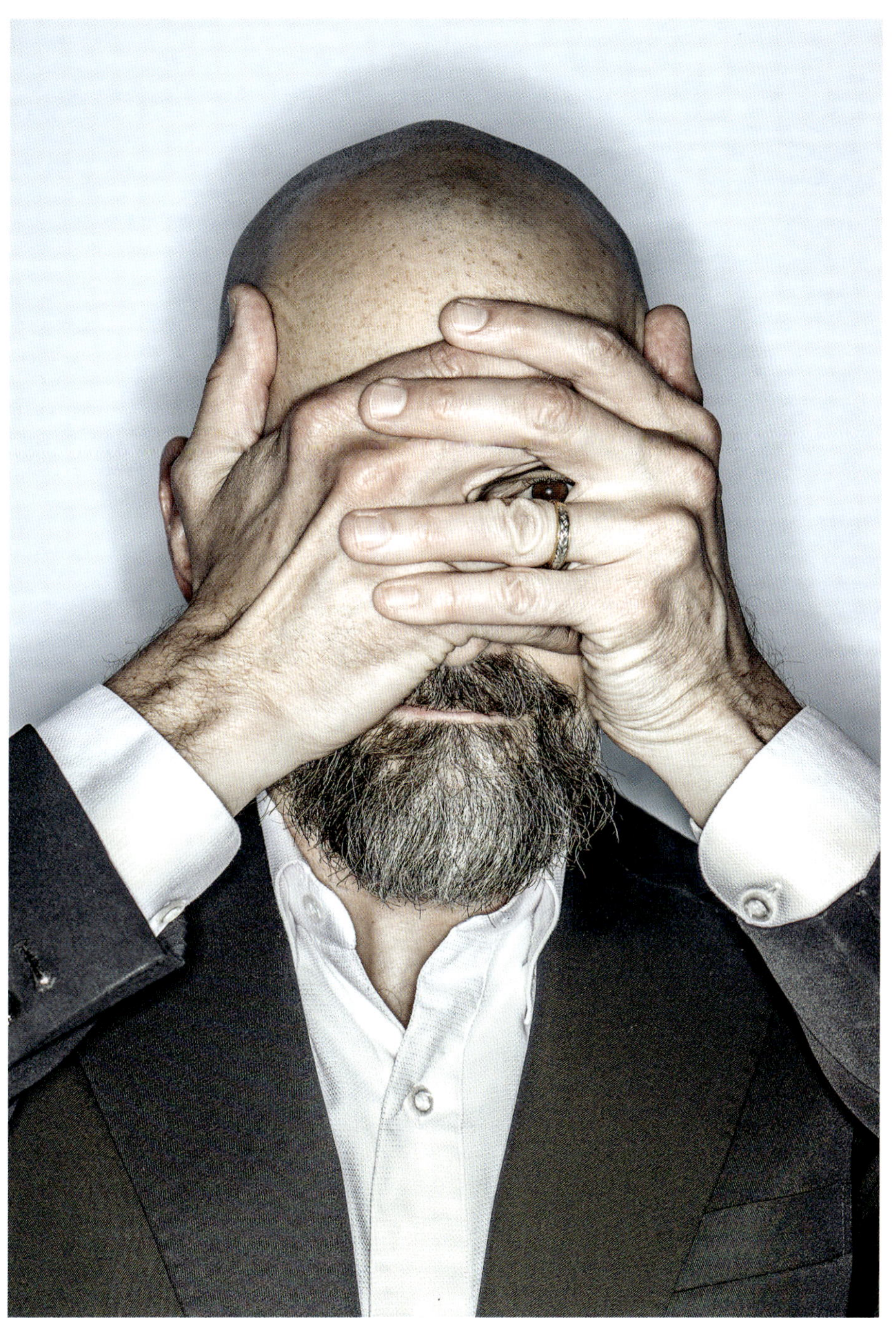

Illustrator Adam Stower came to meet me. Often I know little about where the subjects talents lie but when he told me of his work I suggested bringing one of his creations to life. Being a fan of *Bedknobs and Broomsticks* and *Mary Poppins* I liked the idea of combining photography and illustration.

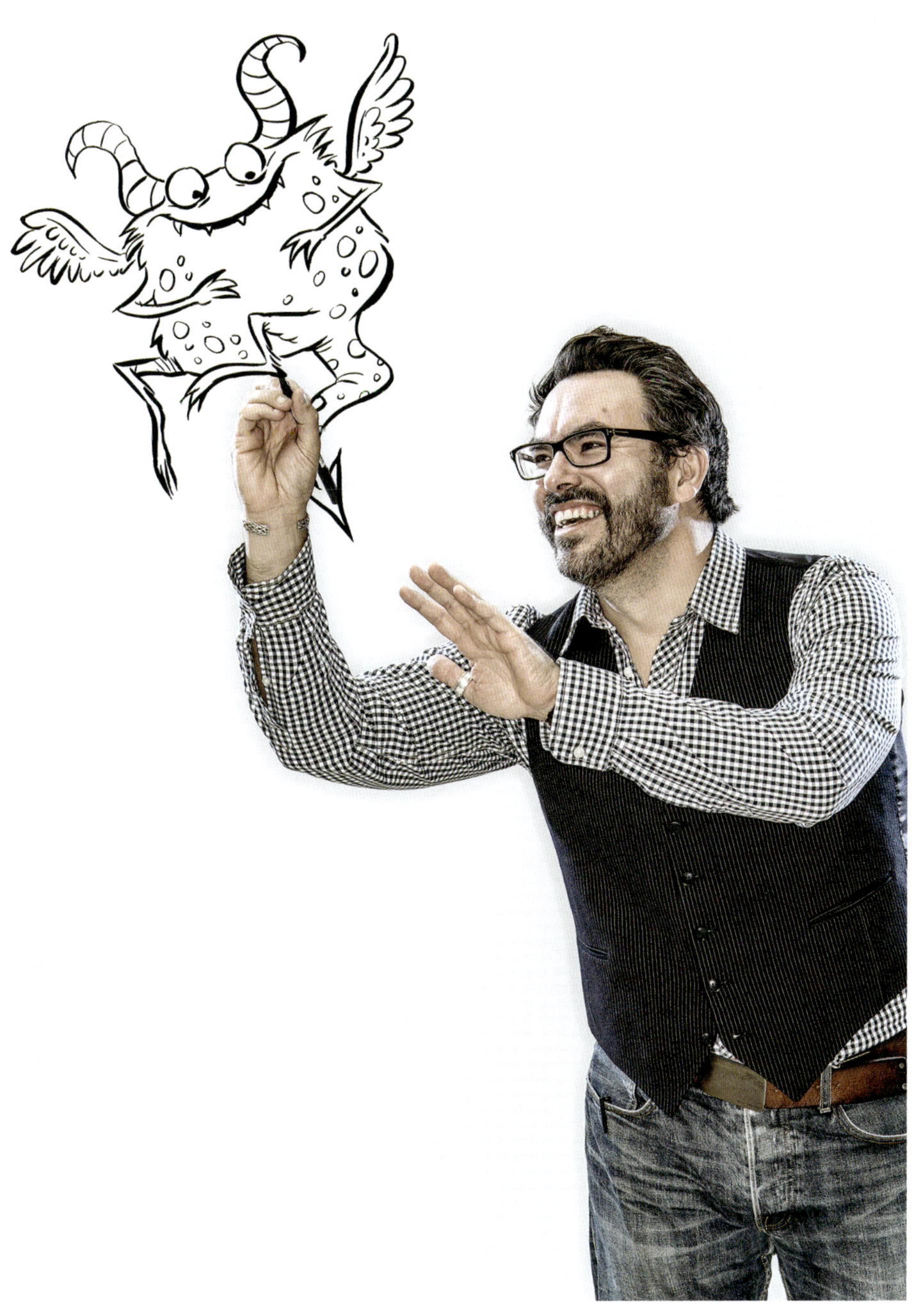

I confess I did not recognise John at first, he was giving an interview to a TV crew but I did think he would photograph well. Ha. This picture was posted to John's Facebook site and received around 25,000 likes. I took one picture and commented he still had it, whatever, 'it' is. Ridiculously photogenic in an annoyingly handsome kind of way, John was very self deprecating about himself stating that it if hadn't been for his looks he would not be where he is now. The days of decadent dcbauchery of Duran Duran at their peak must have been something to behold. The words 'child' and 'sweetshop' spring to mind. I wonder how much of it he can believe himself.

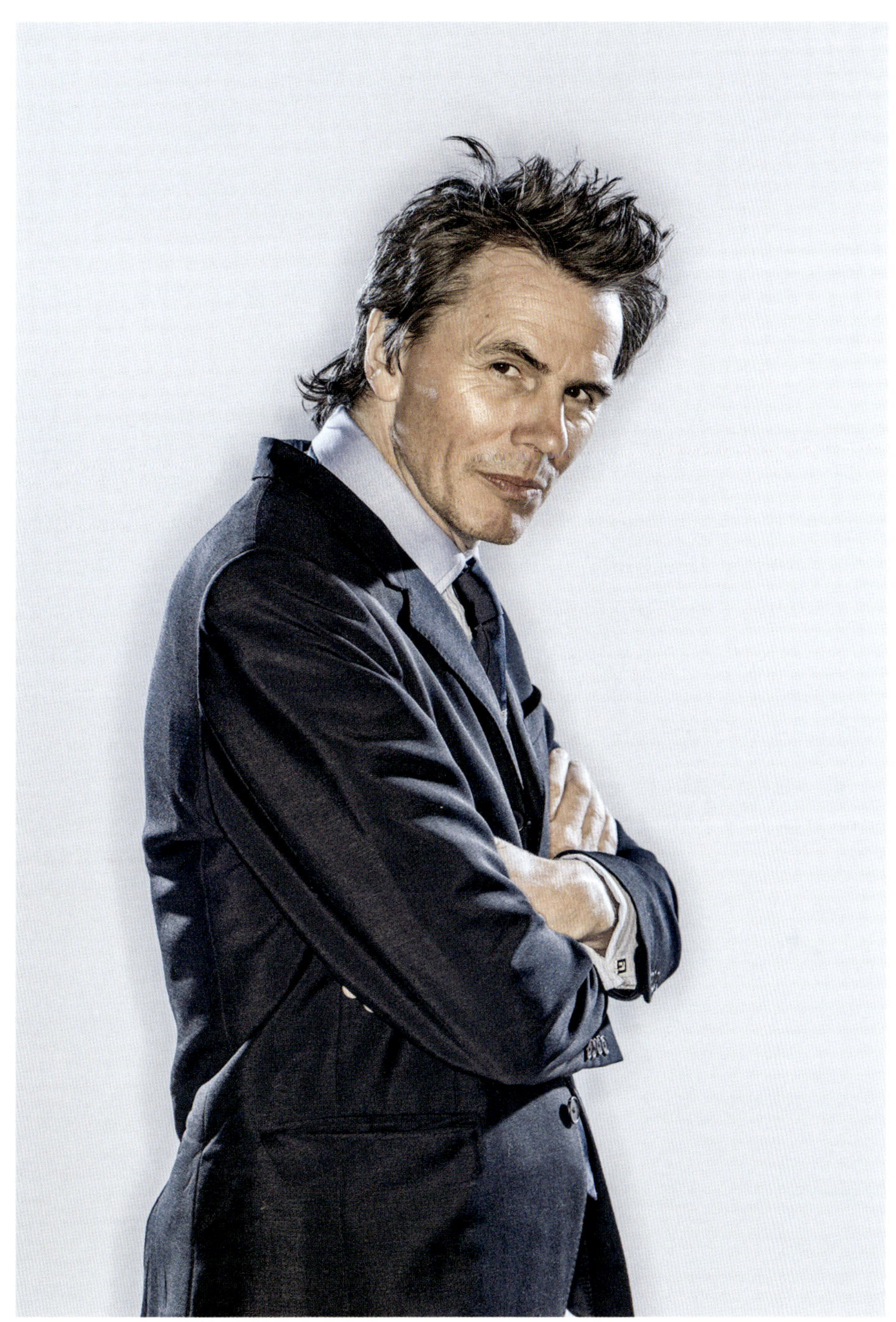

Adam Thirwell

Twice voted the best New Young British novelist by Granta and with a host of other literary awards to his name. I like the engagement in this picture. The body language seems split, with one half saying one thing and the other something else.

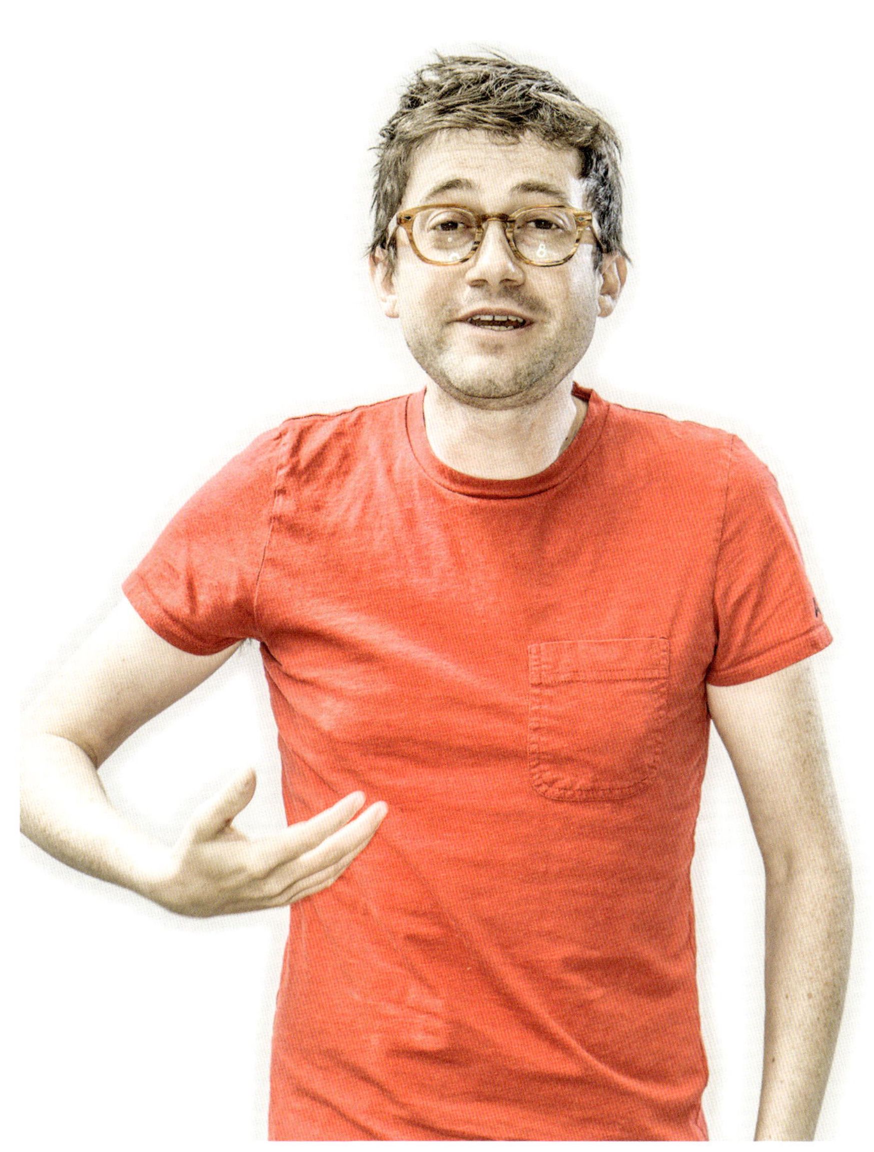

An author, who the arts broadcaster and presenter Melvyn Bragg said he wished he had covered in a South Bank Show special. In one of the pictures Colm was laughing. 'Oh jeez,' he said, 'I can't be seen to smile. My books are all miserable.' He has a face within a face a wonderfully funny man who writes about subjects that often aren't.

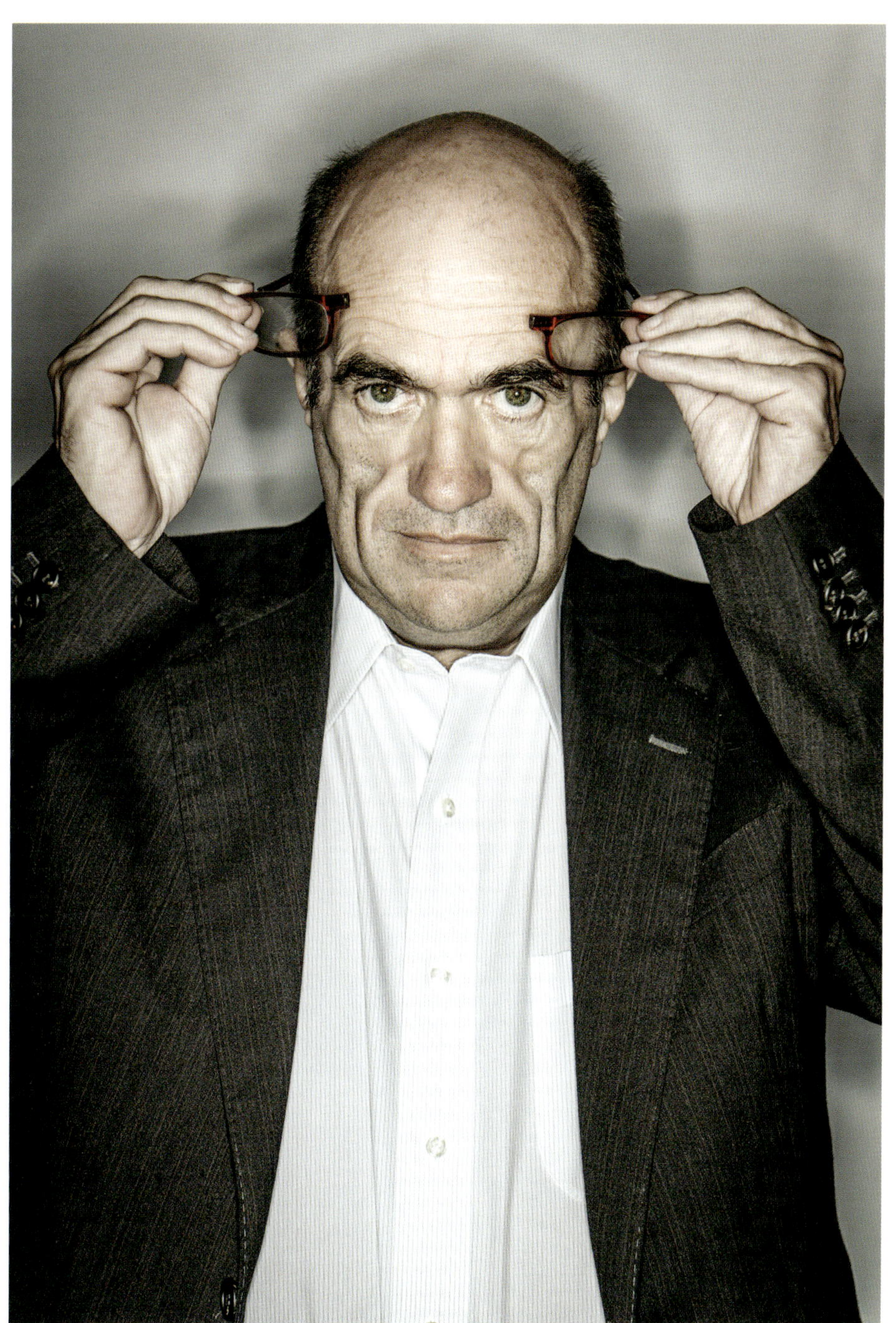

Nigerian born author Chika Unigwe. My pictures try to capture humanity in the subject, not to flatter or deceive and Chika was a delight to photograph. I was being sycophantically flattering (hopefully with tongue in cheek) to Chika which encouraged this reaction. Her husband was nearby enjoying the scene and contributing to the hilarity.

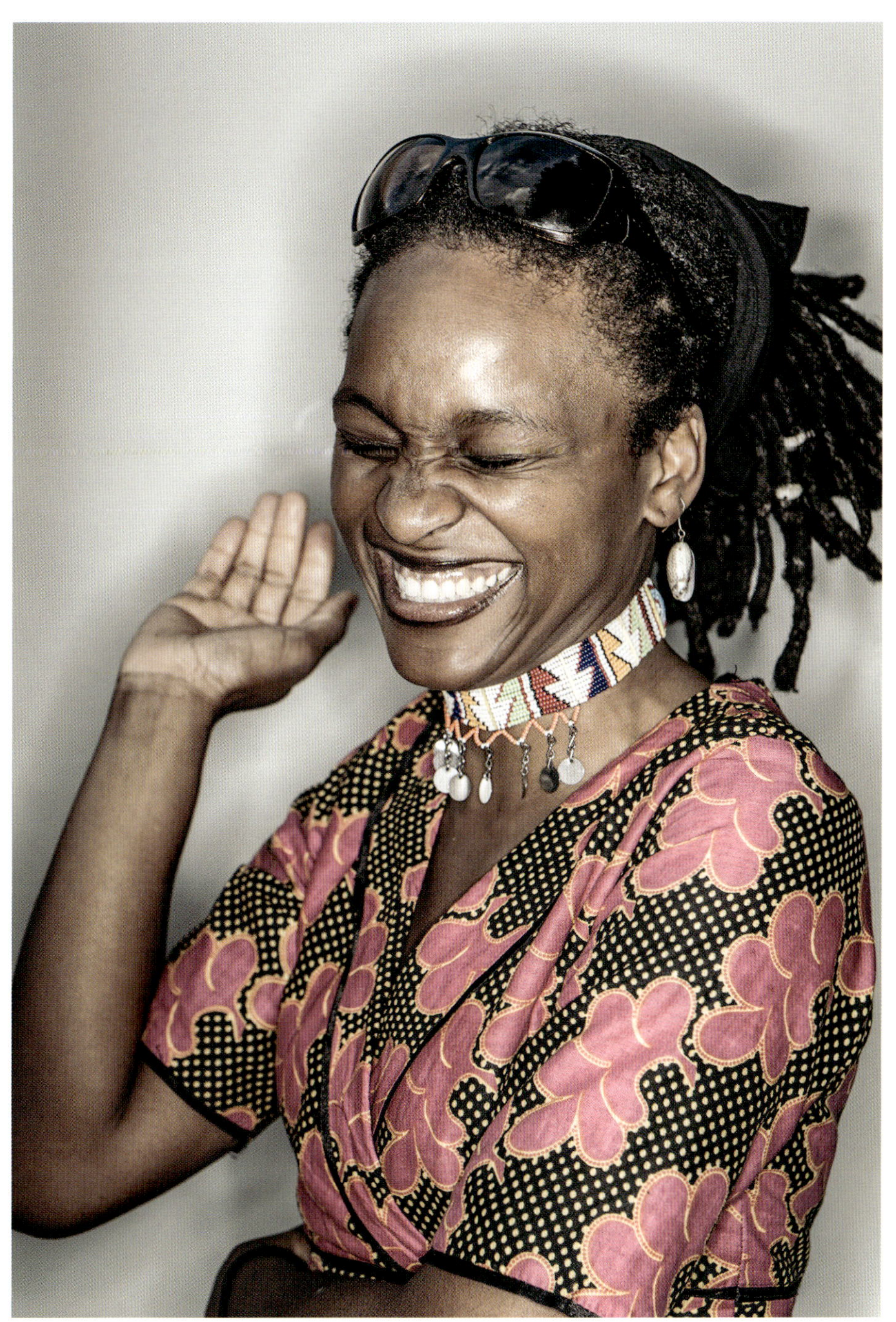

Irvine probably needs little introduction. *Trainspotting, Filth, Skagboys* etc., all deal with the less salubrious side of life. I am not sure he enjoyed having his picture taken. It was night, it was cold and I think he'd rather have been inside having a small sherry(!) and talking about football.

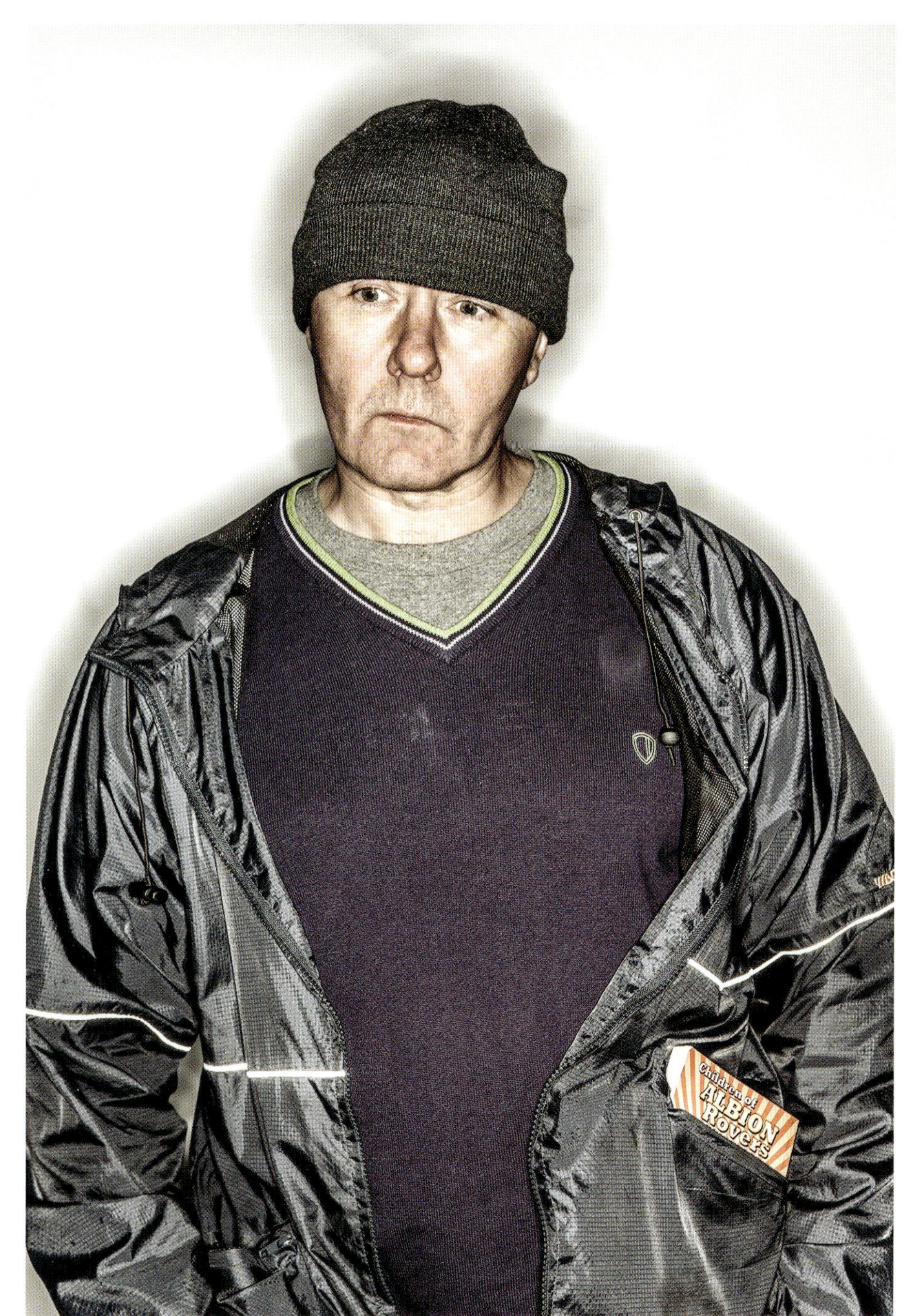

Children of
ALBION
Rovers

What a great name for an author not to mention a fine WW1 moustache. Almost looking as though he belonged in a Spitfire were it not that Tobias is American. Known for writing both short stories and memoirs one of which, *This Boy's Life*, was made into a film directed by Michael Caton-Jones.

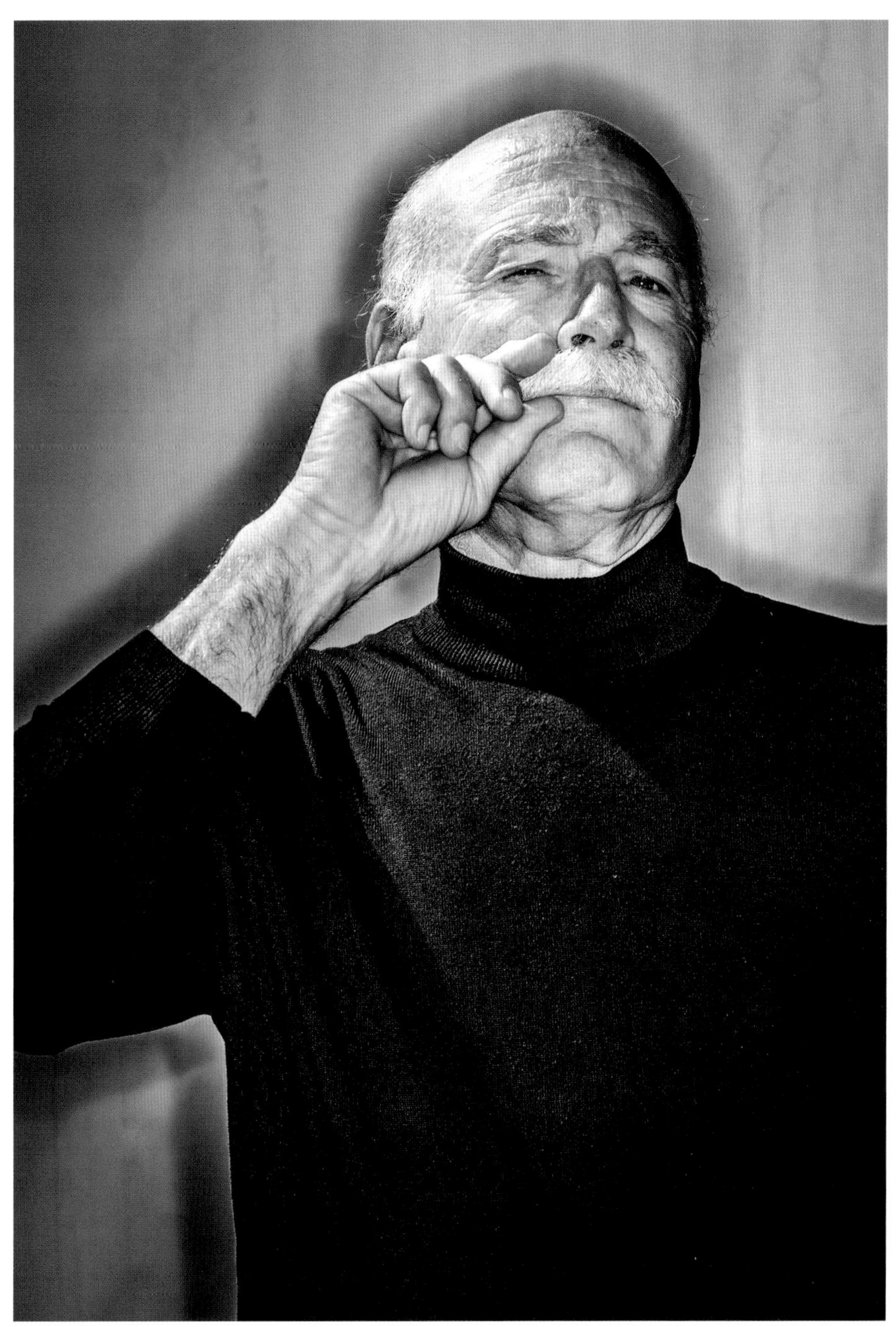